What others in the trenches say about
The Pragmatic Programmer. . .

"The cool thing about this book is that it's great for keeping the programming process fresh. *[The book]* helps you to continue to grow and clearly comes from people who have been there."

▶ **Kent Beck,** author of *Extreme Programming Explained: Embrace Change*

"I found this book to be a great mix of solid advice and wonderful analogies!"

▶ **Martin Fowler,** author of *Refactoring* and *UML Distilled*

"I would buy a copy, read it twice, then tell all my colleagues to run out and grab a copy. This is a book I would never loan because I would worry about it being lost."

▶ **Kevin Ruland,** Management Science, MSG-Logistics

"The wisdom and practical experience of the authors is obvious. The topics presented are relevant and useful. . . . By far its greatest strength for me has been the outstanding analogies—tracer bullets, broken windows, and the fabulous helicopter-based explanation of the need for orthogonality, especially in a crisis situation. I have little doubt that this book will eventually become an excellent source of useful information for journeymen programmers and expert mentors alike."

▶ **John Lakos,** author of *Large-Scale C++ Software Design*

"This is the sort of book I will buy a dozen copies of when it comes out so I can give it to my clients."

▶ **Eric Vought,** Software Engineer

"Most modern books on software development fail to cover the basics of what makes a great software developer, instead spending their time on syntax or technology where in reality the greatest leverage possible for any software team is in having talented developers who really know their craft well. An excellent book."

▶ **Pete McBreen,** Independent Consultant

"Since reading this book, I have implemented many of the practical suggestions and tips it contains. Across the board, they have saved my company time and money while helping me get my job done quicker! This should be a desktop reference for everyone who works with code for a living."

▶ **Jared Richardson,** Senior Software Developer,
iRenaissance, Inc.

"I would like to see this issued to every new employee at my company. . . ."

▶ **Chris Cleeland,** Senior Software Engineer,
Object Computing, Inc.

The Pragmatic Programmer

The Pragmatic Programmer

From Journeyman to Master

Andrew Hunt

David Thomas

ADDISON–WESLEY

Boston • San Francisco • New York • Toronto • Montreal
London • Munich • Paris • Madrid
Capetown • Sydney • Tokyo • Singapore • Mexico City

Lyrics from the song "The Boxer" on page 157 are Copyright © 1968 Paul Simon. Used by permission of the Publisher: Paul Simon Music. Lyrics from the song "Alice's Restaurant" on page 220 are by Arlo Guthrie, ©1966, 1967 (renewed) by APPLESEED MUSIC INC. All Rights Reserved. Used by Permission.

The publisher offers discounts on this book when ordered in quantity for bulk purchases and special sales. For more information, please contact:

U.S. Corporate and Government Sales
(800) 382-3419
corpsales@pearsontechgroup.com

For sales outside of the U.S., please contact:

International Sales
(317) 581-3793
international@pearsontechgroup.com

Visit Addison-Wesley on the Web: www.awprofessional.com

Library of Congress Catalog-in-Publication Data

Hunt, Andrew, 1964 –
    The Pragmatic Programmer / Andrew Hunt, David Thomas.
        p.   cm.
    Includes bibliographical references.
    ISBN 0-201-61622-X
    1. Computer programming I. Thomas, David, 1956–
II. Title.
QA76.6.H857   1999
005.1—dc21
                                                                99–43581
                                                                CIP

ISBN 0-201-61622-X

Text printed in the United States on recycled paper at Donnelley in Crawfordsville, Indiana.
35 16

For Ellie and Juliet,
Elizabeth and Zachary,
Stuart and Henry

Contents

Appendices

Foreword

As a reviewer I got an early opportunity to read the book you are holding. It was great, even in draft form. Dave Thomas and Andy Hunt have something to say, and they know how to say it. I saw what they were doing and I knew it would work. I asked to write this foreword so that I could explain why.

Simply put, this book tells you how to program in a way that you can follow. You wouldn't think that that would be a hard thing to do, but it is. Why? For one thing, not all programming books are written by programmers. Many are compiled by language designers, or the journalists who work with them to promote their creations. Those books tell you how to *talk* in a programming language—which is certainly important, but that is only a small part of what a programmer does.

What does a programmer do besides talk in programming language? Well, that is a deeper issue. Most programmers would have trouble explaining what they do. Programming is a job filled with details, and keeping track of those details requires focus. Hours drift by and the code appears. You look up and there are all of those statements. If you don't think carefully, you might think that programming is just typing statements in a programming language. You would be wrong, of course, but you wouldn't be able to tell by looking around the programming section of the bookstore.

In *The Pragmatic Programmer* Dave and Andy tell us how to program in a way that we can follow. How did they get so smart? Aren't they just as focused on details as other programmers? The answer is that they paid attention to what they were doing while they were doing it—and then they tried to do it better.

Imagine that you are sitting in a meeting. Maybe you are thinking that the meeting could go on forever and that you would rather be programming. Dave and Andy would be thinking about why they were having the meeting, and wondering if there is something else they could do that would take the place of the meeting, and deciding if that something could be automated so that the work of the meeting just happens in the future. Then they would do it.

That is just the way Dave and Andy think. That meeting wasn't something keeping them from programming. It *was* programming. And it was programming that could be improved. I know they think this way because it is tip number two: Think About Your Work.

So imagine that these guys are thinking this way for a few years. Pretty soon they would have a collection of solutions. Now imagine them using their solutions in their work for a few more years, and discarding the ones that are too hard or don't always produce results. Well, that approach just about defines *pragmatic*. Now imagine them taking a year or two more to write their solutions down. You might think, *That information would be a gold mine*. And you would be right.

The authors tell us how they program. And they tell us in a way that we can follow. But there is more to this second statement than you might think. Let me explain.

The authors have been careful to avoid proposing a theory of software development. This is fortunate, because if they had they would be obliged to warp each chapter to defend their theory. Such warping is the tradition in, say, the physical sciences, where theories eventually become laws or are quietly discarded. Programming on the other hand has few (if any) laws. So programming advice shaped around wanna-be laws may sound good in writing, but it fails to satisfy in practice. This is what goes wrong with so many methodology books.

I've studied this problem for a dozen years and found the most promise in a device called a *pattern language*. In short, a *pattern* is a solution, and a pattern language is a system of solutions that reinforce each other. A whole community has formed around the search for these systems.

This book is more than a collection of tips. It is a pattern language in sheep's clothing. I say that because each tip is drawn from experience, told as concrete advice, and related to others to form a system. These are the characteristics that allow us to learn and follow a pattern language. They work the same way here.

You can follow the advice in this book because it is concrete. You won't find vague abstractions. Dave and Andy write directly for you, as if each tip was a vital strategy for energizing your programming career. They make it simple, they tell a story, they use a light touch, and then they follow that up with answers to questions that will come up when you try.

And there is more. After you read ten or fifteen tips you will begin to see an extra dimension to the work. We sometimes call it *QWAN*, short for the *quality without a name*. The book has a philosophy that will ooze into your consciousness and mix with your own. It doesn't preach. It just tells what works. But in the telling more comes through. That's the beauty of the book: It embodies its philosophy, and it does so unpretentiously.

So here it is: an easy to read—and use—book about the whole practice of programming. I've gone on and on about why it works. You probably only care that it does work. It does. You will see.

—Ward Cunningham

Preface

This book will help you become a better programmer.

It doesn't matter whether you are a lone developer, a member of a large project team, or a consultant working with many clients at once. This book will help you, as an individual, to do better work. This book isn't theoretical—we concentrate on practical topics, on using your experience to make more informed decisions. The word *pragmatic* comes from the Latin *pragmaticus*—"skilled in business"—which itself is derived from the Greek πραττειν, meaning "to do." This is a book about doing.

Programming is a craft. At its simplest, it comes down to getting a computer to do what you want it to do (or what your user wants it to do). As a programmer, you are part listener, part advisor, part interpreter, and part dictator. You try to capture elusive requirements and find a way of expressing them so that a mere machine can do them justice. You try to document your work so that others can understand it, and you try to engineer your work so that others can build on it. What's more, you try to do all this against the relentless ticking of the project clock. You work small miracles every day.

It's a difficult job.

There are many people offering you help. Tool vendors tout the miracles their products perform. Methodology gurus promise that their techniques guarantee results. Everyone claims that their programming language is the best, and every operating system is the answer to all conceivable ills.

Of course, none of this is true. There are no easy answers. There is no such thing as a *best* solution, be it a tool, a language, or an operating system. There can only be systems that are more appropriate in a particular set of circumstances.

This is where pragmatism comes in. You shouldn't be wedded to any particular technology, but have a broad enough background and experience base to allow you to choose good solutions in particular situations. Your background stems from an understanding of the basic principles of computer science, and your experience comes from a wide range of practical projects. Theory and practice combine to make you strong.

You adjust your approach to suit the current circumstances and environment. You judge the relative importance of all the factors affecting a project and use your experience to produce appropriate solutions. And you do this continuously as the work progresses. Pragmatic Programmers get the job done, and do it well.

Who Should Read This Book?

This book is aimed at people who want to become more effective and more productive programmers. Perhaps you feel frustrated that you don't seem to be achieving your potential. Perhaps you look at colleagues who seem to be using tools to make themselves more productive than you. Maybe your current job uses older technologies, and you want to know how newer ideas can be applied to what you do.

We don't pretend to have all (or even most) of the answers, nor are all of our ideas applicable in all situations. All we can say is that if you follow our approach, you'll gain experience rapidly, your productivity will increase, and you'll have a better understanding of the entire development process. And you'll write better software.

What Makes a Pragmatic Programmer?

Each developer is unique, with individual strengths and weaknesses, preferences and dislikes. Over time, each will craft his or her own personal environment. That environment will reflect the programmer's individuality just as forcefully as his or her hobbies, clothing, or haircut. However, if you're a Pragmatic Programmer, you'll share many of the following characteristics:

- **Early adopter/fast adapter.** You have an instinct for technologies and techniques, and you love trying things out. When given something new, you can grasp it quickly and integrate it with the rest of your knowledge. Your confidence is born of experience.

- **Inquisitive.** You tend to ask questions. *That's neat—how did you do that? Did you have problems with that library? What's this BeOS I've heard about? How are symbolic links implemented?* You are a pack rat for little facts, each of which may affect some decision years from now.

- **Critical thinker.** You rarely take things as given without first getting the facts. When colleagues say "because that's the way it's done," or a vendor promises the solution to all your problems, you smell a challenge.

- **Realistic.** You try to understand the underlying nature of each problem you face. This realism gives you a good feel for how difficult things are, and how long things will take. Understanding for yourself that a process *should* be difficult or *will* take a while to complete gives you the stamina to keep at it.

- **Jack of all trades.** You try hard to be familiar with a broad range of technologies and environments, and you work to keep abreast of new developments. Although your current job may require you to be a specialist, you will always be able to move on to new areas and new challenges.

We've left the most basic characteristics until last. All Pragmatic Programmers share them. They're basic enough to state as tips:

> **TIP 1**
> Care About Your Craft

We feel that there is no point in developing software unless you care about doing it well.

> **TIP 2**
> Think! About Your Work

In order to be a Pragmatic Programmer, we're challenging you to think about what you're doing while you're doing it. This isn't a one-time audit of current practices—it's an ongoing critical appraisal of every decision you make, every day, and on every development. Never run on auto-pilot. Constantly be thinking, critiquing your work in real time. The old IBM corporate motto, THINK!, is the Pragmatic Programmer's mantra.

If this sounds like hard work to you, then you're exhibiting the *realistic* characteristic. This is going to take up some of your valuable time—time that is probably already under tremendous pressure. The reward is a more active involvement with a job you love, a feeling of mastery over an increasing range of subjects, and pleasure in a feeling of continuous improvement. Over the long term, your time investment will be repaid as you and your team become more efficient, write code that's easier to maintain, and spend less time in meetings.

Individual Pragmatists, Large Teams

Some people feel that there is no room for individuality on large teams or complex projects. "Software construction is an engineering discipline," they say, "that breaks down if individual team members make decisions for themselves."

We disagree.

The construction of software *should* be an engineering discipline. However, this doesn't preclude individual craftsmanship. Think about the large cathedrals built in Europe during the Middle Ages. Each took thousands of person-years of effort, spread over many decades. Lessons learned were passed down to the next set of builders, who advanced the state of structural engineering with their accomplishments. But the carpenters, stonecutters, carvers, and glass workers were all craftspeople, interpreting the engineering requirements to produce a whole that transcended the purely mechanical side of the construction. It was their belief in their individual contributions that sustained the projects:

> *We who cut mere stones must always be envisioning cathedrals.*
> **— Quarry worker's creed**

Within the overall structure of a project there is always room for individuality and craftsmanship. This is particularly true given the current state of software engineering. One hundred years from now, our engineering may seem as archaic as the techniques used by medieval cathedral builders seem to today's civil engineers, while our craftsman-ship will still be honored.

It's a Continuous Process

A tourist visiting England's Eton College asked the gardener how he got the lawns so perfect. "That's easy," he replied, "You just brush off the dew every morning, mow them every other day, and roll them once a week."

"Is that all?" asked the tourist.

"Absolutely," replied the gardener. "Do that for 500 years and you'll have a nice lawn, too."

Great lawns need small amounts of daily care, and so do great pro-grammers. Management consultants like to drop the word *kaizen* in conversations. "Kaizen" is a Japanese term that captures the concept of continuously making many small improvements. It was considered to be one of the main reasons for the dramatic gains in productivity and quality in Japanese manufacturing and was widely copied throughout the world. Kaizen applies to individuals, too. Every day, work to refine the skills you have and to add new tools to your repertoire. Unlike the Eton lawns, you'll start seeing results in a matter of days. Over the years, you'll be amazed at how your experience has blossomed and your skills have grown.

How the Book Is Organized

This book is written as a collection of short sections. Each section is self-contained, and addresses a particular topic. You'll find numerous cross references, which help put each topic in context. Feel free to read the sections in any order—this isn't a book you need to read front-to-back.

Occasionally you'll come across a box labeled *Tip nn* (such as Tip 1, "Care About Your Craft" on page xix). As well as emphasizing points in the text, we feel the tips have a life of their own—we live by them daily. You'll find a summary of all the tips on a pull-out card inside the back cover.

Appendix A contains a set of resources: the book's bibliography, a list of URLs to Web resources, and a list of recommended periodicals, books, and professional organizations. Throughout the book you'll find references to the bibliography and to the list of URLs—such as [KP99] and [URL 18], respectively.

We've included exercises and challenges where appropriate. Exercises normally have relatively straightforward answers, while the challenges are more open-ended. To give you an idea of our thinking, we've included our answers to the exercises in Appendix B, but very few have a single *correct* solution. The challenges might form the basis of group discussions or essay work in advanced programming courses.

What's in a Name?

"When I use a word," Humpty Dumpty said, in rather a scornful tone, "it means just what I choose it to mean—neither more nor less."
▶ **Lewis Carroll, *Through the Looking-Glass***

Scattered throughout the book you'll find various bits of jargon—either perfectly good English words that have been corrupted to mean something technical, or horrendous made-up words that have been assigned meanings by computer scientists with a grudge against the language. The first time we use each of these jargon words, we try to define it, or at least give a hint to its meaning. However, we're sure that some have fallen through the cracks, and others, such as *object* and *relational database,* are in common enough usage that adding a definition would be boring. If you *do* come across a term you haven't seen before, please don't just skip over it. Take time to look it up, perhaps on the Web, or maybe in a computer science textbook. And, if you get a chance, drop us an e-mail and complain, so we can add a definition to the next edition.

Having said all this, we decided to get revenge against the computer scientists. Sometimes, there are perfectly good jargon words for concepts, words that we've decided to ignore. Why? Because the existing jargon is normally restricted to a particular problem domain, or to a particular phase of development. However, one of the basic philosophies of this book is that most of the techniques we're recommending are universal: modularity applies to code, designs, documentation, and team organization, for instance. When we wanted to use the conventional jargon word in a broader context, it got confusing—we couldn't seem to overcome the baggage the original term brought with it. When this happened, we contributed to the decline of the language by inventing our own terms.

Source Code and Other Resources

Most of the code shown in this book is extracted from compilable source files, available for download from our Web site:

> www.pragmaticprogrammer.com

There you'll also find links to resources we find useful, along with updates to the book and news of other Pragmatic Programmer developments.

Send Us Feedback

We'd appreciate hearing from you. Comments, suggestions, errors in the text, and problems in the examples are all welcome. E-mail us at

> ppbook@pragmaticprogrammer.com

Acknowledgments

When we started writing this book, we had no idea how much of a team effort it would end up being.

Addison-Wesley has been brilliant, taking a couple of wet-behind-the-ears hackers and walking us through the whole book-production process, from idea to camera-ready copy. Many thanks to John Wait and Meera Ravindiran for their initial support, Mike Hendrickson, our enthusiastic editor (and a mean cover designer!), Lorraine Ferrier and John Fuller for their help with production, and the indefatigable Julie DeBaggis for keeping us all together.

Then there were the reviewers: Greg Andress, Mark Cheers, Chris Cleeland, Alistair Cockburn, Ward Cunningham, Martin Fowler, Thanh T. Giang, Robert L. Glass, Scott Henninger, Michael Hunter, Brian

Kirby, John Lakos, Pete McBreen, Carey P. Morris, Jared Richardson, Kevin Ruland, Eric Starr, Eric Vought, Chris Van Wyk, and Deborra Zukowski. Without their careful comments and valuable insights, this book would be less readable, less accurate, and twice as long. Thank you all for your time and wisdom.

The second printing of this book benefited greatly from the eagle eyes of our readers. Many thanks to Brian Blank, Paul Boal, Tom Ekberg, Brent Fulgham, Louis Paul Hebert, Henk-Jan Olde Loohuis, Alan Lund, Gareth McCaughan, Yoshiki Shibata, and Volker Wurst, both for finding the mistakes and for having the grace to point them out gently.

Over the years, we have worked with a large number of progressive clients, where we gained and refined the experience we write about here. Recently, we've been fortunate to work with Peter Gehrke on several large projects. His support and enthusiasm for our techniques are much appreciated.

This book was produced using LaTeX, pic, Perl, dvips, ghostview, ispell, GNU make, CVS, Emacs, XEmacs, EGCS, GCC, Java, iContract, and SmallEiffel, using the Bash and zsh shells under Linux. The staggering thing is that all of this tremendous software is freely available. We owe a huge "thank you" to the thousands of Pragmatic Programmers worldwide who have contributed these and other works to us all. We'd particularly like to thank Reto Kramer for his help with iContract.

Last, but in no way least, we owe a huge debt to our families. Not only have they put up with late night typing, huge telephone bills, and our permanent air of distraction, but they've had the grace to read what we've written, time after time. Thank you for letting us dream.

Andy Hunt
Dave Thomas

Chapter 1

A Pragmatic Philosophy

What distinguishes Pragmatic Programmers? We feel it's an attitude, a style, a philosophy of approaching problems and their solutions. They think beyond the immediate problem, always trying to place it in its larger context, always trying to be aware of the bigger picture. After all, without this larger context, how can you be pragmatic? How can you make intelligent compromises and informed decisions?

Another key to their success is that they take responsibility for everything they do, which we discuss in *The Cat Ate My Source Code*. Being responsible, Pragmatic Programmers won't sit idly by and watch their projects fall apart through neglect. In *Software Entropy*, we tell you how to keep your projects pristine.

Most people find change difficult to accept, sometimes for good reasons, sometimes because of plain old inertia. In *Stone Soup and Boiled Frogs*, we look at a strategy for instigating change and (in the interests of balance) present the cautionary tale of an amphibian that ignored the dangers of gradual change.

One of the benefits of understanding the context in which you work is that it becomes easier to know just how good your software has to be. Sometimes near-perfection is the only option, but often there are trade-offs involved. We explore this in *Good-Enough Software*.

Of course, you need to have a broad base of knowledge and experience to pull all of this off. Learning is a continuous and ongoing process. In *Your Knowledge Portfolio*, we discuss some strategies for keeping the momentum up.

Finally, none of us works in a vacuum. We all spend a large amount of time interacting with others. *Communicate!* lists ways we can do this better.

Pragmatic programming stems from a philosophy of pragmatic thinking. This chapter sets the basis for that philosophy.

1 ▶ The Cat Ate My Source Code

The greatest of all weaknesses is the fear of appearing weak.
▶ **J. B. Bossuet, *Politics from Holy Writ*, 1709**

One of the cornerstones of the pragmatic philosophy is the idea of taking responsibility for yourself and your actions in terms of your career advancement, your project, and your day-to-day work. A Pragmatic Programmer takes charge of his or her own career, and isn't afraid to admit ignorance or error. It's not the most pleasant aspect of programming, to be sure, but it will happen—even on the best of projects. Despite thorough testing, good documentation, and solid automation, things go wrong. Deliveries are late. Unforeseen technical problems come up.

These things happen, and we try to deal with them as professionally as we can. This means being honest and direct. We can be proud of our abilities, but we must be honest about our shortcomings—our ignorance as well as our mistakes.

Take Responsibility

Responsibility is something you actively agree to. You make a commitment to ensure that something is done right, but you don't necessarily have direct control over every aspect of it. In addition to doing your own personal best, you must analyze the situation for risks that are beyond your control. You have the right *not* to take on a responsibility for an impossible situation, or one in which the risks are too great. You'll have to make the call based on your own ethics and judgment.

When you *do* accept the responsibility for an outcome, you should expect to be held accountable for it. When you make a mistake (as we all do) or an error in judgment, admit it honestly and try to offer options.

Don't blame someone or something else, or make up an excuse. Don't blame all the problems on a vendor, a programming language, management, or your coworkers. Any and all of these may play a role, but it is up to *you* to provide solutions, not excuses.

If there was a risk that the vendor wouldn't come through for you, then you should have had a contingency plan. If the disk crashes—taking all of your source code with it—and you don't have a backup, it's your fault. Telling your boss "the cat ate my source code" just won't cut it.

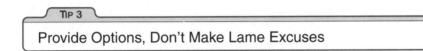

Tip 3

Provide Options, Don't Make Lame Excuses

Before you approach anyone to tell them why something can't be done, is late, or is broken, stop and listen to yourself. Talk to the rubber duck on your monitor, or the cat. Does your excuse sound reasonable, or stupid? How's it going to sound to your boss?

Run through the conversation in your mind. What is the other person likely to say? Will they ask, "Have you tried this..." or "Didn't you consider that?" How will you respond? Before you go and tell them the bad news, is there anything else you can try? Sometimes, you just *know* what they are going to say, so save them the trouble.

Instead of excuses, provide options. Don't say it can't be done; explain what *can* be done to salvage the situation. Does code have to be thrown out? Educate them on the value of refactoring (see *Refactoring*, page 184). Do you need to spend time prototyping to determine the best way to proceed (see *Prototypes and Post-it Notes*, page 53)? Do you need to introduce better testing (see *Code That's Easy to Test*, page 189, and *Ruthless Testing*, page 237) or automation (see *Ubiquitous Automation*, page 230) to prevent it from happening again? Perhaps you need additional resources. Don't be afraid to ask, or to admit that you need help.

Try to flush out the lame excuses before voicing them aloud. If you must, tell your cat first. After all, if little Tiddles is going to take the blame. . . .

Related sections include:
- *Prototypes and Post-it Notes*, page 53
- *Refactoring*, page 184
- *Code That's Easy to Test*, page 189
- *Ubiquitous Automation*, page 230
- *Ruthless Testing*, page 237

Challenges
- How do you react when someone—such as a bank teller, an auto mechanic, or a clerk—comes to you with a lame excuse? What do you think of them and their company as a result?

Software Entropy

While software development is immune from almost all physical laws, *entropy* hits us hard. *Entropy* is a term from physics that refers to the amount of "disorder" in a system. Unfortunately, the laws of thermodynamics guarantee that the entropy in the universe tends toward a maximum. When disorder increases in software, programmers call it "software rot."

There are many factors that can contribute to software rot. The most important one seems to be the psychology, or culture, at work on a project. Even if you are a team of one, your project's psychology can be a very delicate thing. Despite the best laid plans and the best people, a project can still experience ruin and decay during its lifetime. Yet there are other projects that, despite enormous difficulties and constant setbacks, successfully fight nature's tendency toward disorder and manage to come out pretty well.

What makes the difference?

In inner cities, some buildings are beautiful and clean, while others are rotting hulks. Why? Researchers in the field of crime and urban decay discovered a fascinating trigger mechanism, one that very quickly turns a clean, intact, inhabited building into a smashed and abandoned derelict [WK82].

A broken window.

One broken window, left unrepaired for any substantial length of time, instills in the inhabitants of the building a sense of abandonment—a sense that the powers that be don't care about the building. So another window gets broken. People start littering. Graffiti appears. Serious structural damage begins. In a relatively short space of time, the building becomes damaged beyond the owner's desire to fix it, and the sense of abandonment becomes reality.

The "Broken Window Theory" has inspired police departments in New York and other major cities to crack down on the small stuff in order to keep out the big stuff. It works: keeping on top of broken windows, graffiti, and other small infractions has reduced the serious crime level.

TIP 4

Don't Live with Broken Windows

Don't leave "broken windows" (bad designs, wrong decisions, or poor code) unrepaired. Fix each one as soon as it is discovered. If there is insufficient time to fix it properly, then *board it up.* Perhaps you can comment out the offending code, or display a "Not Implemented" message, or substitute dummy data instead. Take *some* action to prevent further damage and to show that you're on top of the situation.

We've seen clean, functional systems deteriorate pretty quickly once windows start breaking. There are other factors that can contribute to software rot, and we'll touch on some of them elsewhere, but neglect *accelerates* the rot faster than any other factor.

You may be thinking that no one has the time to go around cleaning up all the broken glass of a project. If you continue to think like that, then you'd better plan on getting a dumpster, or moving to another neighborhood. Don't let entropy win.

Putting Out Fires

By contrast, there's the story of an obscenely rich acquaintance of Andy's. His house was immaculate, beautiful, loaded with priceless antiques, *objets d'art*, and so on. One day, a tapestry that was hanging a little too close to his living room fireplace caught on fire. The fire department rushed in to save the day—and his house. But before they dragged their big, dirty hoses into the house, they stopped—with the fire raging—to roll out a mat between the front door and the source of the fire.

They didn't want to mess up the carpet.

A pretty extreme case, to be sure, but that's the way it must be with software. One broken window—a badly designed piece of code, a poor management decision that the team must live with for the duration of the project—is all it takes to start the decline. If you find yourself working on a project with quite a few broken windows, it's all too easy to slip into the mindset of "All the rest of this code is crap, I'll just follow suit." It doesn't matter if the project has been fine up to this point. In the original experiment leading to the "Broken Window Theory," an abandoned car sat for a week untouched. But once a single window was broken, the car was stripped and turned upside down within *hours*.

By the same token, if you find yourself on a team and a project where the code is pristinely beautiful—cleanly written, well designed, and elegant—you will likely take extra special care not to mess it up, just like the firefighters. Even if there's a fire raging (deadline, release date, trade show demo, etc.), *you* don't want to be the first one to make a mess.

Related sections include:
- *Stone Soup and Boiled Frogs*, page 7
- *Refactoring*, page 184
- *Pragmatic Teams*, page 224

Challenges
- Help strengthen your team by surveying your computing "neighborhood." Choose two or three "broken windows" and discuss with your colleagues what the problems are and what could be done to fix them.

- Can you tell when a window first gets broken? What is your reaction? If it was the result of someone else's decision, or a management edict, what can you do about it?

▶ Stone Soup and Boiled Frogs

The three soldiers returning home from war were hungry. When they saw the village ahead their spirits lifted—they were sure the villagers would give them a meal. But when they got there, they found the doors locked and the windows closed. After many years of war, the villagers were short of food, and hoarded what they had.

Undeterred, the soldiers boiled a pot of water and carefully placed three stones into it. The amazed villagers came out to watch.

"This is stone soup," the soldiers explained. "Is that all you put in it?" asked the villagers. "Absolutely—although some say it tastes even better with a few carrots...." A villager ran off, returning in no time with a basket of carrots from his hoard.

A couple of minutes later, the villagers again asked "Is that it?"

"Well," said the soldiers, "a couple of potatoes give it body." Off ran another villager.

Over the next hour, the soldiers listed more ingredients that would enhance the soup: beef, leeks, salt, and herbs. Each time a different villager would run off to raid their personal stores.

Eventually they had produced a large pot of steaming soup. The soldiers removed the stones, and they sat down with the entire village to enjoy the first square meal any of them had eaten in months.

There are a couple of morals in the stone soup story. The villagers are tricked by the soldiers, who use the villagers' curiosity to get food from them. But more importantly, the soldiers act as a catalyst, bringing the village together so they can jointly produce something that they couldn't have done by themselves—a synergistic result. Eventually everyone wins.

Every now and then, you might want to emulate the soldiers.

You may be in a situation where you know exactly what needs doing and how to do it. The entire system just appears before your eyes—you know it's right. But ask permission to tackle the whole thing and you'll be met with delays and blank stares. People will form committees, budgets will need approval, and things will get complicated. Everyone will guard their own resources. Sometimes this is called "start-up fatigue."

It's time to bring out the stones. Work out what you *can* reasonably ask for. Develop it well. Once you've got it, show people, and let them marvel. Then say "of course, it *would* be better if we added...." Pretend it's not important. Sit back and wait for them to start asking you to add the functionality you originally wanted. People find it easier to join an ongoing success. Show them a glimpse of the future and you'll get them to rally around.[1]

> TIP 5
> **Be a Catalyst for Change**

The Villagers' Side

On the other hand, the stone soup story is also about gentle and gradual deception. It's about focusing too tightly. The villagers think about the stones and forget about the rest of the world. We all fall for it, every day. Things just creep up on us.

We've all seen the symptoms. Projects slowly and inexorably get totally out of hand. Most software disasters start out too small to notice, and most project overruns happen a day at a time. Systems drift from their specifications feature by feature, while patch after patch gets added to a piece of code until there's nothing of the original left. It's often the accumulation of small things that breaks morale and teams.

> TIP 6
> **Remember the Big Picture**

We've never tried this—honest. But they say that if you take a frog and drop it into boiling water, it will jump straight back out again. However, if you place the frog in a pan of cold water, then gradually heat it, the frog won't notice the slow increase in temperature and will stay put until cooked.

---

1.   While doing this, you may be comforted by the line attributed to Rear Admiral Dr. Grace Hopper: "It's easier to ask forgiveness than it is to get permission."

Note that the frog's problem is different from the broken windows issue discussed in Section 2. In the Broken Window Theory, people lose the will to fight entropy because they perceive that no one else cares. The frog just doesn't notice the change.

Don't be like the frog. Keep an eye on the big picture. Constantly review what's happening around you, not just what you personally are doing.

Related sections include:
- *Software Entropy*, page 4
- *Programming by Coincidence*, page 172
- *Refactoring*, page 184
- *The Requirements Pit*, page 202
- *Pragmatic Teams*, page 224

Challenges
- While reviewing a draft of this book, John Lakos raised the following issue: The soldiers progressively deceive the villagers, but the change they catalyze does them all good. However, by progressively deceiving the frog, you're doing it harm. Can you determine whether you're making stone soup or frog soup when you try to catalyze change? Is the decision subjective or objective?

Good-Enough Software

Striving to better, oft we mar what's well.
► *King Lear* 1.4

There's an old(ish) joke about a U.S. company that places an order for 100,000 integrated circuits with a Japanese manufacturer. Part of the specification was the defect rate: one chip in 10,000. A few weeks later the order arrived: one large box containing thousands of ICs, and a small one containing just ten. Attached to the small box was a label that read: "These are the faulty ones."

If only we really had this kind of control over quality. But the real world just won't let us produce much that's truly perfect, particularly not bug-free software. Time, technology, and temperament all conspire against us.

However, this doesn't have to be frustrating. As Ed Yourdon described in an article in *IEEE Software* [You95], you can discipline yourself to write software that's good enough—good enough for your users, for future maintainers, for your own peace of mind. You'll find that you are more productive and your users are happier. And you may well find that your programs are actually better for their shorter incubation.

Before we go any further, we need to qualify what we're about to say. The phrase "good enough" does not imply sloppy or poorly produced code. All systems must meet their users' requirements to be successful. We are simply advocating that users be given an opportunity to participate in the process of deciding when what you've produced is good enough.

Involve Your Users in the Trade-Off

Normally you're writing software for other people. Often you'll remember to get requirements from them.[2] But how often do you ask them *how good* they want their software to be? Sometimes there'll be no choice. If you're working on pacemakers, the space shuttle, or a low-level library that will be widely disseminated, the requirements will be more stringent and your options more limited. However, if you're working on a brand new product, you'll have different constraints. The marketing people will have promises to keep, the eventual end users may have made plans based on a delivery schedule, and your company will certainly have cash-flow constraints. It would be unprofessional to ignore these users' requirements simply to add new features to the program, or to polish up the code just one more time. We're not advocating panic: it is equally unprofessional to promise impossible time scales and to cut basic engineering corners to meet a deadline.

---

2.   That was supposed to be a joke!

The scope and quality of the system you produce should be specified as part of that system's requirements.

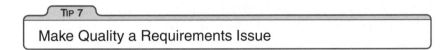

TIP 7

Make Quality a Requirements Issue

Often you'll be in situations where trade-offs are involved. Surprisingly, many users would rather use software with some rough edges *today* than wait a year for the multimedia version. Many IT departments with tight budgets would agree. Great software today is often preferable to perfect software tomorrow. If you give your users something to play with early, their feedback will often lead you to a better eventual solution (see *Tracer Bullets*, page 48).

Know When to Stop

In some ways, programming is like painting. You start with a blank canvas and certain basic raw materials. You use a combination of science, art, and craft to determine what to do with them. You sketch out an overall shape, paint the underlying environment, then fill in the details. You constantly step back with a critical eye to view what you've done. Every now and then you'll throw a canvas away and start again.

But artists will tell you that all the hard work is ruined if you don't know when to stop. If you add layer upon layer, detail over detail, *the painting becomes lost in the paint.*

Don't spoil a perfectly good program by overembellishment and over-refinement. Move on, and let your code stand in its own right for a while. It may not be perfect. Don't worry: it could never be perfect. (In Chapter 6, page 171, we'll discuss philosophies for developing code in an imperfect world.)

Related sections include:
- *Tracer Bullets*, page 48
- *The Requirements Pit*, page 202
- *Pragmatic Teams*, page 224
- *Great Expectations*, page 255

Challenges

- Look at the manufacturers of the software tools and operating systems that you use. Can you find any evidence that these companies are comfortable shipping software they know is not perfect? As a user, would you rather (1) wait for them to get all the bugs out, (2) have complex software and accept some bugs, or (3) opt for simpler software with fewer defects?

- Consider the effect of modularization on the delivery of software. Will it take more or less time to get a monolithic block of software to the required quality compared with a system designed in modules? Can you find commercial examples?

Your Knowledge Portfolio

An investment in knowledge always pays the best interest.
▶ **Benjamin Franklin**

Ah, good old Ben Franklin—never at a loss for a pithy homily. Why, if we could just be early to bed and early to rise, we'd be great programmers—right? The early bird might get the worm, but what happens to the early worm?

In this case, though, Ben really hit the nail on the head. Your knowledge and experience are your most important professional assets.

Unfortunately, they're *expiring assets.*[3] Your knowledge becomes out of date as new techniques, languages, and environments are developed. Changing market forces may render your experience obsolete or irrelevant. Given the speed at which Web-years fly by, this can happen pretty quickly.

As the value of your knowledge declines, so does your value to your company or client. We want to prevent this from ever happening.

---

3. An *expiring asset* is something whose value diminishes over time. Examples include a warehouse full of bananas and a ticket to a ball game.

Your Knowledge Portfolio

We like to think of all the facts programmers know about computing, the application domains they work in, and all their experience as their *Knowledge Portfolios*. Managing a knowledge portfolio is very similar to managing a financial portfolio:

1. Serious investors invest regularly—as a habit.

2. Diversification is the key to long-term success.

3. Smart investors balance their portfolios between conservative and high-risk, high-reward investments.

4. Investors try to buy low and sell high for maximum return.

5. Portfolios should be reviewed and rebalanced periodically.

To be successful in your career, you must manage your knowledge portfolio using these same guidelines.

Building Your Portfolio

- **Invest regularly.** Just as in financial investing, you must invest in your knowledge portfolio *regularly*. Even if it's just a small amount, the habit itself is as important as the sums. A few sample goals are listed in the next section.

- **Diversify.** The more *different* things you know, the more valuable you are. As a baseline, you need to know the ins and outs of the particular technology you are working with currently. But don't stop there. The face of computing changes rapidly—hot technology today may well be close to useless (or at least not in demand) tomorrow. The more technologies you are comfortable with, the better you will be able to adjust to change.

- **Manage risk.** Technology exists along a spectrum from risky, potentially high-reward to low-risk, low-reward standards. It's not a good idea to invest all of your money in high-risk stocks that might collapse suddenly, nor should you invest all of it conservatively and miss out on possible opportunities. Don't put all your technical eggs in one basket.

- **Buy low, sell high.**   Learning an emerging technology before it becomes popular can be just as hard as finding an undervalued stock, but the payoff can be just as rewarding. Learning Java when it first came out may have been risky, but it paid off handsomely for the early adopters who are now at the top of that field.

- **Review and rebalance.**   This is a very dynamic industry. That hot technology you started investigating last month might be stone cold by now. Maybe you need to brush up on that database technology that you haven't used in a while. Or perhaps you could be better positioned for that new job opening if you tried out that other language. . . .

Of all these guidelines, the most important one is the simplest to do:

Tip 8

Invest Regularly in Your Knowledge Portfolio

Goals

Now that you have some guidelines on what and when to add to your knowledge portfolio, what's the best way to go about acquiring intellectual capital with which to fund your portfolio? Here are a few suggestions.

- **Learn at least one new language every year.**   Different languages solve the same problems in different ways. By learning several different approaches, you can help broaden your thinking and avoid getting stuck in a rut. Additionally, learning many languages is far easier now, thanks to the wealth of freely available software on the Internet (see page 267).

- **Read a technical book each quarter.**   Bookstores are full of technical books on interesting topics related to your current project. Once you're in the habit, read a book a month. After you've mastered the technologies you're currently using, branch out and study some that *don't* relate to your project.

- **Read nontechnical books, too.**   It is important to remember that computers are used by *people*—people whose needs you are trying to satisfy. Don't forget the human side of the equation.

- **Take classes.**   Look for interesting courses at your local community college or university, or perhaps at the next trade show that comes to town.

- **Participate in local user groups.**   Don't just go and listen, but actively participate. Isolation can be deadly to your career; find out what people are working on outside of your company.

- **Experiment with different environments.**   If you've worked only in Windows, play with Unix at home (the freely available Linux is perfect for this). If you've used only `makefiles` and an editor, try an IDE, and vice versa.

- **Stay current.**   Subscribe to trade magazines and other journals (see page 262 for recommendations). Choose some that cover technology different from that of your current project.

- **Get wired.**   Want to know the ins and outs of a new language or other technology? Newsgroups are a great way to find out what experiences other people are having with it, the particular jargon they use, and so on. Surf the Web for papers, commercial sites, and any other sources of information you can find.

It's important to continue investing. Once you feel comfortable with some new language or bit of technology, move on. Learn another one.

It doesn't matter whether you ever use any of these technologies on a project, or even whether you put them on your resume. The process of learning will expand your thinking, opening you to new possibilities and new ways of doing things. The cross-pollination of ideas is important; try to apply the lessons you've learned to your current project. Even if your project doesn't use that technology, perhaps you can borrow some ideas. Get familiar with object orientation, for instance, and you'll write plain C programs differently.

Opportunities for Learning

So you're reading voraciously, you're on top of all the latest breaking developments in your field (not an easy thing to do), and somebody asks you a question. You don't have the faintest idea what the answer is, and freely admit as much.

Don't let it stop there. Take it as a personal challenge to find the answer. Ask a guru. (If you don't have a guru in your office, you should be able to find one on the Internet: see the box on on the facing page.) Search the Web. Go to the library.[4]

If you can't find the answer yourself, find out who *can*. Don't let it rest. Talking to other people will help build your personal network, and you may surprise yourself by finding solutions to other, unrelated problems along the way. And that old portfolio just keeps getting bigger. . . .

All of this reading and researching takes time, and time is already in short supply. So you need to plan ahead. Always have something to read in an otherwise dead moment. Time spent waiting for doctors and dentists can be a great opportunity to catch up on your reading—but be sure to bring your own magazine with you, or you might find yourself thumbing through a dog-eared 1973 article about Papua New Guinea.

Critical Thinking

The last important point is to think *critically* about what you read and hear. You need to ensure that the knowledge in your portfolio is accurate and unswayed by either vendor or media hype. Beware of the zealots who insist that their dogma provides the *only* answer—it may or may not be applicable to you and your project.

Never underestimate the power of commercialism. Just because a Web search engine lists a hit first doesn't mean that it's the best match; the content provider can pay to get top billing. Just because a bookstore features a book prominently doesn't mean it's a good book, or even popular; they may have been paid to place it there.

TIP 9

Critically Analyze What You Read and Hear

Unfortunately, there are very few simple answers anymore. But with your extensive portfolio, and by applying some critical analysis to the

---

4. In this era of the Web, many people seem to have forgotten about real live libraries filled with research material and staff.

Care and Cultivation of Gurus

With the global adoption of the Internet, gurus suddenly are as close as your `Enter` key. So, how do you find one, and how do you get one to talk with you?

We find there are some simple tricks.

- Know exactly what you want to ask, and be as specific as you can be.

- Frame your question carefully and politely. Remember that you're asking a favor; don't seem to be demanding an answer.

- Once you've framed your question, stop and look again for the answer. Pick out some keywords and search the Web. Look for appropriate FAQs (lists of frequently asked questions with answers).

- Decide if you want to ask publicly or privately. Usenet newsgroups are wonderful meeting places for experts on just about any topic, but some people are wary of these groups' public nature. Alternatively, you can always e-mail your guru directly. Either way, use a meaningful subject line. ("`Need Help!!!`" doesn't cut it.)

- Sit back and be patient. People are busy, and it may take days to get a specific answer.

Finally, please be sure to thank anyone who responds to you. And if you see people asking questions *you* can answer, play your part and participate.

---

torrent of technical publications you will read, you can understand the *complex* answers.

Challenges

- Start learning a new language this week. Always programmed in C++? Try Smalltalk [URL 13] or Squeak [URL 14]. Doing Java? Try Eiffel [URL 10] or TOM [URL 15]. See page 267 for sources of other free compilers and environments.

- Start reading a new book (but finish this one first!). If you are doing very detailed implementation and coding, read a book on design and architecture. If you are doing high-level design, read a book on coding techniques.

- Get out and talk technology with people who aren't involved in your current project, or who don't work for the same company. Network in your company cafeteria, or maybe seek out fellow enthusiasts at a local user's group meeting.

Communicate!

I believe that it is better to be looked over than it is to be overlooked.
> ▶ **Mae West, *Belle of the Nineties*, 1934**

Maybe we can learn a lesson from Ms. West. It's not just what you've got, but also how you package it. Having the best ideas, the finest code, or the most pragmatic thinking is ultimately sterile unless you can communicate with other people. A good idea is an orphan without effective communication.

As developers, we have to communicate on many levels. We spend hours in meetings, listening and talking. We work with end users, trying to understand their needs. We write code, which communicates our intentions to a machine and documents our thinking for future generations of developers. We write proposals and memos requesting and justifying resources, reporting our status, and suggesting new approaches. And we work daily within our teams to advocate our ideas, modify existing practices, and suggest new ones. A large part of our day is spent communicating, so we need to do it well.

We've put together a list of ideas that we find useful.

Know What You Want to Say

Probably the most difficult part of the more formal styles of communication used in business is working out exactly what it is you want to say. Fiction writers plot out their books in detail before they start, but people writing technical documents are often happy to sit down at a keyboard, enter "1. Introduction," and start typing whatever comes into their heads next.

Plan what you want to say. Write an outline. Then ask yourself, "Does this get across whatever I'm trying to say?" Refine it until it does.

This approach is not just applicable to writing documents. When you're faced with an important meeting or a phone call with a major client, jot down the ideas you want to communicate, and plan a couple of strategies for getting them across.

Know Your Audience

You're communicating only if you're conveying information. To do that, you need to understand the needs, interests, and capabilities of your audience. We've all sat in meetings where a development geek glazes over the eyes of the vice president of marketing with a long monologue on the merits of some arcane technology. This isn't communicating: it's just talking, and it's annoying.[5]

Form a strong mental picture of your audience. The acrostic WISDOM, shown in Figure 1.1 on the following page, may help.

Say you want to suggest a Web-based system to allow your end users to submit bug reports. You can present this system in many different ways, depending on your audience. End users will appreciate that they can submit bug reports 24 hours a day without waiting on the phone. Your marketing department will be able to use this fact to boost sales. Managers in the support department will have two reasons to be happy: fewer staff will be needed, and problem reporting will be automated. Finally, developers may enjoy getting experience with Web-based client-server technologies and a new database engine. By making the appropriate pitch to each group, you'll get them all excited about your project.

Choose Your Moment

It's six o'clock on Friday afternoon, following a week when the auditors have been in. Your boss's youngest is in the hospital, it's pouring rain outside, and the commute home is guaranteed to be a nightmare. This probably isn't a good time to ask her for a memory upgrade for your PC.

As part of understanding what your audience needs to hear, you need to work out what their priorities are. Catch a manager who's just been given a hard time by her boss because some source code got lost, and

---

5.   The word *annoy* comes from the Old French *enui*, which also means "to bore."

Figure 1.1.   The WISDOM acrostic—understanding an audience

What do you want them to learn?
What is their **i**nterest in what you've got to say?
How **s**ophisticated are they?
How much **d**etail do they want?
Whom do you want to **o**wn the information?
How can you **m**otivate them to listen to you?

---

you'll have a more receptive listener to your ideas on source code repositories. Make what you're saying relevant in time, as well as in content. Sometimes all it takes is the simple question "Is this a good time to talk about...?"

Choose a Style

Adjust the style of your delivery to suit your audience. Some people want a formal "just the facts" briefing. Others like a long, wide-ranging chat before getting down to business. When it comes to written documents, some like to receive large bound reports, while others expect a simple memo or e-mail. If in doubt, ask.

Remember, however, that you are half of the communication transaction. If someone says they need a paragraph describing something and you can't see any way of doing it in less than several pages, tell them so. Remember, that kind of feedback is a form of communication, too.

Make It Look Good

Your ideas are important. They deserve a good-looking vehicle to convey them to your audience.

Too many developers (and their managers) concentrate solely on content when producing written documents. We think this is a mistake. Any chef will tell you that you can slave in the kitchen for hours only to ruin your efforts with poor presentation.

There is no excuse today for producing poor-looking printed documents. Modern word processors (along with layout systems such as LaTeX and troff) can produce stunning output. You need to learn just a few basic commands. If your word processor supports style sheets, use them. (Your company may already have defined style sheets that you can use.) Learn how to set page headers and footers. Look at the sample documents included with your package to get ideas on style and layout. *Check the spelling,* first automatically and then by hand. After awl, their are spelling miss steaks that the chequer can knot ketch.

Involve Your Audience

We often find that the documents we produce end up being less important than the process we go through to produce them. If possible, involve your readers with early drafts of your document. Get their feedback, and pick their brains. You'll build a good working relationship, and you'll probably produce a better document in the process.

Be a Listener

There's one technique that you must use if you want people to listen to you: *listen to them.* Even if this is a situation where you have all the information, even if this is a formal meeting with you standing in front of 20 suits—if you don't listen to them, they won't listen to you.

Encourage people to talk by asking questions, or have them summarize what you tell them. Turn the meeting into a dialog, and you'll make your point more effectively. Who knows, you might even learn something.

Get Back to People

If you ask someone a question, you feel they're impolite if they don't respond. But how often do you fail to get back to people when they send you an e-mail or a memo asking for information or requesting some action? In the rush of everyday life, it's easy to forget. Always respond to e-mails and voice mails, even if the response is simply "I'll get back to you later." Keeping people informed makes them far more forgiving of the occasional slip, and makes them feel that you haven't forgotten them.

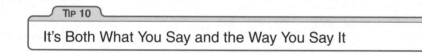

TIP 10

It's Both What You Say and the Way You Say It

Unless you work in a vacuum, you need to be able to communicate. The more effective that communication, the more influential you become.

E-Mail Communication

Everything we've said about communicating in writing applies equally to electronic mail. E-mail has evolved to the point where it is a mainstay of intra- and intercorporate communications. E-mail is used to discuss contracts, to settle disputes, and as evidence in court. But for some reason, people who would never send out a shabby paper document are happy to fling nasty-looking e-mail around the world.

Our e-mail tips are simple:

- Proofread before you hit SEND.

- Check the spelling.

- Keep the format simple. Some people read e-mail using proportional fonts, so the ASCII art pictures you laboriously created will look to them like hen-scratchings.

- Use rich-text or HTML formatted mail only if you know that all your recipients can read it. Plain text is universal.

- Try to keep quoting to a minimum. No one likes to receive back their own 100-line e-mail with "I agree" tacked on.

- If you're quoting other people's e-mail, be sure to attribute it, and quote it inline (rather than as an attachment).

- Don't flame unless you want it to come back and haunt you later.

- Check your list of recipients before sending. A recent *Wall Street Journal* article described an employee who took to distributing criticisms of his boss over departmental e-mail, without realizing that his boss was included on the distribution list.

- Archive and organize your e-mail—both the important stuff you receive and the mail you send.

As various Microsoft and Netscape employees discovered during the 1999 Department of Justice investigation, e-mail is forever. Try to give the same attention and care to e-mail as you would to any written memo or report.

Summary
- Know what you want to say.
- Know your audience.
- Choose your moment.
- Choose a style.
- Make it look good.
- Involve your audience.
- Be a listener.
- Get back to people.

Related sections include:
- *Prototypes and Post-it Notes*, page 53
- *Pragmatic Teams*, page 224

Challenges
- There are several good books that contain sections on communications within development teams [Bro95, McC95, DL99]. Make it a point to try to read all three over the next 18 months. In addition, the book *Dinosaur Brains* [Ber96] discusses the emotional baggage we all bring to the work environment.

- The next time you have to give a presentation, or write a memo advocating some position, try working through the WISDOM acrostic on page 20 before you start. See if it helps you understand how to position what you say. If appropriate, talk to your audience afterward and see how accurate your assessment of their needs was.

Chapter 2

A Pragmatic Approach

There are certain tips and tricks that apply at all levels of software development, ideas that are almost axiomatic, and processes that are virtually universal. However, these approaches are rarely documented as such; you'll mostly find them written down as odd sentences in discussions of design, project management, or coding.

In this chapter we'll bring these ideas and processes together. The first two sections, *The Evils of Duplication* and *Orthogonality*, are closely related. The first warns you not to duplicate knowledge throughout your systems, the second not to split any one piece of knowledge across multiple system components.

As the pace of change increases, it becomes harder and harder to keep our applications relevant. In *Reversibility*, we'll look at some techniques that help insulate your projects from their changing environment.

The next two sections are also related. In *Tracer Bullets*, we talk about a style of development that allows you to gather requirements, test designs, and implement code at the same time. If this sounds too good to be true, it is: tracer bullet developments are not always applicable. When they're not, *Prototypes and Post-it Notes* shows you how to use prototyping to test architectures, algorithms, interfaces, and ideas.

As computer science slowly matures, designers are producing increasingly higher-level languages. While the compiler that accepts "make it so" hasn't yet been invented, in *Domain Languages* we present some more modest suggestions that you can implement for yourself.

Finally, we all work in a world of limited time and resources. You can survive both of these scarcities better (and keep your bosses happier) if you get good at working out how long things will take, which we cover in *Estimating*.

By keeping these fundamental principles in mind during development, you can write code that's better, faster, and stronger. You can even make it look easy.

The Evils of Duplication

Giving a computer two contradictory pieces of knowledge was Captain James T. Kirk's preferred way of disabling a marauding artificial intelligence. Unfortunately, the same principle can be effective in bringing down *your* code.

As programmers, we collect, organize, maintain, and harness knowledge. We document knowledge in specifications, we make it come alive in running code, and we use it to provide the checks needed during testing.

Unfortunately, knowledge isn't stable. It changes—often rapidly. Your understanding of a requirement may change following a meeting with the client. The government changes a regulation and some business logic gets outdated. Tests may show that the chosen algorithm won't work. All this instability means that we spend a large part of our time in maintenance mode, reorganizing and reexpressing the knowledge in our systems.

Most people assume that maintenance begins when an application is released, that maintenance means fixing bugs and enhancing features. We think these people are wrong. Programmers are constantly in maintenance mode. Our understanding changes day by day. New requirements arrive as we're designing or coding. Perhaps the environment changes. Whatever the reason, maintenance is not a discrete activity, but a routine part of the entire development process.

When we perform maintenance, we have to find and change the representations of things—those capsules of knowledge embedded in the application. The problem is that it's easy to duplicate knowledge in the specifications, processes, and programs that we develop, and when we do so, we invite a maintenance nightmare—one that starts well before the application ships.

We feel that the only way to develop software reliably, and to make our developments easier to understand and maintain, is to follow what we call the *DRY* principle:

> EVERY PIECE OF KNOWLEDGE MUST HAVE A SINGLE, UNAMBIGUOUS, AUTHORITATIVE REPRESENTATION WITHIN A SYSTEM.

Why do we call it *DRY*?

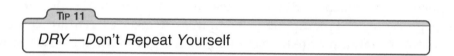

TIP 11

DRY—Don't Repeat Yourself

The alternative is to have the same thing expressed in two or more places. If you change one, you have to remember to change the others, or, like the alien computers, your program will be brought to its knees by a contradiction. It isn't a question of whether you'll remember: it's a question of when you'll forget.

You'll find the *DRY* principle popping up time and time again throughout this book, often in contexts that have nothing to do with coding. We feel that it is one of the most important tools in the Pragmatic Programmer's tool box.

In this section we'll outline the problems of duplication and suggest general strategies for dealing with it.

How Does Duplication Arise?

Most of the duplication we see falls into one of the following categories:

- **Imposed duplication.** Developers feel they have no choice—the environment seems to require duplication.

- **Inadvertent duplication.** Developers don't realize that they are duplicating information.

- **Impatient duplication.** Developers get lazy and duplicate because it seems easier.

- **Interdeveloper duplication.** Multiple people on a team (or on different teams) duplicate a piece of information.

Let's look at these four *i*'s of duplication in more detail.

Imposed Duplication

Sometimes, duplication seems to be forced on us. Project standards may require documents that contain duplicated information, or documents that duplicate information in the code. Multiple target platforms each require their own programming languages, libraries, and development environments, which makes us duplicate shared definitions and procedures. Programming languages themselves require certain structures that duplicate information. We have all worked in situations where we felt powerless to avoid duplication. And yet often there are ways of keeping each piece of knowledge in one place, honoring the *DRY* principle, and making our lives easier at the same time. Here are some techniques:

Multiple representations of information. At the coding level, we often need to have the same information represented in different forms. Maybe we're writing a client-server application, using different languages on the client and server, and need to represent some shared structure on both. Perhaps we need a class whose attributes mirror the schema of a database table. Maybe you're writing a book and want to include excerpts of programs that you also will compile and test.

With a bit of ingenuity you can normally remove the need for duplication. Often the answer is to write a simple filter or code generator. Structures in multiple languages can be built from a common metadata representation using a simple code generator each time the software is built (an example of this is shown in Figure 3.4, page 106). Class definitions can be generated automatically from the online database schema, or from the metadata used to build the schema in the first place. The code extracts in this book are inserted by a preprocessor each time we format the text. The trick is to make the process active: this cannot be a one-time conversion, or we're back in a position of duplicating data.

Documentation in code. Programmers are taught to comment their code: good code has lots of comments. Unfortunately, they are never taught *why* code needs comments: bad code *requires* lots of comments.

The *DRY* principle tells us to keep the low-level knowledge in the code, where it belongs, and reserve the comments for other, high-level explanations. Otherwise, we're duplicating knowledge, and every change means changing both the code and the comments. The comments will inevitably become out of date, and untrustworthy comments are worse than no comments at all. (See *It's All Writing*, page 248, for more information on comments.)

Documentation and code. You write documentation, then you write code. Something changes, and you amend the documentation and update the code. The documentation and code both contain representations of the same knowledge. And we all know that in the heat of the moment, with deadlines looming and important clients clamoring, we tend to defer the updating of documentation.

Dave once worked on an international telex switch. Quite understandably, the client demanded an exhaustive test specification and required that the software pass all tests on each delivery. To ensure that the tests accurately reflected the specification, the team generated them programmatically from the document itself. When the client amended their specification, the test suite changed automatically. Once the team convinced the client that the procedure was sound, generating acceptance tests typically took only a few seconds.

Language issues. Many languages impose considerable duplication in the source. Often this comes about when the language separates a module's interface from its implementation. C and C++ have header files that duplicate the names and type information of exported variables, functions, and (for C++) classes. Object Pascal even duplicates this information in the same file. If you are using remote procedure calls or CORBA [URL 29], you'll duplicate interface information between the interface specification and the code that implements it.

There is no easy technique for overcoming the requirements of a language. While some development environments hide the need for header files by generating them automatically, and Object Pascal allows you to abbreviate repeated function declarations, you are generally stuck with what you're given. At least with most language-based issues, a header file that disagrees with the implementation will generate some form of compilation or linkage error. You can still get things wrong, but at least you'll be told about it fairly early on.

Think also about comments in header and implementation files. There is absolutely no point in duplicating a function or class header comment between the two files. Use the header files to document interface issues, and the implementation files to document the nitty-gritty details that users of your code don't need to know.

Inadvertent Duplication

Sometimes, duplication comes about as the result of mistakes in the design.

Let's look at an example from the distribution industry. Say our analysis reveals that, among other attributes, a truck has a type, a license number, and a driver. Similarly, a delivery route is a combination of a route, a truck, and a driver. We code up some classes based on this understanding.

But what happens when Sally calls in sick and we have to change drivers? Both Truck and DeliveryRoute contain a driver. Which one do we change? Clearly this duplication is bad. Normalize it according to the underlying business model—does a truck really have a driver as part of its underlying attribute set? Does a route? Or maybe there needs to be a third object that knits together a driver, a truck, and a route. Whatever the eventual solution, avoid this kind of unnormalized data.

There is a slightly less obvious kind of unnormalized data that occurs when we have multiple data elements that are mutually dependent. Let's look at a class representing a line:

```
class Line {
 public:
   Point  start;
   Point  end;
   double length;
};
```

At first sight, this class might appear reasonable. A line clearly has a start and end, and will always have a length (even if it's zero). But we have duplication. The length is defined by the start and end points: change one of the points and the length changes. It's better to make the length a calculated field:

```
class Line {
 public:
   Point   start;
   Point   end;
   double length() { return start.distanceTo(end); }
};
```

Later on in the development process, you may choose to violate the *DRY* principle for performance reasons. Frequently this occurs when you need to cache data to avoid repeating expensive operations. The trick is to localize the impact. The violation is not exposed to the outside world: only the methods within the class have to worry about keeping things straight.

```
class Line {
 private:
   bool    changed;
   double length;
   Point   start;
   Point   end;
 public:
   void setStart(Point p) { start = p; changed = true; }
   void setEnd(Point p)   { end   = p; changed = true; }

   Point getStart(void)   { return start; }
   Point getEnd(void)     { return end;   }

   double getLength() {
     if (changed) {
       length  = start.distanceTo(end);
       changed = false;
     }
     return length;
   }
};
```

This example also illustrates an important issue for object-oriented languages such as Java and C++. Where possible, always use accessor functions to read and write the attributes of objects.[1] It will make it easier to add functionality, such as caching, in the future.

---

1. The use of accessor functions ties in with Meyer's *Uniform Access principle* [Mey97b], which states that "All services offered by a module should be available through a uniform notation, which does not betray whether they are implemented through storage or through computation."

Impatient Duplication

Every project has time pressures—forces that can drive the best of us to take shortcuts. Need a routine similar to one you've written? You'll be tempted to copy the original and make a few changes. Need a value to represent the maximum number of points? If I change the header file, the whole project will get rebuilt. Maybe I should just use a literal number here; and here; and here. Need a class like one in the Java runtime? The source is available, so why not just copy it and make the changes you need (license provisions notwithstanding)?

If you feel this temptation, remember the hackneyed aphorism "short cuts make for long delays." You may well save some seconds now, but at the potential loss of hours later. Think about the issues surrounding the Y2K fiasco. Many were caused by the laziness of developers not parameterizing the size of date fields or implementing centralized libraries of date services.

Impatient duplication is an easy form to detect and handle, but it takes discipline and a willingness to spend time up front to save pain later.

Interdeveloper Duplication

On the other hand, perhaps the hardest type of duplication to detect and handle occurs between different developers on a project. Entire sets of functionality may be inadvertently duplicated, and that duplication could go undetected for years, leading to maintenance problems. We heard firsthand of a U.S. state whose governmental computer systems were surveyed for Y2K compliance. The audit turned up more than 10,000 programs, each containing its own version of Social Security number validation.

At a high level, deal with the problem by having a clear design, a strong technical project leader (see page 228 in *Pragmatic Teams*), and a well-understood division of responsibilities within the design. However, at the module level, the problem is more insidious. Commonly needed functionality or data that doesn't fall into an obvious area of responsibility can get implemented many times over.

We feel that the best way to deal with this is to encourage active and frequent communication between developers. Set up forums to discuss common problems. (On past projects, we have set up private Usenet newsgroups to allow developers to exchange ideas and ask questions. This provides a nonintrusive way of communicating—even across multiple sites—while retaining a permanent history of everything said.) Appoint a team member as the project librarian, whose job is to facilitate the exchange of knowledge. Have a central place in the source tree where utility routines and scripts can be deposited. And make a point of reading other people's source code and documentation, either informally or during code reviews. You're not snooping—you're learning from them. And remember, the access is reciprocal—don't get twisted about other people poring (pawing?) through *your* code, either.

Tip 12

Make It Easy to Reuse

What you're trying to do is foster an environment where it's easier to find and reuse existing stuff than to write it yourself. *If it isn't easy, people won't do it.* And if you fail to reuse, you risk duplicating knowledge.

Related sections include:

Orthogonality

8 ▶

Orthogonality is a critical concept if you want to produce systems that are easy to design, build, test, and extend. However, the concept of orthogonality is rarely taught directly. Often it is an implicit feature of various other methods and techniques you learn. This is a mistake. Once you learn to apply the principle of orthogonality directly, you'll notice an immediate improvement in the quality of systems you produce.

What Is Orthogonality?

"Orthogonality" is a term borrowed from geometry. Two lines are orthogonal if they meet at right angles, such as the axes on a graph. In vector terms, the two lines are *independent*. Move along one of the lines, and your position projected onto the other doesn't change.

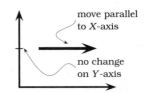

move parallel to X-axis

no change on Y-axis

In computing, the term has come to signify a kind of independence or decoupling. Two or more things are orthogonal if changes in one do not affect any of the others. In a well-designed system, the database code will be orthogonal to the user interface: you can change the interface without affecting the database, and swap databases without changing the interface.

Before we look at the benefits of orthogonal systems, let's first look at a system that isn't orthogonal.

A Nonorthogonal System

You're on a helicopter tour of the Grand Canyon when the pilot, who made the obvious mistake of eating fish for lunch, suddenly groans and faints. Fortunately, he left you hovering 100 feet above the ground. You rationalize that the collective pitch lever[2] controls overall lift, so lower-

---

2. Helicopters have four basic controls. The *cyclic* is the stick you hold in your right hand. Move it, and the helicopter moves in the corresponding direction. Your left hand holds the *collective pitch lever*. Pull up on this and you increase the pitch on all the blades, generating lift. At the end of the pitch lever is the *throttle*. Finally you have two foot *pedals*, which vary the amount of tail rotor thrust and so help turn the helicopter.

ing it slightly will start a gentle descent to the ground. However, when you try it, you discover that life isn't that simple. The helicopter's nose drops, and you start to spiral down to the left. Suddenly you discover that you're flying a system where every control input has secondary effects. Lower the left-hand lever and you need to add compensating backward movement to the right-hand stick and push the right pedal. But then each of these changes affects all of the other controls again. Suddenly you're juggling an unbelievably complex system, where every change impacts all the other inputs. Your workload is phenomenal: your hands and feet are constantly moving, trying to balance all the interacting forces.

Helicopter controls are decidedly not orthogonal.

Benefits of Orthogonality

As the helicopter example illustrates, nonorthogonal systems are inherently more complex to change and control. When components of any system are highly interdependent, there is no such thing as a local fix.

Tip 13

Eliminate Effects Between Unrelated Things

We want to design components that are self-contained: independent, and with a single, well-defined purpose (what Yourdon and Constantine call *cohesion* [YC86]). When components are isolated from one another, you know that you can change one without having to worry about the rest. As long as you don't change that component's external interfaces, you can be comfortable that you won't cause problems that ripple through the entire system.

You get two major benefits if you write orthogonal systems: increased productivity and reduced risk.

Gain Productivity

- Changes are localized, so development time and testing time are reduced. It is easier to write relatively small, self-contained components than a single large block of code. Simple components can be designed, coded, unit tested, and then forgotten—there is no need to keep changing existing code as you add new code.

- An orthogonal approach also promotes reuse. If components have specific, well-defined responsibilities, they can be combined with new components in ways that were not envisioned by their original implementors. The more loosely coupled your systems, the easier they are to reconfigure and reengineer.

- There is a fairly subtle gain in productivity when you combine orthogonal components. Assume that one component does M distinct things and another does N things. If they are orthogonal and you combine them, the result does $M \times N$ things. However, if the two components are not orthogonal, there will be overlap, and the result will do less. You get more functionality per unit effort by combining orthogonal components.

Reduce Risk

An orthogonal approach reduces the risks inherent in any development.

- Diseased sections of code are isolated. If a module is sick, it is less likely to spread the symptoms around the rest of the system. It is also easier to slice it out and transplant in something new and healthy.

- The resulting system is less fragile. Make small changes and fixes to a particular area, and any problems you generate will be restricted to that area.

- An orthogonal system will probably be better tested, because it will be easier to design and run tests on its components.

- You will not be as tightly tied to a particular vendor, product, or platform, because the interfaces to these third-party components will be isolated to smaller parts of the overall development.

Let's look at some of the ways you can apply the principle of orthogonality to your work.

Project Teams

Have you noticed how some project teams are efficient, with everyone knowing what to do and contributing fully, while the members of other teams are constantly bickering and don't seem able to get out of each other's way?

Often this is an orthogonality issue. When teams are organized with lots of overlap, members are confused about responsibilities. Every change needs a meeting of the entire team, because any one of them *might* be affected.

How do you organize teams into groups with well-defined responsibilities and minimal overlap? There's no simple answer. It depends partly on the project and your analysis of the areas of potential change. It also depends on the people you have available. Our preference is to start by separating infrastructure from application. Each major infrastructure component (database, communications interface, middleware layer, and so on) gets its own subteam. Each obvious division of application functionality is similarly divided. Then we look at the people we have (or plan to have) and adjust the groupings accordingly.

You can get an informal measure of the orthogonality of a project team's structure. Simply see how many people *need* to be involved in discussing each change that is requested. The larger the number, the less orthogonal the group. Clearly, an orthogonal team is more efficient. (Having said this, we also encourage subteams to communicate constantly with each other.)

Design

Most developers are familiar with the need to design orthogonal systems, although they may use words such as *modular*, *component-based*, and *layered* to describe the process. Systems should be composed of a set of cooperating modules, each of which implements functionality independent of the others. Sometimes these components are organized into layers, each providing a level of abstraction. This layered approach is a powerful way to design orthogonal systems. Because each layer uses only the abstractions provided by the layers below it, you have great flexibility in changing underlying implementations without affecting code. Layering also reduces the risk of runaway dependencies between modules. You'll often see layering expressed in diagrams such as Figure 2.1 on the next page.

There is an easy test for orthogonal design. Once you have your components mapped out, ask yourself: *If I dramatically change the require-*

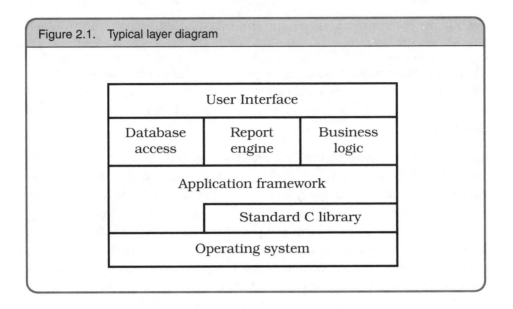

Figure 2.1. Typical layer diagram

ments behind a particular function, how many modules are affected? In an orthogonal system, the answer should be "one."[3] Moving a button on a GUI panel should not require a change in the database schema. Adding context-sensitive help should not change the billing subsystem.

Let's consider a complex system for monitoring and controlling a heating plant. The original requirement called for a graphical user interface, but the requirements were changed to add a voice response system with touchtone telephone control of the plant. In an orthogonally designed system, you would need to change only those modules associated with the user interface to handle this: the underlying logic of controlling the plant would remain unchanged. In fact, if you structure your system carefully, you should be able to support both interfaces with the same underlying code base. *It's Just a View*, page 157, talks about writing decoupled code using the Model-View-Controller (MVC) paradigm, which works well in this situation.

---

3.   In reality, this is naive. Unless you are remarkably lucky, most real-world requirements changes will affect multiple functions in the system. However, if you analyze the change in terms of functions, each functional change should still ideally affect just one module.

Also ask yourself how decoupled your design is from changes in the real world. Are you using a telephone number as a customer identifier? What happens when the phone company reassigns area codes? *Don't rely on the properties of things you can't control.*

Toolkits and Libraries

Be careful to preserve the orthogonality of your system as you introduce third-party toolkits and libraries. Choose your technologies wisely.

We once worked on a project that required that a certain body of Java code run both locally on a server machine and remotely on a client machine. The alternatives for distributing classes this way were RMI and CORBA. If a class were made remotely accessible using RMI, every call to a remote method in that class could potentially throw an exception, which means that a naive implementation would require us to handle the exception whenever our remote classes were used. Using RMI here is clearly not orthogonal: code calling our remote classes should not have to be aware of their locations. The alternative—using CORBA—did not impose that restriction: we could write code that was unaware of our classes' locations.

When you bring in a toolkit (or even a library from other members of your team), ask yourself whether it imposes changes on your code that shouldn't be there. If an object persistence scheme is transparent, then it's orthogonal. If it requires you to create or access objects in a special way, then it's not. Keeping such details isolated from your code has the added benefit of making it easier to change vendors in the future.

The Enterprise Java Beans (EJB) system is an interesting example of orthogonality. In most transaction-oriented systems, the application code has to delineate the start and end of each transaction. With EJB, this information is expressed declaratively as metadata, outside any code. The same application code can run in different EJB transaction environments with no change. This is likely to be a model for many future environments.

Another interesting twist on orthogonality is Aspect-Oriented Programming (AOP), a research project at Xerox Parc ([KLM+97] and [URL 49]). AOP lets you express in one place behavior that would otherwise be distributed throughout your source code. For example, log messages are normally generated by sprinkling explicit calls to some log function throughout your source. With AOP, you implement logging orthogonally to the things being logged. Using the Java version of AOP, you could write a log message when entering any method of class Fred by coding the *aspect*:

```
aspect Trace {
  advise * Fred.*(..) {
    static before {
      Log.write("-> Entering " + thisJoinPoint.methodName);
    }
  }
}
```

If you *weave* this aspect into your code, trace messages will be generated. If you don't, you'll see no messages. Either way, your original source is unchanged.

Coding

Every time you write code you run the risk of reducing the orthogonality of your application. Unless you constantly monitor not just what you are doing but also the larger context of the application, you might unintentionally duplicate functionality in some other module, or express existing knowledge twice.

There are several techniques you can use to maintain orthogonality:

- **Keep your code decoupled.**   Write shy code—modules that don't reveal anything unnecessary to other modules and that don't rely on other modules' implementations. Try the Law of Demeter [LH89], which we discuss in *Decoupling and the Law of Demeter*, page 138. If you need to change an object's state, get the object to do it for you. This way your code remains isolated from the other code's implementation and increases the chances that you'll remain orthogonal.

- **Avoid global data.**   Every time your code references global data, it ties itself into the other components that share that data. Even globals that you intend only to read can lead to trouble (for example, if you suddenly need to change your code to be multithreaded). In general, your code is easier to understand and maintain if you explicitly pass any required context into your modules. In object-oriented applications, context is often passed as parameters to objects' constructors. In other code, you can create structures containing the context and pass around references to them.

The Singleton pattern in *Design Patterns* [GHJV95] is a way of ensuring that there is only one instance of an object of a particular class. Many people use these singleton objects as a kind of global variable (particularly in languages, such as Java, that otherwise do not support the concept of globals). Be careful with singletons—they can also lead to unnecessary linkage.

- **Avoid similar functions.** Often you'll come across a set of functions that all look similar—maybe they share common code at the start and end, but each has a different central algorithm. Duplicate code is a symptom of structural problems. Have a look at the Strategy pattern in *Design Patterns* for a better implementation.

Get into the habit of being constantly critical of your code. Look for any opportunities to reorganize it to improve its structure and orthogonality. This process is called *refactoring*, and it's so important that we've dedicated a section to it (see *Refactoring*, page 184).

Testing

An orthogonally designed and implemented system is easier to test. Because the interactions between the system's components are formalized and limited, more of the system testing can be performed at the individual module level. This is good news, because module level (or unit) testing is considerably easier to specify and perform than integration testing. In fact, we suggest that every module have its own unit test built into its code, and that these tests be performed automatically as part of the regular build process (see *Code That's Easy to Test*, page 189).

Building unit tests is itself an interesting test of orthogonality. What does it take to build and link a unit test? Do you have to drag in a large percentage of the rest of the system just to get a test to compile or link? If so, you've found a module that is not well decoupled from the rest of the system.

Bug fixing is also a good time to assess the orthogonality of the system as a whole. When you come across a problem, assess how localized the fix is. Do you change just one module, or are the changes scattered throughout the entire system? When you make a change, does it fix everything, or do other problems mysteriously arise? This is a good opportunity to bring automation to bear. If you use a source code control system (and you will after reading *Source Code Control*, page 86), tag bug fixes when you check the code back in after testing. You can then run monthly reports analyzing trends in the number of source files affected by each bug fix.

Documentation

Perhaps surprisingly, orthogonality also applies to documentation. The axes are content and presentation. With truly orthogonal documentation, you should be able to change the appearance dramatically without changing the content. Modern word processors provide style sheets and macros that help (see *It's All Writing*, page 248).

Living with Orthogonality

Orthogonality is closely related to the *DRY* principle introduced on page 27. With *DRY*, you're looking to minimize duplication within a system, whereas with orthogonality you reduce the interdependency among the system's components. It may be a clumsy word, but if you use the principle of orthogonality, combined closely with the *DRY* principle, you'll find that the systems you develop are more flexible, more understandable, and easier to debug, test, and maintain.

If you're brought into a project where people are desperately struggling to make changes, and where every change seems to cause four other things to go wrong, remember the nightmare with the helicopter. The project probably is not orthogonally designed and coded. It's time to refactor.

And, if you're a helicopter pilot, don't eat the fish....

Related sections include:
- *The Evils of Duplication*, page 26
- *Source Code Control*, page 86
- *Design by Contract*, page 109
- *Decoupling and the Law of Demeter*, page 138

Challenges

- Consider the difference between large GUI-oriented tools typically found on Windows systems and small but combinable command line utilities used at shell prompts. Which set is more orthogonal, and why? Which is easier to use for exactly the purpose for which it was intended? Which set is easier to combine with other tools to meet new challenges?

- C++ supports multiple inheritance, and Java allows a class to implement multiple interfaces. What impact does using these facilities have on orthogonality? Is there a difference in impact between using multiple inheritance and multiple interfaces? Is there a difference between using delegation and using inheritance?

Exercises

1. You are writing a class called `Split`, which splits input lines into fields. Which of the following two Java class signatures is the more orthogonal design?

   Answer on p. 279

```
class Split1 {
  public Split1(InputStreamReader rdr) { ...
  public void readNextLine() throws IOException { ...
  public int numFields() { ...
  public String getField(int fieldNo) { ...
}
class Split2 {
  public Split2(String line) { ...
  public int numFields()     { ...
  public String getField(int fieldNo) { ...
}
```

2. Which will lead to a more orthogonal design: modeless or modal dialog boxes?

   Answer on p. 279

3. How about procedural languages versus object technology? Which results in a more orthogonal system?

   Answer on p. 280

Reversibility

Nothing is more dangerous than an idea if it's the only one you have.
▶ **Emil-Auguste Chartier, *Propos sur la religion*, 1938**

Engineers prefer simple, single solutions to problems. Math tests that allow you to proclaim with great confidence that $x = 2$ are much more comfortable than fuzzy, warm essays about the myriad causes of the French Revolution. Management tends to agree with the engineers: single, easy answers fit nicely on spreadsheets and project plans.

If only the real world would cooperate! Unfortunately, while x is 2 today, it may need to be 5 tomorrow, and 3 next week. Nothing is forever—and if you rely heavily on some fact, you can almost guarantee that it *will* change.

There is always more than one way to implement something, and there is usually more than one vendor available to provide a third-party product. If you go into a project hampered by the myopic notion that there is only *one* way to do it, you may be in for an unpleasant surprise. Many project teams have their eyes forcibly opened as the future unfolds:

> *"But you said we'd use database XYZ! We are 85% done coding the project, we can't change now!" the programmer protested. "Sorry, but our company decided to standardize on database PDQ instead—for all projects. It's out of my hands. We'll just have to recode. All of you will be working weekends until further notice."*

Changes don't have to be that Draconian, or even that immediate. But as time goes by, and your project progresses, you may find yourself stuck in an untenable position. With every critical decision, the project team commits to a smaller target—a narrower version of reality that has fewer options.

By the time many critical decisions have been made, the target becomes so small that if it moves, or the wind changes direction, or a butterfly in Tokyo flaps its wings, you miss.[4] And you may miss by a huge amount.

---

4. Take a nonlinear, or chaotic, system and apply a small change to one of its inputs. You may get a large and often unpredictable result. The clichéd butterfly flapping its wings in Tokyo could be the start of a chain of events that ends up generating a tornado in Texas. Does this sound like any projects you know?

The problem is that critical decisions aren't easily reversible.

Once you decide to use this vendor's database, or that architectural pattern, or a certain deployment model (client-server versus stand-alone, for instance), you are committed to a course of action that cannot be undone, except at great expense.

Reversibility

Many of the topics in this book are geared to producing flexible, adaptable software. By sticking to their recommendations—especially the *DRY* principle (page 26), decoupling (page 138), and use of metadata (page 144)—we don't have to make as many critical, irreversible decisions. This is a good thing, because we don't always make the best decisions the first time around. We commit to a certain technology only to discover we can't hire enough people with the necessary skills. We lock in a certain third-party vendor just before they get bought out by their competitor. Requirements, users, and hardware change faster than we can get the software developed.

Suppose you decide, early in the project, to use a relational database from vendor A. Much later, during performance testing, you discover that the database is simply too slow, but that the object database from vendor B is faster. With most conventional projects, you'd be out of luck. Most of the time, calls to third-party products are entangled throughout the code. But if you *really* abstracted the idea of a database out—to the point where it simply provides persistence as a service—then you have the flexibility to change horses in midstream.

Similarly, suppose the project begins as a client-server model, but then, late in the game, marketing decides that servers are too expensive for some clients, and they want a stand-alone version. How hard would that be for you? Since it's just a deployment issue, *it shouldn't take more than a few days*. If it would take longer, then you haven't thought about reversibility. The other direction is even more interesting. What if the stand-alone product you are making needs to be deployed in a client-server or *n*-tier fashion? *That shouldn't be hard either.*

The mistake lies in assuming that any decision is cast in stone—and in not preparing for the contingencies that might arise. Instead of carving

decisions in stone, think of them more as being written in the sand at
the beach. A big wave can come along and wipe them out at any time.

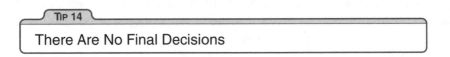

TIP 14

There Are No Final Decisions

Flexible Architecture

While many people try to keep their *code* flexible, you also need to think
about maintaining flexibility in the areas of architecture, deployment,
and vendor integration.

Technologies such as CORBA can help insulate portions of a project
from changes in development language or platform. Is the performance
of Java on that platform not up to expectations? Recode the client in
C++, and nothing else needs to change. Is the rules engine in C++
not flexible enough? Switch over to a Smalltalk version. With a CORBA
architecture, you have to take a hit only for the component you are
replacing; the other components shouldn't be affected.

Are you developing for Unix? Which one? Do you have all of the porta-
bility concerns addressed? Are you developing for a particular version
of Windows? Which one—3.1, 95, 98, NT, CE, or 2000? How hard will
it be to support other versions? If you keep decisions soft and pliable,
it won't be hard at all. If you have poor encapsulation, high coupling,
and hard-coded logic or parameters in the code, it might be impossible.

Not sure how marketing wants to deploy the system? Think about it up
front and you can support a stand-alone, client-server, or *n*-tier model
just by changing a configuration file. We've written programs that do
just that.

Normally, you can simply hide a third-party product behind a well-
defined, abstract interface. In fact, we've always been able to do so
on any project we've worked on. But suppose you couldn't isolate it
that cleanly. What if you had to sprinkle certain statements liberally
throughout the code? Put that requirement in metadata, and use some
automatic mechanism, such as Aspects (see page 39) or Perl, to insert
the necessary statements into the code itself. Whatever mechanism you

use, *make it reversible*. If something is added automatically, it can be taken out automatically as well.

No one knows what the future may hold, especially not us! So enable your code to rock-n-roll: to "rock on" when it can, to roll with the punches when it must.

Related sections include:
- *Decoupling and the Law of Demeter*, page 138
- *Metaprogramming*, page 144
- *It's Just a View*, page 157

Challenges
- Time for a little quantum mechanics with Schrödinger's cat. Suppose you have a cat in a closed box, along with a radioactive particle. The particle has exactly a 50% chance of fissioning into two. If it does, the cat will be killed. If it doesn't, the cat will be okay. So, is the cat dead or alive? According to Schrödinger, the correct answer is *both*. Every time a sub-nuclear reaction takes place that has two possible outcomes, the universe is cloned. In one, the event occurred, in the other it didn't. The cat's alive in one universe, dead in another. Only when you open the box do you know which universe *you* are in.

  No wonder coding for the future is difficult.

  But think of code evolution along the same lines as a box full of Schrödinger's cats: every decision results in a different version of the future. How many possible futures can your code support? Which ones are more likely? How hard will it be to support them when the time comes?

  Dare you open the box?

▶10 Tracer Bullets

Ready, fire, aim...

There are two ways to fire a machine gun in the dark.[5] You can find out exactly where your target is (range, elevation, and azimuth). You can determine the environmental conditions (temperature, humidity, air pressure, wind, and so on). You can determine the precise specifications of the cartridges and bullets you are using, and their interactions with the actual gun you are firing. You can then use tables or a firing computer to calculate the exact bearing and elevation of the barrel. If everything works exactly as specified, your tables are correct, and the environment doesn't change, your bullets should land close to their target.

Or you could use tracer bullets.

Tracer bullets are loaded at intervals on the ammo belt alongside regular ammunition. When they're fired, their phosphorus ignites and leaves a pyrotechnic trail from the gun to whatever they hit. If the tracers are hitting the target, then so are the regular bullets.

Not surprisingly, tracer bullets are preferred to the labor of calculation. The feedback is immediate, and because they operate in the same environment as the real ammunition, external effects are minimized.

The analogy might be violent, but it applies to new projects, particularly when you're building something that hasn't been built before. Like the gunners, you're trying to hit a target in the dark. Because your users have never seen a system like this before, their requirements may be vague. Because you may be using algorithms, techniques, languages, or libraries you aren't familiar with, you face a large number of unknowns. And because projects take time to complete, you can pretty much guarantee the environment you're working in will change before you're done.

The classic response is to specify the system to death. Produce reams of paper itemizing every requirement, tying down every unknown, and

---

5. To be pedantic, there are many ways of firing a machine gun in the dark, including closing your eyes and spraying out bullets. But this is an analogy, and we're allowed to take liberties.

constraining the environment. Fire the gun using dead reckoning. One big calculation up front, then shoot and hope.

Pragmatic Programmers, however, tend to prefer using tracer bullets.

Code That Glows in the Dark

Tracer bullets work because they operate in the same environment and under the same constraints as the real bullets. They get to the target fast, so the gunner gets immediate feedback. And from a practical standpoint they're a relatively cheap solution.

To get the same effect in code, we're looking for something that gets us from a requirement to some aspect of the final system quickly, visibly, and repeatably.

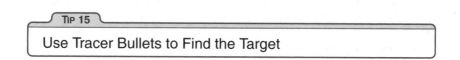

TIP 15

Use Tracer Bullets to Find the Target

We once undertook a complex client-server database marketing project. Part of its requirement was the ability to specify and execute temporal queries. The servers were a range of relational and specialized databases. The client GUI, written in Object Pascal, used a set of C libraries to provide an interface to the servers. The user's query was stored on the server in a Lisp-like notation before being converted to optimized SQL just prior to execution. There were many unknowns and many different environments, and no one was too sure how the GUI should behave.

This was a great opportunity to use tracer code. We developed the framework for the front end, libraries for representing the queries, and a structure for converting a stored query into a database-specific query. Then we put it all together and checked that it worked. For that initial build, all we could do was submit a query that listed all the rows in a table, but it proved that the UI could talk to the libraries, the libraries could serialize and unserialize a query, and the server could generate SQL from the result. Over the following months we gradually fleshed out this basic structure, adding new functionality by augmenting each component of the tracer code in parallel. When the UI added a new query type, the library grew and the SQL generation was made more sophisticated.

Tracer code is not disposable: you write it for keeps. It contains all the error checking, structuring, documentation, and self-checking that any piece of production code has. It simply is not fully functional. However, once you have achieved an end-to-end connection among the components of your system, you can check how close to the target you are, adjusting if necessary. Once you're on target, adding functionality is easy.

Tracer development is consistent with the idea that a project is never finished: there will always be changes required and functions to add. It is an incremental approach.

The conventional alternative is a kind of heavy engineering approach: code is divided into modules, which are coded in a vacuum. Modules are combined into subassemblies, which are then further combined, until one day you have a complete application. Only then can the application as a whole be presented to the user and tested.

The tracer code approach has many advantages:

- **Users get to see something working early.** If you have successfully communicated what you are doing (see *Great Expectations*, page 255), your users will know they are seeing something immature. They won't be disappointed by a lack of functionality; they'll be ecstatic to see some visible progress toward their system. They also get to contribute as the project progresses, increasing their buy-in. These same users will likely be the people who'll tell you how close to the target each iteration is.

- **Developers build a structure to work in.** The most daunting piece of paper is the one with nothing written on it. If you have worked out all the end-to-end interactions of your application, and have embodied them in code, then your team won't need to pull as much out of thin air. This makes everyone more productive, and encourages consistency.

- **You have an integration platform.** As the system is connected end-to-end, you have an environment to which you can add new pieces of code once they have been unit-tested. Rather than attempting a big-bang integration, you'll be integrating every day (often many times a day). The impact of each new change is more apparent, and the interactions are more limited, so debugging and testing are faster and more accurate.

- **You have something to demonstrate.** Project sponsors and top brass have a tendency to want to see demos at the most inconvenient times. With tracer code, you'll always have something to show them.

- **You have a better feel for progress.** In a tracer code development, developers tackle use cases one by one. When one is done, they move to the next. It is far easier to measure performance and to demonstrate progress to your user. Because each individual development is smaller, you avoid creating those monolithic blocks of code that are reported as 95% complete week after week.

Tracer Bullets Don't Always Hit Their Target

Tracer bullets show what you're hitting. This may not always be the target. You then adjust your aim until they're on target. That's the point.

It's the same with tracer code. You use the technique in situations where you're not 100% certain of where you're going. You shouldn't be surprised if your first couple of attempts miss: the user says "that's not what I meant," or data you need isn't available when you need it, or performance problems seem likely. Work out how to change what you've got to bring it nearer the target, and be thankful that you've used a lean development methodology. A small body of code has low inertia—it is easy and quick to change. You'll be able to gather feedback on your application and generate a new, more accurate version faster and at less cost than with any other method. And because every major application component is represented in your tracer code, your users can be confident that what they're seeing is based on reality, not just a paper specification.

Tracer Code versus Prototyping

You might think that this tracer code concept is nothing more than prototyping under an aggressive name. There is a difference. With a prototype, you're aiming to explore specific aspects of the final system. With a true prototype, you will throw away whatever you lashed together when trying out the concept, and recode it properly using the lessons you've learned.

For example, say you're producing an application that helps shippers determine how to pack odd-sized boxes into containers. Among other problems, the user interface needs to be intuitive and the algorithms you use to determine optimal packing are very complex.

You could prototype a user interface for your end users in a GUI tool. You code only enough to make the interface responsive to user actions. Once they've agreed to the layout, you might throw it away and recode it, this time with the business logic behind it, using the target language. Similarly, you might want to prototype a number of algorithms that perform the actual packing. You might code functional tests in a high-level, forgiving language such as Perl, and code low-level performance tests in something closer to the machine. In any case, once you'd made your decision, you'd start again and code the algorithms in their final environment, interfacing to the real world. This is *prototyping*, and it is very useful.

The tracer code approach addresses a different problem. You need to know how the application as a whole hangs together. You want to show your users how the interactions will work in practice, and you want to give your developers an architectural skeleton on which to hang code. In this case, you might construct a tracer consisting of a trivial implementation of the container packing algorithm (maybe something like first-come, first-served) and a simple but working user interface. Once you have all the components in the application plumbed together, you have a framework to show your users and your developers. Over time, you add to this framework with new functionality, completing stubbed routines. But the framework stays intact, and you know the system will continue to behave the way it did when your first tracer code was completed.

The distinction is important enough to warrant repeating. Prototyping generates disposable code. Tracer code is lean but complete, and forms part of the skeleton of the final system. Think of prototyping as the reconnaissance and intelligence gathering that takes place before a single tracer bullet is fired.

Related sections include:

▶ Prototypes and Post-it Notes

Many different industries use prototypes to try out specific ideas; prototyping is much cheaper than full-scale production. Car makers, for example, may build many different prototypes of a new car design. Each one is designed to test a specific aspect of the car—the aerodynamics, styling, structural characteristics, and so on. Perhaps a clay model will be built for wind tunnel testing, maybe a balsa wood and duct tape model will do for the art department, and so on. Some car companies take this a step further, and now do a great deal of modeling work on the computer, reducing costs even further. In this way, risky or uncertain elements can be tried out without committing to building the real item.

We build software prototypes in the same fashion, and for the same reasons—to analyze and expose risk, and to offer chances for correction at a greatly reduced cost. Like the car makers, we can target a prototype to test one or more specific aspects of a project.

We tend to think of prototypes as code-based, but they don't always have to be. Like the car makers, we can build prototypes out of different materials. Post-it notes are great for prototyping dynamic things such as workflow and application logic. A user interface can be prototyped as a drawing on a whiteboard, as a nonfunctional mock-up drawn with a paint program, or with an interface builder.

Prototypes are designed to answer just a few questions, so they are much cheaper and faster to develop than applications that go into production. The code can ignore unimportant details—unimportant to you at the moment, but probably very important to the user later on. If you are prototyping a GUI, for instance, you can get away with incorrect results or data. On the other hand, if you're just investigating computational or performance aspects, you can get away with a pretty poor GUI, or perhaps even no GUI at all.

But if you find yourself in an environment where you *cannot* give up the details, then you need to ask yourself if you are really building a prototype at all. Perhaps a tracer bullet style of development would be more appropriate in this case (see *Tracer Bullets*, page 48).

Things to Prototype

What sorts of things might you choose to investigate with a prototype? Anything that carries risk. Anything that hasn't been tried before, or that is absolutely critical to the final system. Anything unproven, experimental, or doubtful. Anything you aren't comfortable with. You can prototype

- Architecture
- New functionality in an existing system
- Structure or contents of external data
- Third-party tools or components
- Performance issues
- User interface design

Prototyping is a learning experience. Its value lies not in the code produced, but in the lessons learned. That's really the point of prototyping.

> **TIP 16**
>
> Prototype to Learn

How to Use Prototypes

When building a prototype, what details can you ignore?

- **Correctness.** You may be able to use dummy data where appropriate.

- **Completeness.** The prototype may function only in a very limited sense, perhaps with only one preselected piece of input data and one menu item.

- **Robustness.** Error checking is likely to be incomplete or missing entirely. If you stray from the predefined path, the prototype may crash and burn in a glorious display of pyrotechnics. That's okay.

- **Style.** It is painful to admit this in print, but prototype code probably doesn't have much in the way of comments or documentation. You may produce reams of documentation as a result of your experience with the prototype, but comparatively very little on the prototype system itself.

Since a prototype should gloss over details, and focus in on specific aspects of the system being considered, you may want to implement prototypes using a very high-level language—higher than the rest of the project (maybe a language such as Perl, Python, or Tcl). A high-level scripting language lets you defer many details (including specifying data types) and still produce a functional (albeit incomplete or slow) piece of code.[6] If you need to prototype user interfaces, investigate tools such as Tcl/Tk, Visual Basic, Powerbuilder, or Delphi.

Scripting languages work well as the "glue" to combine low-level pieces into new combinations. Under Windows, Visual Basic can glue together COM controls. More generally, you can use languages such as Perl and Python to bind together low-level C libraries—either by hand, or automatically with tools such as the freely available SWIG [URL 28]. Using this approach, you can rapidly assemble existing components into new configurations to see how things work.

Prototyping Architecture

Many prototypes are constructed to model the entire system under consideration. As opposed to tracer bullets, none of the individual modules in the prototype system need to be particularly functional. In fact, you may not even need to code in order to prototype architecture—you can prototype on a whiteboard, with Post-it notes or index cards. What you are looking for is how the system hangs together as a whole, again deferring details. Here are some specific areas you may want to look for in the architectural prototype:

- Are the responsibilities of the major components well defined and appropriate?

- Are the collaborations between major components well defined?

- Is coupling minimized?

- Can you identify potential sources of duplication?

- Are interface definitions and constraints acceptable?

---

6.   If you are investigating absolute (instead of relative) performance, you will need to stick to a language that is close in performance to the target language.

- Does every module have an access path to the data it needs during execution? Does it have that access *when* it needs it?

This last item tends to generate the most surprises and the most valuable results from the prototyping experience.

How *Not* to Use Prototypes

Before you embark on any code-based prototyping, make sure that everyone understands that you are writing disposable code. Prototypes can be deceptively attractive to people who don't know that they are just prototypes. You must make it *very* clear that this code is disposable, incomplete, and unable to be completed.

It's easy to become misled by the apparent completeness of a demonstrated prototype, and project sponsors or management may insist on deploying the prototype (or its progeny) if you don't set the right expectations. Remind them that you can build a great prototype of a new car out of balsa wood and duct tape, but you wouldn't try to drive it in rush-hour traffic!

If you feel there is a strong possibility in your environment or culture that the purpose of prototype code may be misinterpreted, you may be better off with the tracer bullet approach. You'll end up with a solid framework on which to base future development.

When used properly, a prototype can save you huge amounts of time, money, pain, and suffering by identifying and correcting potential problem spots early in the development cycle—the time when fixing mistakes is both cheap and easy.

Related sections include:
- *The Cat Ate My Source Code*, page 2
- *Communicate!*, page 18
- *Tracer Bullets*, page 48
- *Great Expectations*, page 255

Exercises

Answer on p. 280

4. Marketing would like to sit down and brainstorm a few Web-page designs with you. They are thinking of clickable image maps to take you to other pages, and so on. But they can't decide on a model for the image—maybe

it's a car, or a phone, or a house. You have a list of target pages and content; they'd like to see a few prototypes. Oh, by the way, you have 15 minutes. What tools might you use?

Domain Languages

The limits of language are the limits of one's world.
▶ **Ludwig Wittgenstein**

Computer languages influence *how* you think about a problem, and how you think about communicating. Every language comes with a list of features—buzzwords such as static versus dynamic typing, early versus late binding, inheritance models (single, multiple, or none)—all of which may suggest or obscure certain solutions. Designing a solution with Lisp in mind will produce different results than a solution based on C-style thinking, and vice versa. Conversely, and we think more importantly, the language of the problem domain may also suggest a programming solution.

We always try to write code using the vocabulary of the application domain (see *The Requirements Pit*, page 210, where we suggest using a project glossary). In some cases, we can go to the next level and actually program using the vocabulary, syntax, and semantics—the language—of the domain.

When you listen to users of a proposed system, they might be able to tell you exactly how the system should work:

> *Listen for transactions defined by ABC Regulation 12.3 on a set of X.25 lines, translate them to XYZ Company's format 43B, retransmit them on the satellite uplink, and store for future analysis.*

If your users have a number of such well-bounded statements, you can invent a mini-language tailored to the application domain that expresses exactly what they want:

```
From X25LINE1 (Format=ABC123) {
  Put TELSTAR1 (Format=XYZ43B);
  Store DB;
}
```

This language need not be executable. Initially, it could be simply a way of capturing the user's requirements—a specification. However, you may want to consider taking this a step further and actually implementing the language. Your specification has become executable code.

After you've written the application, the users give you a new requirement: transactions with negative balances shouldn't be stored, and should be sent back on the X.25 lines in the original format:

```
From X25LINE1 (Format=ABC123) {
  if (ABC123.balance < 0) {
    Put X25LINE1 (Format=ABC123);
  }
  else {
    Put TELSTAR1 (Format=XYZ43B);
    Store DB;
  }
}
```

That was easy, wasn't it? With the proper support in place, you can program much closer to the application domain. We're not suggesting that your end users actually program in these languages. Instead, you're giving yourself a tool that lets you work closer to their domain.

TIP 17

Program Close to the Problem Domain

Whether it's a simple language to configure and control an application program, or a more complex language to specify rules or procedures, we think you should consider ways of moving your project closer to the problem domain. By coding at a higher level of abstraction, you are free to concentrate on solving domain problems, and can ignore petty implementation details.

Remember that there are many users of an application. There's the end user, who understands the business rules and the required outputs. There are also secondary users: operations staff, configuration and test managers, support and maintenance programmers, and future generations of developers. Each of these users has their own problem domain, and you can generate mini-environments and languages for all of them.

Domain-Specific Errors

If you are writing in the problem domain, you can also perform domain-specific validation, reporting problems in terms your users can understand. Take our switching application on on the facing page. Suppose the user misspelled the format name:

```
From X25LINE1 (Format=AB123)
```

If this happened in a standard, general-purpose programming language, you might receive a standard, general-purpose error message:

```
Syntax error: undeclared identifier
```

But with a mini-language, you would instead be able to issue an error message using the vocabulary of the domain:

```
"AB123" is not a format. Known formats are ABC123,
        XYZ43B, PDQB, and 42.
```

Implementing a Mini-Language

At its simplest, a mini-language may be in a line-oriented, easily parsed format. In practice, we probably use this form more than any other. It can be parsed simply using `switch` statements, or using regular expressions in scripting languages such as Perl. The answer to Exercise 5 on page 281 shows a simple implementation in C.

You can also implement a more complex language, with a more formal syntax. The trick here is to define the syntax first using a notation such as BNF.[7] Once you have your grammar specified, it is normally trivial to convert it into the input syntax for a parser generator. C and C++ programmers have been using `yacc` (or its freely available implementation, `bison` [URL 27]) for years. These programs are documented in detail in the book *Lex and Yacc* [LMB92]. Java programmers can try `javaCC`, which can be found at [URL 26]. The answer to Exercise 7 on page 282

---

7. BNF, or Backus-Naur Form, lets you specify *context-free* grammars recursively. Any good book on compiler construction or parsing will cover BNF in (exhaustive) detail.

shows a parser written using `bison`. As it shows, once you know the syntax, it's really not a lot of work to write simple mini-languages.

There's another way of implementing a mini-language: extend an existing one. For example, you could integrate application-level functionality with (say) Python [URL 9] and write something like[8]

```
record = X25LINE1.get(format=ABC123)
if (record.balance < 0):
        X25LINE1.put(record, format=ABC123)
else:
        TELSTAR1.put(record, format=XYZ43B)
        DB.store(record)
```

Data Languages and Imperative Languages

The languages you implement can be used in two different ways.

Data languages produce some form of data structure used by an application. These languages are often used to represent configuration information.

For example, the `sendmail` program is used throughout the world for routing e-mail over the Internet. It has many excellent features and benefits, which are controlled by a thousand-line configuration file, written using `sendmail`'s own configuration language:

```
Mlocal, P=/usr/bin/procmail,
        F=lsDFMAw5:/|@qSPfhn9,
        S=10/30, R=20/40,
        T=DNS/RFC822/X-Unix,
        A=procmail -Y -a $h -d $u
```

Obviously, readability is not one of `sendmail`'s strengths.

For years, Microsoft has been using a data language that can describe menus, widgets, dialog boxes, and other Windows resources. Figure 2.2 on the next page shows an excerpt from a typical resource file. This is far easier to read than the `sendmail` example, but it is used in exactly the same way—it is compiled to generate a data structure.

Imperative languages take this a step further. Here the language is actually executed, and so can contain statements, control constructs, and the like (such as the script on page 58).

---

8.   Thanks to Eric Vought for this example.

Figure 2.2.   Windows .rc file

```
MAIN_MENU MENU
{
 POPUP "&File"
 {
  MENUITEM "&New", CM_FILENEW
  MENUITEM "&Open...", CM_FILEOPEN
  MENUITEM "&Save", CM_FILESAVE
 }
}
MY_DIALOG_BOX DIALOG 6, 15, 292, 287
STYLE DS_MODALFRAME | WS_POPUP | WS_VISIBLE |
                     WS_CAPTION | WS_SYSMENU
CAPTION "My Dialog Box"
FONT 8, "MS Sans Serif"
{
 DEFPUSHBUTTON "OK", ID_OK, 232, 16, 50, 14
 PUSHBUTTON "Help", ID_HELP, 232, 52, 50, 14
 CONTROL "Edit Text Control", ID_EDIT1,
         "EDIT", WS_BORDER | WS_TABSTOP, 16, 16, 80, 56
 CHECKBOX "Checkbox", ID_CHECKBOX1, 153, 65, 42, 38,
         BS_AUTOCHECKBOX | WS_TABSTOP
}
```

You can also use your own imperative languages to ease program maintenance. For example, you may be asked to integrate information from a legacy application into your new GUI development. A common way of achieving this is by *screen scraping*; your application connects to the mainframe application as if it were a regular human user, issuing keystrokes and "reading" the responses it gets back. You could script the interaction using a mini-language.[9]

```
locate prompt "SSN:"
type "%s" social_security_number
type enter

waitfor keyboardunlock

if text_at(10,14) is "INVALID SSN" return bad_ssn
if text_at(10,14) is "DUPLICATE SSN" return dup_ssn
# etc...
```

When the application determines it is time to enter a Social Security number, it invokes the interpreter on this script, which then controls

---

9.   In fact, you can buy tools that support just this kind of scripting. You can also investigate open-source packages such as Expect, which provide similar capabilities [URL 24].

the transaction. If the interpreter is embedded within the application, the two can even share data directly (for example, via a callback mechanism).

Here you're programming in the maintenance programmer's domain. When the mainframe application changes, and the fields move around, the programmer can simply update your high-level description, rather than groveling around in the details of C code.

Stand-Alone and Embedded Languages

A mini-language doesn't have to be used directly by the application to be useful. Many times we may use a specification language to create artifacts (including metadata) that are compiled, read-in, or otherwise used by the program itself (see *Metaprogramming*, page 144).

For example, on page 100 we describe a system in which we used Perl to generate a large number of derivations from an original schema specification. We invented a common language to express the database schema, and then generated all the forms of it we needed—SQL, C, Web pages, XML, and others. The application didn't use the specification directly, but it relied on the output produced from it.

It is common to embed high-level imperative languages directly into your application, so that they execute when your code runs. This is clearly a powerful capability; you can change your application's behavior by changing the scripts it reads, all without compiling. This can significantly simplify maintenance in a dynamic application domain.

Easy Development or Easy Maintenance?

We've looked at several different grammars, ranging from simple line-oriented formats to more complex grammars that look like real languages. Since it takes extra effort to implement, why would you choose a more complex grammar?

The trade-off is extendibility and maintenance. While the code for parsing a "real" language may be harder to write, it will be much easier for people to understand, and to extend in the future with new features and functionality. Languages that are too simple may be easy to parse, but can be cryptic—much like the sendmail example on page 60.

Given that most applications exceed their expected lifetimes, you're probably better off biting the bullet and adopting the more complex and readable language up front. The initial effort will be repaid many times in reduced support and maintenance costs.

Related sections include:
- *Metaprogramming*, page 144

Challenges
- Could some of the requirements of your current project be expressed in a domain-specific language? Would it be possible to write a compiler or translator that could generate most of the code required?

- If you decide to adopt mini-languages as a way of programming closer to the problem domain, you're accepting that some effort will be required to implement them. Can you see ways in which the framework you develop for one project can be reused in others?

Exercises

5. We want to implement a mini-language to control a simple drawing package (perhaps a turtle-graphics system). The language consists of single-letter commands. Some commands are followed by a single number. For example, the following input would draw a rectangle.

Answer on p. 281

```
P 2   # select pen 2
D     # pen down
W 2   # draw west 2cm
N 1   # then north 1
E 2   # then east 2
S 1   # then back south
U     # pen up
```

Implement the code that parses this language. It should be designed so that it is simple to add new commands.

6. Design a BNF grammar to parse a time specification. All of the following examples should be accepted.

Answer on p. 282

```
4pm, 7:38pm, 23:42, 3:16, 3:16am
```

7. Implement a parser for the BNF grammar in Exercise 6 using yacc, bison, or a similar parser-generator.

Answer on p. 282

8. Implement the time parser using Perl. [*Hint:* Regular expressions make good parsers.]

Answer on p. 283

▷ Estimating

Quick! How long will it take to send *War and Peace* over a 56k modem line? How much disk space will you need for a million names and addresses? How long does a 1,000-byte block take to pass through a router? How many months will it take to deliver your project?

At one level, these are all meaningless questions—they are all missing information. And yet they can all be answered, as long as you are comfortable estimating. And, in the process of producing an estimate, you'll come to understand more about the world your programs inhabit.

By learning to estimate, and by developing this skill to the point where you have an intuitive feel for the magnitudes of things, you will be able to show an apparent magical ability to determine their feasibility. When someone says "we'll send the backup over an ISDN line to the central site," you'll be able to know intuitively whether this is practical. When you're coding, you'll be able to know which subsystems need optimizing and which ones can be left alone.

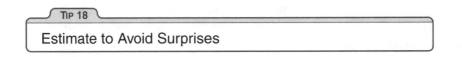

TIP 18

Estimate to Avoid Surprises

As a bonus, at the end of this section we'll reveal the single correct answer to give whenever anyone asks you for an estimate.

How Accurate Is Accurate Enough?

To some extent, all answers are estimates. It's just that some are more accurate than others. So the first question you have to ask yourself when someone asks you for an estimate is the context in which your answer will be taken. Do they need high accuracy, or are they looking for a ballpark figure?

- If your grandmother asks when you will arrive, she's probably wondering whether to make you lunch or dinner. On the other hand, a diver trapped underwater and running out of air is probably interested in an answer down to the second.

- What's the value of π? If you're wondering how much edging to buy to put around a circular flower bed, then "3" is probably good enough.[10] If you're in school, then maybe "$\frac{22}{7}$" is a good approximation. If you're in NASA, then maybe 12 decimal places will do.

One of the interesting things about estimating is that the units you use make a difference in the interpretation of the result. If you say that something will take about 130 working days, then people will be expecting it to come in pretty close. However, if you say "Oh, about six months," then they know to look for it any time between five and seven months from now. Both numbers represent the same duration, but "130 days" probably implies a higher degree of accuracy than you feel. We recommend that you scale time estimates as follows:

Duration	Quote estimate in
1–15 days	days
3–8 weeks	weeks
8–30 weeks	months
30+ weeks	think hard before giving an estimate

So, if after doing all the necessary work, you decide that a project will take 125 working days (25 weeks), you might want to deliver an estimate of "about six months."

The same concepts apply to estimates of any quantity: choose the units of your answer to reflect the accuracy you intend to convey.

Where Do Estimates Come From?

All estimates are based on models of the problem. But before we get too deeply into the techniques of building models, we have to mention a basic estimating trick that always gives good answers: ask someone who's already done it. Before you get too committed to model building, cast around for someone who's been in a similar situation in the past.

---

10. "3" is also apparently good enough if you are a legislator. In 1897, Indiana State Legislature House Bill No. 246 attempted to decree that henceforth π should have the value of "3". The Bill was tabled indefinitely at its second reading when a mathematics professor pointed out that their powers did not quite extend to passing laws of nature.

See how their problem got solved. It's unlikely you'll ever find an exact match, but you'd be surprised how many times you can successfully draw on other's experiences.

Understand What's Being Asked

The first part of any estimation exercise is building an understanding of what's being asked. As well as the accuracy issues discussed above, you need to have a grasp of the scope of the domain. Often this is implicit in the question, but you need to make it a habit to think about the scope before starting to guess. Often, the scope you choose will form part of the answer you give: "Assuming there are no traffic accidents and there's gas in the car, I should be there in 20 minutes."

Build a Model of the System

This is the fun part of estimating. From your understanding of the question being asked, build a rough and ready bare-bones mental model. If you're estimating response times, your model may involve a server and some kind of arriving traffic. For a project, the model may be the steps that your organization uses during development, along with a very rough picture of how the system might be implemented.

Model building can be both creative and useful in the long term. Often, the process of building the model leads to discoveries of underlying patterns and processes that weren't apparent on the surface. You may even want to reexamine the original question: "You asked for an estimate to do X. However, it looks like Y, a variant of X, could be done in about half the time, and you lose only one feature."

Building the model introduces inaccuracies into the estimating process. This is inevitable, and also beneficial. You are trading off model simplicity for accuracy. Doubling the effort on the model may give you only a slight increase in accuracy. Your experience will tell you when to stop refining.

Break the Model into Components

Once you have a model, you can decompose it into components. You'll need to discover the mathematical rules that describe how these components interact. Sometimes a component contributes a single value that is added into the result. Some components may supply multiplying factors, while others may be more complicated (such as those that simulate the arrival of traffic at a node).

You'll find that each component will typically have parameters that affect how it contributes to the overall model. At this stage, simply identify each parameter.

Give Each Parameter a Value

Once you have the parameters broken out, you can go through and assign each one a value. You expect to introduce some errors in this step. The trick is to work out which parameters have the most impact on the result, and concentrate on getting them about right. Typically, parameters whose values are added into a result are less significant than those that are multiplied or divided. Doubling a line speed may double the amount of data received in an hour, while adding a 5 ms transit delay will have no noticeable effect.

You should have a justifiable way of calculating these critical parameters. For the queuing example, you might want to measure the actual transaction arrival rate of the existing system, or find a similar system to measure. Similarly, you could measure the current time taken to serve a request, or come up with an estimate using the techniques described in this section. In fact, you'll often find yourself basing an estimate on other subestimates. This is where your largest errors will creep in.

Calculate the Answers

Only in the simplest of cases will an estimate have a single answer. You might be happy to say "I can walk five cross-town blocks in 15 minutes." However, as the systems get more complex, you'll want to hedge your answers. Run multiple calculations, varying the values of the critical parameters, until you work out which ones really drive the model. A spreadsheet can be a big help. Then couch your answer in terms of these parameters. "The response time is roughly three quarters of a second if the system has a SCSI bus and 64MB memory, and one second with 48MB memory." (Notice how "three quarters of a second" conveys a different feeling of accuracy than 750 ms.)

During the calculation phase, you may start getting answers that seem strange. Don't be too quick to dismiss them. If your arithmetic is correct, your understanding of the problem or your model is probably wrong. This is valuable information.

Keep Track of Your Estimating Prowess

We think it's a great idea to record your estimates so you can see how close you were. If an overall estimate involved calculating subestimates, keep track of these as well. Often you'll find your estimates are pretty good—in fact, after a while, you'll come to expect this.

When an estimate turns out wrong, don't just shrug and walk away. Find out why it differed from your guess. Maybe you chose some parameters that didn't match the reality of the problem. Maybe your model was wrong. Whatever the reason, take some time to uncover what happened. If you do, your next estimate will be better.

Estimating Project Schedules

The normal rules of estimating can break down in the face of the complexities and vagaries of a sizable application development. We find that often the only way to determine the timetable for a project is by gaining experience on that same project. This needn't be a paradox if you practice incremental development, repeating the following steps.

- Check requirements
- Analyze risk
- Design, implement, integrate
- Validate with the users

Initially, you may have only a vague idea of how many iterations will be required, or how long they may be. Some methods require you to nail this down as part of the initial plan, but for all but the most trivial of projects this is a mistake. Unless you are doing an application similar to a previous one, with the same team and the same technology, you'd just be guessing.

So you complete the coding and testing of the initial functionality and mark this as the end of the first increment. Based on that experience, you can refine your initial guess on the number of iterations and what can be included in each. The refinement gets better and better each time, and confidence in the schedule grows along with it.

> **TIP 19**
>
> Iterate the Schedule with the Code

This may not be popular with management, who typically want a single, hard-and-fast number before the project even starts. You'll have to help them understand that the team, their productivity, and the environment will determine the schedule. By formalizing this, and refining the schedule as part of each iteration, you'll be giving them the most accurate scheduling estimates you can.

What to Say When Asked for an Estimate

You say *"I'll get back to you."*

You almost always get better results if you slow the process down and spend some time going through the steps we describe in this section. Estimates given at the coffee machine will (like the coffee) come back to haunt you.

Related sections include:
- *Algorithm Speed*, page 177

Challenges
- Start keeping a log of your estimates. For each, track how accurate you turned out to be. If your error was greater than 50%, try to find out where your estimate went wrong.

Exercises
9. You are asked "Which has a higher bandwidth: a 1Mbps communications line or a person walking between two computers with a full 4GB tape in their pocket?" What constraints will you put on your answer to ensure that the scope of your response is correct? (For example, you might say that the time taken to access the tape is ignored.)

Answer on p. 283

10. So, which has the higher bandwidth?

Answer on p. 284

Chapter 3

The Basic Tools

Every craftsman starts his or her journey with a basic set of good-quality tools. A woodworker might need rules, gauges, a couple of saws, some good planes, fine chisels, drills and braces, mallets, and clamps. These tools will be lovingly chosen, will be built to last, will perform specific jobs with little overlap with other tools, and, perhaps most importantly, will feel right in the budding woodworker's hands.

Then begins a process of learning and adaptation. Each tool will have its own personality and quirks, and will need its own special handling. Each must be sharpened in a unique way, or held just so. Over time, each will wear according to use, until the grip looks like a mold of the woodworker's hands and the cutting surface aligns perfectly with the angle at which the tool is held. At this point, the tools become conduits from the craftsman's brain to the finished product—they have become extensions of his or her hands. Over time, the woodworker will add new tools, such as biscuit cutters, laser-guided miter saws, dovetail jigs—all wonderful pieces of technology. But you can bet that he or she will be happiest with one of those original tools in hand, feeling the plane sing as it slides through the wood.

Tools amplify your talent. The better your tools, and the better you know how to use them, the more productive you can be. Start with a basic set of generally applicable tools. As you gain experience, and as you come across special requirements, you'll add to this basic set. Like the craftsman, expect to add to your toolbox regularly. Always be on the lookout for better ways of doing things. If you come across a situation where you feel your current tools can't cut it, make a note to look for something different or more powerful that would have helped. Let need drive your acquisitions.

Many new programmers make the mistake of adopting a single power tool, such as a particular integrated development environment (IDE), and never leave its cozy interface. This really is a mistake. We need to be comfortable beyond the limits imposed by an IDE. The only way to do this is to keep the basic tool set sharp and ready to use.

In this chapter we'll talk about investing in your own basic toolbox. As with any good discussion on tools, we'll start (in *The Power of Plain Text*) by looking at your raw materials, the stuff you'll be shaping. From there we'll move to the workbench, or in our case the computer. How can you use your computer to get the most out of the tools you use? We'll discuss this in *Shell Games*. Now that we have material and a bench to work on, we'll turn to the tool you'll probably use more than any other, your editor. In *Power Editing*, we'll suggest ways of making you more efficient.

To ensure that we never lose any of our precious work, we should always use a *Source Code Control* system—even for things such as our personal address book! And, since Mr. Murphy was really an optimist after all, you can't be a great programmer until you become highly skilled at *Debugging*.

You'll need some glue to bind much of the magic together. We discuss some possibilities, such as awk, Perl, and Python, in *Text Manipulation*.

Just as woodworkers sometimes build jigs to guide the construction of complex pieces, programmers can write code that itself writes code. We discuss this in *Code Generators*.

Spend time learning to use these tools, and at some point you'll be surprised to discover your fingers moving over the keyboard, manipulating text without conscious thought. The tools will have become extensions of your hands.

The Power of Plain Text

As Pragmatic Programmers, our base material isn't wood or iron, it's knowledge. We gather requirements as knowledge, and then express that knowledge in our designs, implementations, tests, and documents. And we believe that the best format for storing knowledge persistently is *plain text*. With plain text, we give ourselves the ability to manipulate knowledge, both manually and programmatically, using virtually every tool at our disposal.

What Is Plain Text?

Plain text is made up of printable characters in a form that can be read and understood directly by people. For example, although the following snippet is made up of printable characters, it is meaningless.

```
Field19=467abe
```

The reader has no idea what the significance of 467abe may be. A better choice would be to make it *understandable* to humans.

```
DrawingType=UMLActivityDrawing
```

Plain text doesn't mean that the text is unstructured; XML, SGML, and HTML are great examples of plain text that has a well-defined structure. You can do everything with plain text that you could do with some binary format, including versioning.

Plain text tends to be at a higher level than a straight binary encoding, which is usually derived directly from the implementation. Suppose you wanted to store a property called uses_menus that can be either TRUE or FALSE. Using text, you might write this as

```
myprop.uses_menus=FALSE
```

Contrast this with 0010010101110101.

The problem with most binary formats is that the context necessary to understand the data is separate from the data itself. You are artificially divorcing the data from its meaning. The data may as well be encrypted; it is absolutely meaningless without the application logic to parse it. With plain text, however, you can achieve a self-describing data stream that is independent of the application that created it.

┌─ TIP 20 ─────────────────────────────────────┐
│   │
│ Keep Knowledge in Plain Text   │
│   │
└───┘

Drawbacks

There are two major drawbacks to using plain text: (1) It may take more space to store than a compressed binary format, and (2) it may be computationally more expensive to interpret and process a plain text file.

Depending on your application, either or both of these situations may be unacceptable—for example, when storing satellite telemetry data, or as the internal format of a relational database.

But even in these situations, it may be acceptable to store *metadata* about the raw data in plain text (see *Metaprogramming*, page 144).

Some developers may worry that by putting metadata in plain text, they're exposing it to the system's users. This fear is misplaced. Binary data may be more obscure than plain text, but it is no more secure. If you worry about users seeing passwords, encrypt them. If you don't want them changing configuration parameters, include a *secure hash*[1] of all the parameter values in the file as a checksum.

The Power of Text

Since *larger* and *slower* aren't the most frequently requested features from users, why bother with plain text? What *are* the benefits?

- Insurance against obsolescence
- Leverage
- Easier testing

Insurance Against Obsolescence

Human-readable forms of data, and self-describing data, will outlive all other forms of data and the applications that created them. Period.

---

1. MD5 is often used for this purpose. For an excellent introduction to the wonderful world of cryptography, see [Sch95].

As long as the data survives, you will have a chance to be able to use it—potentially long after the original application that wrote it is defunct.

You can parse such a file with only partial knowledge of its format; with most binary files, you must know all the details of the entire format in order to parse it successfully.

Consider a data file from some legacy system[2] that you are given. You know little about the original application; all that's important to you is that it maintained a list of clients' Social Security numbers, which you need to find and extract. Among the data, you see

```
<FIELD10>123-45-6789</FIELD10>
...
<FIELD10>567-89-0123</FIELD10>
...
<FIELD10>901-23-4567</FIELD10>
```

Recognizing the format of a Social Security number, you can quickly write a small program to extract that data—even if you have no information on anything else in the file.

But imagine if the file had been formatted this way instead:

```
AC27123456789B11P
...
XY43567890123QTYL
...
6T2190123456788AM
```

You may not have recognized the significance of the numbers quite as easily. This is the difference between *human readable* and *human understandable*.

While we're at it, FIELD10 doesn't help much either. Something like

```
<SSNO>123-45-6789</SSNO>
```

makes the exercise a no-brainer—and ensures that the data will outlive any project that created it.

Leverage

Virtually every tool in the computing universe, from source code management systems to compiler environments to editors and stand-alone filters, can operate on plain text.

---

2. All software becomes legacy as soon as it's written.

> **The Unix Philosophy**
>
> Unix is famous for being designed around the philosophy of small, sharp tools, each intended to do one thing well. This philosophy is enabled by using a common underlying format—the line-oriented, plain text file. Databases used for system administration (users and passwords, networking configuration, and so on) are all kept as plain text files. (Some systems, such as Solaris, also maintain a binary form of certain databases as a performance optimization. The plain text version is kept as an interface to the binary version.)
>
> When a system crashes, you may be faced with only a minimal environment to restore it (you may not be able to access graphics drivers, for instance). Situations such as this can really make you appreciate the simplicity of plain text.

For instance, suppose you have a production deployment of a large application with a complex site-specific configuration file (`sendmail` comes to mind). If this file is in plain text, you could place it under a source code control system (see *Source Code Control*, page 86), so that you automatically keep a history of all changes. File comparison tools such as `diff` and `fc` allow you to see at a glance what changes have been made, while `sum` allows you to generate a checksum to monitor the file for accidental (or malicious) modification.

Easier Testing

If you use plain text to create synthetic data to drive system tests, then it is a simple matter to add, update, or modify the test data *without having to create any special tools to do so.* Similarly, plain text output from regression tests can be trivially analyzed (with `diff`, for instance) or subjected to more thorough scrutiny with Perl, Python, or some other scripting tool.

Lowest Common Denominator

Even in the future of XML-based intelligent agents that travel the wild and dangerous Internet autonomously, negotiating data interchange among themselves, the ubiquitous text file will still be there. In fact, in heterogeneous environments the advantages of plain text can outweigh all of the drawbacks. You need to ensure that all parties can communicate using a common standard. Plain text is that standard.

Related sections include:
- *Source Code Control*, page 86
- *Code Generators*, page 102
- *Metaprogramming*, page 144
- *Blackboards*, page 165
- *Ubiquitous Automation*, page 230
- *It's All Writing*, page 248

Challenges
- Design a small address book database (name, phone number, and so on) using a straightforward binary representation in your language of choice. Do this before reading the rest of this challenge.

  1. Translate that format into a plain text format using XML.

  2. For each version, add a new, variable-length field called *directions* in which you might enter directions to each person's house.

  What issues come up regarding versioning and extensibility? Which form was easier to modify? What about converting existing data?

 # Shell Games

Every woodworker needs a good, solid, reliable workbench, somewhere to hold work pieces at a convenient height while he or she works them. The workbench becomes the center of the wood shop, the craftsman returning to it time and time again as a piece takes shape.

For a programmer manipulating files of text, that workbench is the command shell. From the shell prompt, you can invoke your full repertoire of tools, using pipes to combine them in ways never dreamt of by their original developers. From the shell, you can launch applications, debuggers, browsers, editors, and utilities. You can search for files, query the status of the system, and filter output. And by programming the shell, you can build complex macro commands for activities you perform often.

For programmers raised on GUI interfaces and integrated development environments (IDEs), this might seem an extreme position. After all, can't you do everything equally well by pointing and clicking?

The simple answer is "no." GUI interfaces are wonderful, and they can be faster and more convenient for some simple operations. Moving files, reading MIME-encoded e-mail, and typing letters are all things that you might want to do in a graphical environment. But if you do all your work using GUIs, you are missing out on the full capabilities of your environment. You won't be able to automate common tasks, or use the full power of the tools available to you. And you won't be able to combine your tools to create customized *macro tools*. A benefit of GUIs is WYSIWYG—what you see is what you get. The disadvantage is WYSIAYG—what you see is *all* you get.

GUI environments are normally limited to the capabilities that their designers intended. If you need to go beyond the model the designer provided, you are usually out of luck—and more often than not, you *do* need to go beyond the model. Pragmatic Programmers don't just cut code, or develop object models, or write documentation, or automate the build process—we do *all* of these things. The scope of any one tool is usually limited to the tasks that the tool is expected to perform. For instance, suppose you need to integrate a code preprocessor (to implement design-by-contract, or multi-processing pragmas, or some such) into your IDE. Unless the designer of the IDE explicitly provided hooks for this capability, you can't do it.

You may already be comfortable working from the command prompt, in which case you can safely skip this section. Otherwise, you may need to be convinced that the shell is your friend.

As a Pragmatic Programmer, you will constantly want to perform ad hoc operations—things that the GUI may not support. The command line is better suited when you want to quickly combine a couple of commands to perform a query or some other task. Here are a few examples.

Find all .c files modified more recently than your Makefile.

Shell...   `find . -name '*.c' -newer Makefile -print`

GUI.....   Open the Explorer, navigate to the correct directory, click on the Makefile, and note the modification time. Then bring up Tools/Find, and enter `*.c` for the file specification. Select the date tab, and enter the date you noted for the Makefile in the first date field. Then hit OK.

Construct a zip/tar archive of my source.

Shell...   `zip archive.zip *.h *.c`   *– or –*
               `tar cvf archive.tar *.h *.c`

GUI.....   Bring up a ZIP utility (such as the shareware WinZip [URL 41]), select "Create New Archive," enter its name, select the source directory in the add dialog, set the filter to "`*.c`", click "Add," set the filter to "`*.h`", click "Add," then close the archive.

Which Java files have not been changed in the last week?

Shell...   `find . -name '*.java' -mtime +7 -print`

GUI.....   Click and navigate to "Find files," click the "Named" field and type in "*.java", select the "Date Modified" tab. Then select "Between." Click on the starting date and type in the starting date of the beginning of the project. Click on the ending date and type in the date of a week ago today (be sure to have a calendar handy). Click on "Find Now."

Of those files, which use the awt libraries?

Shell...   `find . -name '*.java' -mtime +7 -print |`
               `xargs grep 'java.awt'`

GUI.....   Load each file in the list from the previous example into an editor and search for the string "java.awt". Write down the name of each file containing a match.

Clearly the list could go on. The shell commands may be obscure or terse, but they are powerful and concise. And, because shell commands can be combined into script files (or command files under Windows systems), you can build sequences of commands to automate things you do often.

Use the Power of Command Shells

Gain familiarity with the shell, and you'll find your productivity soaring. Need to create a list of all the unique package names explicitly imported by your Java code? The following stores it in a file called "list."

```
grep '^import ' *.java |
   sed -e's/.*import  *//' -e's/;.*$//' |
   sort -u >list
```

If you haven't spent much time exploring the capabilities of the command shell on the systems you use, this might appear daunting. However, invest some energy in becoming familiar with your shell and things will soon start falling into place. Play around with your command shell, and you'll be surprised at how much more productive it makes you.

Shell Utilities and Windows Systems

Although the command shells provided with Windows systems are improving gradually, Windows command-line utilities are still inferior to their Unix counterparts. However, all is not lost.

Cygnus Solutions has a package called Cygwin [URL 31]. As well as providing a Unix compatibility layer for Windows, Cygwin comes with a collection of more than 120 Unix utilities, including such favorites as ls, grep, and find. The utilities and libraries may be downloaded and used for free, but be sure to read their license.[3] The Cygwin distribution comes with the Bash shell.

3.　The GNU General Public License [URL 57] is a kind of legal virus that Open Source developers use to protect their (and your) rights. You should spend some time reading it. In essence, it says that you can use and modify GPL'd software, but if you distribute any modifications they must be licensed according to the GPL (and marked as such), and you must make source available. That's the virus part—whenever you derive a work from a GPL'd work, your derived work must also be GPL'd. However, it does not limit you in any way when simply using the tools—the ownership and licensing of software developed using the tools are up to you.

Using Unix Tools Under Windows

We love the availability of high-quality Unix tools under Windows, and use them daily. However, be aware that there are integration issues. Unlike their MS-DOS counterparts, these utilities are sensitive to the case of filenames, so `ls a*.bat` won't find AUTOEXEC.BAT. You may also come across problems with filenames containing spaces, and with differences in path separators. Finally, there are interesting problems when running MS-DOS programs that expect MS-DOS–style arguments under the Unix shells. For example, the Java utilities from JavaSoft use a colon as their CLASSPATH separator under Unix, but use a semicolon under MS-DOS. As a result, a Bash or ksh script that runs on a Unix box will run identically under Windows, but the command line it passes to Java will be interpreted incorrectly.

Alternatively, David Korn (of Korn shell fame) has put together a package called UWIN. This has the same aims as the Cygwin distribution—it is a Unix development environment under Windows. UWIN comes with a version of the Korn shell. Commercial versions are available from Global Technologies, Ltd. [URL 30]. In addition, AT&T allows free downloading of the package for evaluation and academic use. Again, read their license before using.

Finally, Tom Christiansen is (at the time of writing) putting together *Perl Power Tools*, an attempt to implement all the familiar Unix utilities portably, in Perl [URL 32].

Related sections include:
- *Ubiquitous Automation*, page 230

Challenges
- Are there things that you're currently doing manually in a GUI? Do you ever pass instructions to colleagues that involve a number of individual "click this button," "select this item" steps? Could these be automated?

- Whenever you move to a new environment, make a point of finding out what shells are available. See if you can bring your current shell with you.

- Investigate alternatives to your current shell. If you come across a problem your shell can't address, see if an alternative shell would cope better.

Power Editing

We've talked before about tools being an extension of your hand. Well, this applies to editors more than to any other software tool. You need to be able to manipulate text as effortlessly as possible, because text is the basic raw material of programming. Let's look at some common features and functions that help you get the most from your editing environment.

One Editor

We think it is better to know one editor very well, and use it for all editing tasks: code, documentation, memos, system administration, and so on. Without a single editor, you face a potential modern day Babel of confusion. You may have to use the built-in editor in each language's IDE for coding, and an all-in-one office product for documentation, and maybe a different built-in editor for sending e-mail. Even the keystrokes you use to edit command lines in the shell may be different.[4] It is difficult to be proficient in any of these environments if you have a different set of editing conventions and commands in each.

You need to be proficient. Simply typing linearly and using a mouse to cut and paste is not enough. You just can't be as effective that way as you can with a powerful editor under your fingers. Typing ⟨←⟩ or ⟨BACKSPACE⟩ ten times to move the cursor left to the beginning of a line isn't as efficient as typing a single key such as ⟨^A⟩, ⟨Home⟩, or ⟨0⟩.

> TIP 22
> **Use a Single Editor Well**

Choose an editor, know it thoroughly, and use it for all editing tasks. If you use a single editor (or set of keybindings) across all text editing activities, you don't have to stop and think to accomplish text manipulation: the necessary keystrokes will be a reflex. The editor will be

---

4. Ideally, the shell you use should have keybindings that match the ones used by your editor. Bash, for instance, supports both vi and emacs keybindings.

an extension of your hand; the keys will sing as they slice their way through text and thought. That's our goal.

Make sure that the editor you choose is available on all platforms you use. Emacs, vi, CRiSP, Brief, and others are available across multiple platforms, often in both GUI and non-GUI (text screen) versions.

Editor Features

Beyond whatever features you find particularly useful and comfortable, here are some basic abilities that we think every decent editor should have. If your editor falls short in any of these areas, then this may be the time to consider moving on to a more advanced one.

- **Configurable.** All aspects of the editor should be configurable to your preferences, including fonts, colors, window sizes, and key-stroke bindings (which keys perform what commands). Using only keystrokes for common editing operations is more efficient than mouse or menu-driven commands, because your hands never leave the keyboard.

- **Extensible.** An editor shouldn't be obsolete just because a new programming language comes out. It should be able to integrate with whatever compiler environment you are using. You should be able to "teach" it the nuances of any new language or text format (XML, HTML version 9, and so on).

- **Programmable.** You should be able to program the editor to perform complex, multistep tasks. This can be done with macros or with a built-in scripting programming language (Emacs uses a variant of Lisp, for instance).

In addition, many editors support features that are specific to a particular programming language, such as:

- Syntax highlighting
- Auto-completion
- Auto-indentation
- Initial code or document boilerplate
- Tie-in to help systems
- IDE-like features (compile, debug, and so on)

Figure 3.1.   Sorting lines in an editor

```
import java.util.Vector;      emacs: M-x sort-lines      import java.awt.*;
import java.util.Stack;            ─────────▶           import java.net.URL;
import java.net.URL;               ─────────▶           import java.util.Stack;
import java.awt.*;              vi: :.,+3!sort           import java.util.Vector;
```

A feature such as syntax highlighting may sound like a frivolous extra, but in reality it can be very useful and enhance your productivity. Once you get used to seeing keywords appear in a different color or font, a mistyped keyword that *doesn't* appear that way jumps out at you long before you fire up the compiler.

Having the ability to compile and navigate directly to errors within the editor environment is very handy on big projects. Emacs in particular is adept at this style of interaction.

Productivity

A surprising number of people we've met use the Windows notepad utility to edit their source code. This is like using a teaspoon as a shovel—simply typing and using basic mouse-based cut and paste is not enough.

What sort of things will you need to do that *can't* be done in this way?

Well, there's cursor movement, to start with. Single keystrokes that move you in units of words, lines, blocks, or functions are far more efficient than repeatedly typing a keystroke that moves you character by character or line by line.

Or suppose you are writing Java code. You like to keep your import statements in alphabetical order, and someone else has checked in a few files that don't adhere to this standard (this may sound extreme, but on a large project it can save you a lot of time scanning through a long list of import statements). You'd like to go quickly through a few files and sort a small section of them. In editors such as vi and Emacs you can do this easily (see Figure 3.1). Try *that* in notepad.

Some editors can help streamline common operations. For instance, when you create a new file in a particular language, the editor can supply a template for you. It might include:

- Name of the class or module filled in (derived from the filename)

- Your name and/or copyright statements

- Skeletons for constructs in that language (constructor and destructor declarations, for example)

Another useful feature is auto-indenting. Rather than having to indent manually (by using space or tab), the editor automatically indents for you at the appropriate time (after typing an open brace, for example). The nice part about this feature is that you can use the editor to provide a consistent indentation style for your project.[5]

Where to Go from Here

This sort of advice is particularly hard to write because virtually every reader is at a different level of comfort and expertise with the editor(s) they are currently using. So, to summarize, and to provide some guidance on where to go next, find yourself in the left-hand column of the chart, and look at the right-hand column to see what we think you should do.

If this sounds like you...	**Then think about**...
I use only basic features of many different editors.	Pick a powerful editor and learn it well.
I have a favorite editor, but I don't use all of its features.	Learn them. Cut down the number of keystrokes you need to type.
I have a favorite editor and use it where possible.	Try to expand and use it for more tasks than you do already.
I think you are nuts. Notepad is the best editor ever made.	As long as you are happy and productive, go for it! But if you find yourself subject to "editor envy," you may need to reevaluate your position.

---

5. The Linux kernel is developed this way. Here you have geographically dispersed developers, many working on the same pieces of code. There is a published list of settings (in this case, for Emacs) that describes the required indentation style.

What Editors Are Available?

Having recommended that you master a decent editor, which one do we recommend? Well, we're going to duck that question; your choice of editor is a personal one (some would even say a religious one!). However, in Appendix A, page 266, we list a number of popular editors and where to get them.

Challenges

- Some editors use full-blown languages for customization and scripting. Emacs, for example, uses Lisp. As one of the new languages you are going to learn this year, learn the language your editor uses. For anything you find yourself doing repeatedly, develop a set of macros (or equivalent) to handle it.

- Do you know everything your editor is capable of doing? Try to stump your colleagues who use the same editor. Try to accomplish any given editing task in as few keystrokes as possible.

Source Code Control

Progress, far from consisting in change, depends on retentiveness. Those who cannot remember the past are condemned to repeat it.

▶ **George Santayana, *Life of Reason***

One of the important things we look for in a user interface is the UNDO key—a single button that forgives us our mistakes. It's even better if the environment supports multiple levels of undo and redo, so you can go back and recover from something that happened a couple of minutes ago. But what if the mistake happened last week, and you've turned your computer on and off ten times since then? Well, that's one of the many benefits of using a source code control system: it's a giant UNDO key—a project-wide time machine that can return you to those halcyon days of last week, when the code actually compiled and ran.

Source code control systems, or the more widely scoped *configuration management* systems, keep track of every change you make in your source code and documentation. The better ones can keep track of compiler and OS versions as well. With a properly configured source code control system, *you can always go back to a previous version of your software.*

But a source code control system (SCCS[6]) does far more than undo mistakes. A good SCCS will let you track changes, answering questions such as: Who made changes in this line of code? What's the difference between the current version and last week's? How many lines of code did we change in this release? Which files get changed most often? This kind of information is invaluable for bug-tracking, audit, performance, and quality purposes.

An SCCS will also let you identify releases of your software. Once identified, you will always be able to go back and regenerate the release, independent of changes that may have occurred later.

We often use an SCCS to manage branches in the development tree. For example, once you have released some software, you'll normally want to continue developing for the next release. At the same time, you'll need to deal with bugs in the current release, shipping fixed versions to clients. You'll want these bug fixes rolled into the next release (if appropriate), but you don't want to ship code under development to clients. With an SCCS you can generate branches in the development tree each time you generate a release. You apply bug fixes to code in the branch, and continue developing on the main trunk. Since the bug fixes may be relevant to the main trunk as well, some systems allow you to merge selected changes from the branch back into the main trunk automatically.

Source code control systems may keep the files they maintain in a central repository—a great candidate for archiving.

Finally, some products may allow two or more users to be working concurrently on the same set of files, even making concurrent changes in the same file. The system then manages the merging of these changes when the files are sent back to the repository. Although seemingly risky, such systems work well in practice on projects of all sizes.

---

6.   We use the uppercase SCCS to refer to generic source code control systems. There is also a specific system called "sccs," originally released with AT&T System V Unix.

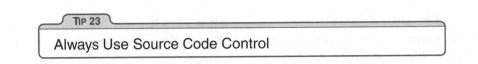

TIP 23

Always Use Source Code Control

Always. Even if you are a single-person team on a one-week project. Even if it's a "throw-away" prototype. Even if the stuff you're working on isn't source code. Make sure that *everything* is under source code control—documentation, phone number lists, memos to vendors, makefiles, build and release procedures, that little shell script that burns the CD master—everything. We routinely use source code control on just about everything we type (including the text of this book). Even if we're not working on a project, our day-to-day work is secured in a repository.

Source Code Control and Builds

There is a tremendous hidden benefit in having an entire project under the umbrella of a source code control system: you can have product builds that are *automatic* and *repeatable*.

The project build mechanism can pull the latest source out of the repository automatically. It can run in the middle of the night after everyone's (hopefully) gone home. You can run automatic regression tests to ensure that the day's coding didn't break anything. The automation of the build ensures consistency—there are no manual procedures, and you won't need developers remembering to copy code into some special build area.

The build is repeatable because you can always rebuild the source as it existed on a given date.

But My Team Isn't Using Source Code Control

Shame on them! Sounds like an opportunity to do some evangelizing! However, while you wait for them to see the light, perhaps you should implement your own private source control. Use one of the freely available tools we list in Appendix A, and make a point of keeping your personal work safely tucked into a repository (as well as doing whatever your project requires). Although this may seem to be duplication of effort, we can pretty much guarantee it will save you grief (and save your project money) the first time you need to answer questions such as "What did you do to the *xyz* module?" and "What broke the build?" This approach may also help convince your management that source code control really works.

Don't forget that an SCCS is equally applicable to the things you do outside of work.

Source Code Control Products

Appendix A, page 271, gives URLs for representative source code control systems, some commercial and others freely available. And many more products are available—look for pointers to the configuration management FAQ. For an introduction to the freely-available CVS version control system, see our book *Pragmatic Version Control* [TH03].

Related sections include:
- *Orthogonality*, page 34
- *The Power of Plain Text*, page 73
- *It's All Writing*, page 248

Challenges
- Even if you are not able to use an SCCS at work, install RCS or CVS on a personal system. Use it to manage your pet projects, documents you write, and (possibly) configuration changes applied to the computer system itself.

- Take a look at some of the Open Source projects for which publicly accessible archives are available on the Web (such as Mozilla [URL 51], KDE [URL 54], and the Gimp [URL 55]). How do you get updates of the source? How do you make changes—does the project regulate access or arbitrate the inclusion of changes?

Debugging

It is a painful thing
To look at your own trouble and know
That you yourself and no one else has made it
► **Sophocles, *Ajax***

The word *bug* has been used to describe an "object of terror" ever since the fourteenth century. Rear Admiral Dr. Grace Hopper, the inventor of COBOL, is credited with observing the first *computer bug*—literally, a moth caught in a relay in an early computer system. When asked to explain why the machine wasn't behaving as intended, a technician reported that there was "a bug in the system," and dutifully taped it—wings and all—into the log book.

Regrettably, we still have "bugs" in the system, albeit not the flying kind. But the fourteenth century meaning—a bogeyman—is perhaps even more applicable now than it was then. Software defects manifest themselves in a variety of ways, from misunderstood requirements to coding errors. Unfortunately, modern computer systems are still limited to doing what you *tell* them to do, not necessarily what you *want* them to do.

No one writes perfect software, so it's a given that debugging will take up a major portion of your day. Let's look at some of the issues involved in debugging and some general strategies for finding elusive bugs.

Psychology of Debugging

Debugging itself is a sensitive, emotional subject for many developers. Instead of attacking it as a puzzle to be solved, you may encounter denial, finger pointing, lame excuses, or just plain apathy.

Embrace the fact that debugging is just *problem solving*, and attack it as such.

Having found someone else's bug, you can spend time and energy laying blame on the filthy culprit who created it. In some workplaces this is part of the culture, and may be cathartic. However, in the technical arena, you want to concentrate on fixing the *problem*, not the blame.

> TIP 24
>
> Fix the Problem, Not the Blame

It doesn't really matter whether the bug is your fault or someone else's. It is still your problem.

A Debugging Mindset

The easiest person to deceive is one's self.
► **Edward Bulwer-Lytton, *The Disowned***

Before you start debugging, it's important to adopt the right mindset. You need to turn off many of the defenses you use each day to protect your ego, tune out any project pressures you may be under, and get yourself comfortable. Above all, remember the first rule of debugging:

> TIP 25
>
> Don't Panic

It's easy to get into a panic, especially if you are facing a deadline, or have a nervous boss or client breathing down your neck while you are trying to find the cause of the bug. But it is very important to step back a pace, and actually *think* about what could be causing the symptoms that you believe indicate a bug.

If your first reaction on witnessing a bug or seeing a bug report is "that's impossible," you are plainly wrong. Don't waste a single neuron on the train of thought that begins "but that can't happen" because quite clearly it *can*, and has.

Beware of myopia when debugging. Resist the urge to fix just the symptoms you see: it is more likely that the actual fault may be several steps removed from what you are observing, and may involve a number of other related things. Always try to discover the root cause of a problem, not just this particular appearance of it.

Where to Start

Before you *start* to look at the bug, make sure that you are working on code that compiled cleanly—without warnings. We routinely set compiler warning levels as high as possible. It doesn't make sense to waste time trying to find a problem that the compiler could find for you! We need to concentrate on the harder problems at hand.

When trying to solve any problem, you need to gather all the relevant data. Unfortunately, bug reporting isn't an exact science. It's easy to be misled by coincidences, and you can't afford to waste time debugging coincidences. You first need to be accurate in your observations.

Accuracy in bug reports is further diminished when they come through a third party—you may actually need to *watch* the user who reported the bug in action to get a sufficient level of detail.

Andy once worked on a large graphics application. Nearing release, the testers reported that the application crashed every time they painted a stroke with a particular brush. The programmer responsible argued that there was nothing wrong with it; he had tried painting with it, and it worked just fine. This dialog went back and forth for several days, with tempers rapidly rising.

Finally, we got them together in the same room. The tester selected the brush tool and painted a stroke from the upper right corner to the lower left corner. The application exploded. "Oh," said the programmer, in a small voice, who then sheepishly admitted that he had made test strokes only from the lower left to the upper right, which did not expose the bug.

There are two points to this story:

- You may need to interview the user who reported the bug in order to gather more data than you were initially given.

- Artificial tests (such as the programmer's single brush stroke from bottom to top) don't exercise enough of an application. You must brutally test both boundary conditions and realistic end-user usage patterns. You need to do this systematically (see *Ruthless Testing*, page 237).

Debugging Strategies

Once *you* think you know what is going on, it's time to find out what the *program* thinks is going on.

> ### Bug Reproduction
>
> No, our bugs aren't really multiplying (although some of them are probably old enough to do it legally). We're talking about a different kind of reproduction.
>
> The best way to start fixing a bug is to make it reproducible. After all, if you can't reproduce it, how will you know if it is ever fixed?
>
> But we want more than a bug that can be reproduced by following some long series of steps; we want a bug that can be reproduced with a *single command*. It's a lot harder to fix a bug if you have to go through 15 steps to get to the point where the bug shows up. Sometimes by forcing yourself to isolate the circumstances that display the bug, you'll even gain an insight on how to fix it.
>
> See *Ubiquitous Automation,* page 230, for other ideas along these lines.

Visualize Your Data

Often, the easiest way to discern what a program is doing—or what it is going to do—is to get a good look at the data it is operating on. The simplest example of this is a straightforward "`variable name = data value`" approach, which may be implemented as printed text, or as fields in a GUI dialog box or list.

But you can gain a much deeper insight into your data by using a debugger that allows you to *visualize* your data and all of the inter-relationships that exist. There are debuggers that can represent your data as a 3D fly-over through a virtual reality landscape, or as a 3D waveform plot, or just as simple structural diagrams, as shown in Figure 3.2 on the next page. As you single-step through your program, pictures like these can be worth much more than a thousand words, as the bug you've been hunting suddenly jumps out at you.

Even if your debugger has limited support for visualizing data, you can still do it yourself—either by hand, with paper and pencil, or with external plotting programs.

The DDD debugger has some visualization capabilities, and is freely available (see [URL 19]). It is interesting to note that DDD works with

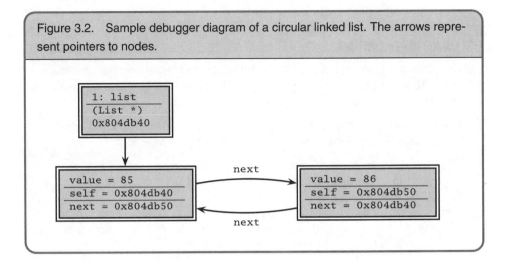

Figure 3.2.   Sample debugger diagram of a circular linked list. The arrows represent pointers to nodes.

multiple languages, including Ada, C, C++, Fortran, Java, Modula, Pascal, Perl, and Python (clearly an orthogonal design).

Tracing

Debuggers generally focus on the state of the program *now*. Sometimes you need more—you need to watch the state of a program or a data structure over time. Seeing a stack trace can only tell you how you got here directly. It can't tell you what you were doing prior to this call chain, especially in event-based systems.

Tracing statements are those little diagnostic messages you print to the screen or to a file that say things such as "got here" and "value of x = 2." It's a primitive technique compared with IDE-style debuggers, but it is peculiarly effective at diagnosing several classes of errors that debuggers can't. Tracing is invaluable in any system where time itself is a factor: concurrent processes, real-time systems, and event-based applications.

You can use tracing statements to "drill down" into the code. That is, you can add tracing statements as you descend the call tree.

Trace messages should be in a regular, consistent format; you may want to parse them automatically. For instance, if you needed to track down a resource leak (such as unbalanced file opens/closes), you could trace each open and each close in a log file. By processing the log

> ### Corrupt Variables? Check Their Neighborhood
>
> Sometimes you'll examine a variable, expecting to see a small integer value, and instead get something like `0x6e69614d`. Before you roll up your sleeves for some serious debugging, have a quick look at the memory around this corrupted variable. Often it will give you a clue. In our case, examining the surrounding memory as characters shows us
>
> ```
> 20333231 6e69614d 2c745320 746f4e0a
>  1 2 3    M a i n    S t ,  \n N o t
> 2c6e776f 2058580a 31323433 00000a33
>  o w n ,  \n X X    3 4 2 1  3 \n \0 \0
> ```
>
> Looks like someone sprayed a street address over our counter. Now we know where to look.

file with Perl, you could easily identify where the offending open was occurring.

Rubber Ducking

A very simple but particularly useful technique for finding the cause of a problem is simply to explain it to someone else. The other person should look over your shoulder at the screen, and nod his or her head constantly (like a rubber duck bobbing up and down in a bathtub). They do not need to say a word; the simple act of explaining, step by step, what the code is supposed to do often causes the problem to leap off the screen and announce itself.[7]

It sounds simple, but in explaining the problem to another person you must explicitly state things that you may take for granted when going through the code yourself. By having to verbalize some of these assumptions, you may suddenly gain new insight into the problem.

---

7. Why "rubber ducking"? While an undergraduate at Imperial College in London, Dave did a lot of work with a research assistant named Greg Pugh, one of the best developers Dave has known. For several months Greg carried around a small yellow rubber duck, which he'd place on his terminal while coding. It was a while before Dave had the courage to ask. . . .

Process of Elimination

In most projects, the code you are debugging may be a mixture of application code written by you and others on your project team, third-party products (database, connectivity, graphical libraries, specialized communications or algorithms, and so on) and the platform environment (operating system, system libraries, and compilers).

It is possible that a bug exists in the OS, the compiler, or a third-party product—but this should not be your first thought. It is much more likely that the bug exists in the application code under development. It is generally more profitable to assume that the application code is incorrectly calling into a library than to assume that the library itself is broken. Even if the problem *does* lie with a third party, you'll still have to eliminate your code before submitting the bug report.

We worked on a project where a senior engineer was convinced that the `select` system call was broken on Solaris. No amount of persuasion or logic could change his mind (the fact that every other networking application on the box worked fine was irrelevant). He spent weeks writing work-arounds, which, for some odd reason, didn't seem to fix the problem. When finally forced to sit down and read the documentation on `select`, he discovered the problem and corrected it in a matter of minutes. We now use the phrase "select is broken" as a gentle reminder whenever one of us starts blaming the system for a fault that is likely to be our own.

TIP 26

"select" Isn't Broken

Remember, if you see hoof prints, think horses—not zebras. The OS is probably not broken. And the database is probably just fine.

If you "changed only one thing" and the system stopped working, that one thing was likely to be responsible, directly or indirectly, no matter how farfetched it seems. Sometimes the thing that changed is outside of your control: new versions of the OS, compiler, database, or other third-party software can wreak havoc with previously correct code. New bugs might show up. Bugs for which you had a work-around get fixed, breaking the work-around. APIs change, functionality changes; in short, it's a whole new ball game, and you must retest the system under these new conditions. So keep a close eye on the schedule when considering an upgrade; you may want to wait until *after* the next release.

If, however, you have no obvious place to start looking, you can always rely on a good old-fashioned binary search. See if the symptoms are present at either of two far away spots in the code. Then look in the middle. If the problem is present, then the bug lies between the start and the middle point; otherwise, it is between the middle point and the end. You can continue in this fashion until you narrow down the spot sufficiently to identify the problem.

The Element of Surprise

When you find yourself surprised by a bug (perhaps even muttering "that's impossible" under your breath where we can't hear you), you must reevaluate truths you hold dear. In that linked list routine—the one you knew was bulletproof and couldn't possibly be the cause of this bug—did you test *all* the boundary conditions? That other piece of code you've been using for years—it couldn't possibly still have a bug in it. Could it?

Of course it can. The amount of surprise you feel when something goes wrong is directly proportional to the amount of trust and faith you have in the code being run. That's why, when faced with a "surprising" failure, you must realize that one or more of your assumptions is wrong. Don't gloss over a routine or piece of code involved in the bug because you "know" it works. Prove it. Prove it in *this* context, with *this* data, with *these* boundary conditions.

> TIP 27
>
> Don't Assume It—Prove It

When you come across a surprise bug, beyond merely fixing it, you need to determine why this failure wasn't caught earlier. Consider whether you need to amend the unit or other tests so that they would have caught it.

Also, if the bug is the result of bad data that was propagated through a couple of levels before causing the explosion, see if better parameter checking in those routines would have isolated it earlier (see the discussions on crashing early and assertions on pages 120 and 122, respectively).

While you're at it, are there any other places in the code that may be susceptible to this same bug? Now is the time to find and fix them. Make sure that *whatever* happened, you'll know if it happens again.

If it took a long time to fix this bug, ask yourself why. Is there anything you can do to make fixing this bug easier the next time around? Perhaps you could build in better testing hooks, or write a log file analyzer.

Finally, if the bug is the result of someone's wrong assumption, discuss the problem with the whole team: if one person misunderstands, then it's possible many people do.

Do all this, and hopefully you won't be surprised next time.

Debugging Checklist

- Is the problem being reported a direct result of the underlying bug, or merely a symptom?

- Is the bug *really* in the compiler? Is it in the OS? Or is it in your code?

- If you explained this problem in detail to a coworker, what would you say?

- If the suspect code passes its unit tests, are the tests complete enough? What happens if you run the unit test with *this* data?

- Do the conditions that caused this bug exist anywhere else in the system?

Related sections include:
- *Assertive Programming*, page 122
- *Programming by Coincidence*, page 172
- *Ubiquitous Automation*, page 230
- *Ruthless Testing*, page 237

Challenges
- Debugging is challenge enough.

▶ Text Manipulation

Pragmatic Programmers manipulate text the same way woodworkers shape wood. In previous sections we discussed some specific tools—shells, editors, debuggers—that we use. These are similar to a woodworker's chisels, saws, and planes—tools specialized to do one or two jobs well. However, every now and then we need to perform some transformation not readily handled by the basic tool set. We need a general-purpose text manipulation tool.

Text manipulation languages are to programming what routers[8] are to woodworking. They are noisy, messy, and somewhat brute force. Make mistakes with them, and entire pieces can be ruined. Some people swear they have no place in the toolbox. But in the right hands, both routers and text manipulation languages can be incredibly powerful and versatile. You can quickly trim something into shape, make joints, and carve. Used properly, these tools have surprising finesse and subtlety. But they take time to master.

There is a growing number of good text manipulation languages. Unix developers often like to use the power of their command shells, augmented with tools such as awk and sed. People who prefer a more structured tool like the object-oriented nature of Python [URL 9]. Some people use Tcl [URL 23] as their tool of choice. We happen to prefer Ruby [TFH04] and Perl [URL 8] for hacking out short scripts.

These languages are important enabling technologies. Using them, you can quickly hack up utilities and prototype ideas—jobs that might take five or ten times as long using conventional languages. And that multiplying factor is crucially important to the kind of experimenting that we do. Spending 30 minutes trying out a crazy idea is a whole lot better than spending five hours. Spending a day automating important components of a project is acceptable; spending a week might not be. In their book *The Practice of Programming* [KP99], Kernighan and Pike built the same program in five different languages. The Perl version was the shortest (17 lines, compared with C's 150). With Perl you can

---

8.   Here *router* means the tool that spins cutting blades very, very fast, not a device for interconnecting networks.

manipulate text, interact with programs, talk over networks, drive Web pages, perform arbitrary precision arithmetic, and write programs that look like Snoopy swearing.

TIP 28

Learn a Text Manipulation Language

To show the wide-ranging applicability of text manipulation languages, here's a sample of some applications we've developed over the last few years.

- **Database schema maintenance.** A set of Perl scripts took a plain text file containing a database schema definition and from it generated:

  - The SQL statements to create the database
  - Flat data files to populate a data dictionary
  - C code libraries to access the database
  - Scripts to check database integrity
  - Web pages containing schema descriptions and diagrams
  - An XML version of the schema

- **Java property access.** It is good OO programming style to restrict access to an object's properties, forcing external classes to get and set them via methods. However, in the common case where a property is represented inside the class by a simple member variable, creating a `get` and `set` method for each variable is tedious and mechanical. We have a Perl script that modifies the source files and inserts the correct method definitions for all appropriately flagged variables.

- **Test data generation.** We had tens of thousands of records of test data, spread over several different files and formats, that needed to be knitted together and converted into a form suitable for loading into a relational database. Perl did it in a couple of hours (and in the process found a couple of consistency errors in the original data).

- **Book writing.** We think it is important that any code presented in a book should have been tested first. Most of the code in this book has been. However, using the *DRY* principle (see *The Evils of Duplication*, page 26) we didn't want to copy and paste lines of code from the tested programs into the book. That would have meant that the code was duplicated, virtually guaranteeing that we'd forget to update an example when the corresponding program was changed. For some examples, we also didn't want to bore you with all the framework code needed to make our example compile and run. We turned to Perl. A relatively simple script is invoked when we format the book—it extracts a named segment of a source file, does syntax highlighting, and converts the result into the typesetting language we use.

- **C to Object Pascal interface.** A client had a team of developers writing Object Pascal on PCs. Their code needed to interface to a body of code written in C. We developed a short Perl script that parsed the C header files, extracting the definitions of all exported functions and the data structures they used. We then generated Object Pascal units with Pascal records for all the C structures, and imported procedure definitions for all the C functions. This generation process became part of the build, so that whenever the C header changed, a new Object Pascal unit would be constructed automatically.

- **Generating Web documentation.** Many project teams are publishing their documentation to internal Web sites. We have written many Perl programs that analyze database schemas, C or C++ source files, makefiles, and other project sources to produce the required HTML documentation. We also use Perl to wrap the documents with standard headers and footers, and to transfer them to the Web site.

We use text manipulation languages almost every day. Many of the ideas in this book can be implemented more simply in them than in any other language of which we're aware. These languages make it easy to write code generators, which we'll look at next.

Related sections include:
- *The Evils of Duplication*, page 26

Exercises

Answer on p. 285

11. Your C program uses an enumerated type to represent one of 100 states. You'd like to be able to print out the state as a string (as opposed to a number) for debugging purposes. Write a script that reads from standard input a file containing

```
name
state_a
state_b
  :      :
```

Produce the file *name.h*, which contains

```
extern const char* NAME_names[];
typedef enum {
    state_a,
    state_b,
      :      :
  } NAME;
```

and the file *name.c*, which contains

```
const char* NAME_names[] = {
    "state_a",
    "state_b",
      :        :
  };
```

Answer on p. 286

12. Halfway through writing this book, we realized that we hadn't put the use strict directive into many of our Perl examples. Write a script that goes through the .pl files in a directory and adds a use strict at the end of the initial comment block to all files that don't already have one. Remember to keep a backup of all files you change.

Code Generators

When woodworkers are faced with the task of producing the same thing over and over, they cheat. They build themselves a jig or a template. If they get the jig right once, they can reproduce a piece of work time after time. The jig takes away complexity and reduces the chances of making mistakes, leaving the craftsman free to concentrate on quality.

As programmers, we often find ourselves in a similar position. We need to achieve the same functionality, but in different contexts. We need to repeat information in different places. Sometimes we just need to protect ourselves from carpal tunnel syndrome by cutting down on repetitive typing.

In the same way a woodworker invests the time in a jig, a programmer can build a code generator. Once built, it can be used throughout the life of the project at virtually no cost.

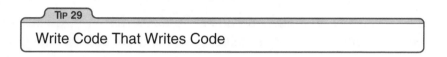

TIP 29

Write Code That Writes Code

There are two main types of code generators:

1. *Passive code generators* are run once to produce a result. From that point forward, the result becomes freestanding—it is divorced from the code generator. The wizards discussed in *Evil Wizards*, page 198, along with some CASE tools, are examples of passive code generators.

2. *Active code generators* are used each time their results are required. The result is a throw-away—it can always be reproduced by the code generator. Often, active code generators read some form of script or control file to produce their results.

Passive Code Generators

Passive code generators save typing. They are basically parameterized templates, generating a given output from a set of inputs. Once the result is produced, it becomes a full-fledged source file in the project; it will be edited, compiled, and placed under source control just like any other file. Its origins will be forgotten.

Passive code generators have many uses:

- *Creating new source files.* A passive code generator can produce templates, source code control directives, copyright notices, and standard comment blocks for each new file in a project. We have our editors set up to do this whenever we create a new file: edit a new Java program, and the new editor buffer will automatically contain a comment block, package directive, and the outline class declaration, already filled in.

- *Performing one-off conversions* among programming languages. We started writing this book using the troff system, but we switched to LaTeX after 15 sections had been completed. We wrote a code generator that read the troff source and converted it to LaTeX. It was about 90% accurate; the rest we did by hand. This is an interesting feature of passive code generators: they don't have to be totally accurate. You get to choose how much effort you put into the generator, compared with the energy you spend fixing up its output.

- *Producing lookup tables and other resources* that are expensive to compute at runtime. Instead of calculating trigonometric functions, many early graphics systems used precomputed tables of sine and cosine values. Typically, these tables were produced by a passive code generator and then copied into the source.

Active Code Generators

While passive code generators are simply a convenience, their active cousins are a necessity if you want to follow the *DRY* principle. With an active code generator, you can take a single representation of some piece of knowledge and convert it into all the forms your application needs. This *is not* duplication, because the derived forms are disposable, and are generated as needed by the code generator (hence the word *active*).

Whenever you find yourself trying to get two disparate environments to work together, you should consider using active code generators.

Perhaps you're developing a database application. Here, you're dealing with two environments—the database and the programming language you are using to access it. You have a schema, and you need to define low-level structures mirroring the layout of certain database tables. You could just code these directly, but this violates the *DRY* principle: knowledge of the schema would then be expressed in two places. When the schema changes, you need to remember to change the corresponding code. If a column is removed from a table, but the code base is not changed, you might not even get a compilation error. The first you'll know about it is when your tests start failing (or when the user calls).

An alternative is to use an active code generator—take the schema and use it to generate the source code for the structures, as shown in Figure 3.3. Now, whenever the schema changes, the code used to access it also changes, automatically. If a column is removed, then its corresponding field in the structure will disappear, and any higher-level code that uses that column will fail to compile. You've caught the error at compile time,

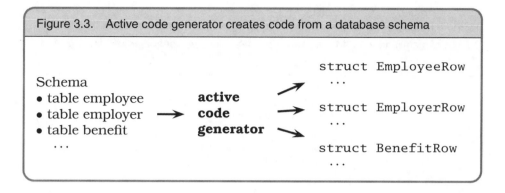

Figure 3.3.   Active code generator creates code from a database schema

not in production. Of course, this scheme works only if you make the code generation part of the build process itself.[9]

Another example of melding environments using code generators happens when different programming languages are used in the same application. In order to communicate, each code base will need some information in common—data structures, message formats, and field names, for example. Rather than duplicate this information, use a code generator. Sometimes you can parse the information out of the source files of one language and use it to generate code in a second language. Often, though, it is simpler to express it in a simpler, language-neutral representation and generate the code for both languages, as shown in Figure 3.4 on the following page. Also see the answer to Exercise 13 on page 286 for an example of how to separate the parsing of the flat file representation from code generation.

Code Generators Needn't Be Complex

All this talk of *active* this and *passive* that may leave you with the impression that code generators are complex beasts. They needn't be. Normally the most complex part is the parser, which analyzes the input file. Keep the input format simple, and the code generator becomes

9.   Just *how* do you go about building code from a database schema? There are several ways. If the schema is held in a flat file (for example, as `create table` statements), then a relatively simple script can parse it and generate the source. Alternatively, if you use a tool to create the schema directly in the database, then you should be able to extract the information you need directly from the database's data dictionary. Perl provides libraries that give you access to most major databases.

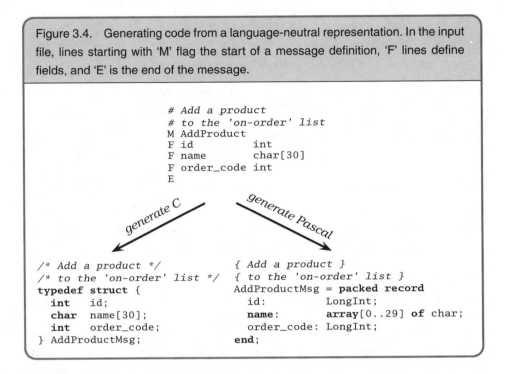

Figure 3.4. Generating code from a language-neutral representation. In the input file, lines starting with 'M' flag the start of a message definition, 'F' lines define fields, and 'E' is the end of the message.

simple. Have a look at the answer to Exercise 13 (page 286): the actual code generation is basically `print` statements.

Code Generators Needn't Generate Code

Although many of the examples in this section show code generators that produce program source, this needn't always be the case. You can use code generators to write just about any output: HTML, XML, plain text—any text that might be an input somewhere else in your project.

Related sections include:
- *The Evils of Duplication*, page 26
- *The Power of Plain Text*, page 73
- *Evil Wizards*, page 198
- *Ubiquitous Automation*, page 230

Exercises

Answer on p. 286

13. Write a code generator that takes the input file in Figure 3.4, and generates output in two languages of your choice. Try to make it easy to add new languages.

Chapter 4

Pragmatic Paranoia

> **Tip 30**
>
> You Can't Write Perfect Software

Did that hurt? It shouldn't. Accept it as an axiom of life. Embrace it. Celebrate it. Because perfect software doesn't exist. No one in the brief history of computing has ever written a piece of perfect software. It's unlikely that you'll be the first. And unless you accept this as a fact, you'll end up wasting time and energy chasing an impossible dream.

So, given this depressing reality, how does a Pragmatic Programmer turn it into an advantage? That's the topic of this chapter.

Everyone knows that they personally are the only good driver on Earth. The rest of the world is out there to get them, blowing through stop signs, weaving between lanes, not indicating turns, talking on the telephone, reading the paper, and just generally not living up to our standards. So we drive defensively. We look out for trouble before it happens, anticipate the unexpected, and never put ourselves into a position from which we can't extricate ourselves.

The analogy with coding is pretty obvious. We are constantly interfacing with other people's code—code that might not live up to our high standards—and dealing with inputs that may or may not be valid. So we are taught to code defensively. If there's any doubt, we validate all information we're given. We use assertions to detect bad data. We check for consistency, put constraints on database columns, and generally feel pretty good about ourselves.

But Pragmatic Programmers take this a step further. *They don't trust themselves, either.* Knowing that no one writes perfect code, including themselves, Pragmatic Programmers code in defenses against their own mistakes. We describe the first defensive measure in *Design by Contract*: clients and suppliers must agree on rights and responsibilities.

In *Dead Programs Tell No Lies*, we want to ensure that we do no damage while we're working the bugs out. So we try to check things often and terminate the program if things go awry.

Assertive Programming describes an easy method of checking along the way—write code that actively verifies your assumptions.

Exceptions, like any other technique, can cause more harm than good if not used properly. We'll discuss the issues in *When to Use Exceptions*.

As your programs get more dynamic, you'll find yourself juggling system resources—memory, files, devices, and the like. In *How to Balance Resources*, we'll suggest ways of ensuring that you don't drop any of the balls.

In a world of imperfect systems, ridiculous time scales, laughable tools, and impossible requirements, let's play it safe.

When everybody actually is out to get you, paranoia is just good thinking.
   ▶ **Woody Allen**

Design by Contract

Nothing astonishes men so much as common sense and plain dealing.
▶ **Ralph Waldo Emerson, *Essays***

Dealing with computer systems is hard. Dealing with people is even harder. But as a species, we've had longer to figure out issues of human interactions. Some of the solutions we've come up with during the last few millennia can be applied to writing software as well. One of the best solutions for ensuring plain dealing is the *contract*.

A contract defines your rights and responsibilities, as well as those of the other party. In addition, there is an agreement concerning repercussions if either party fails to abide by the contract.

Maybe you have an employment contract that specifies the hours you'll work and the rules of conduct you must follow. In return, the company pays you a salary and other perks. Each party meets its obligations and everyone benefits.

It's an idea used the world over—both formally and informally—to help humans interact. Can we use the same concept to help software modules interact? The answer is "yes."

DBC

Bertrand Meyer [Mey97b] developed the concept of *Design by Contract* for the language Eiffel.[1] It is a simple yet powerful technique that focuses on documenting (and agreeing to) the rights and responsibilities of software modules to ensure program correctness. What is a correct program? One that does no more and no less than it claims to do. Documenting and verifying that claim is the heart of *Design by Contract* (DBC, for short).

Every function and method in a software system *does something*. Before it starts that *something*, the routine may have some expectation of the state of the world, and it may be able to make a statement about the state of the world when it concludes. Meyer describes these expectations and claims as follows:

---

1. Based in part on earlier work by Dijkstra, Floyd, Hoare, Wirth, and others. For more information on Eiffel itself, see [URL 10] and [URL 11].

- **Preconditions.** What must be true in order for the routine to be called; the routine's requirements. A routine should never get called when its preconditions would be violated. It is the caller's responsibility to pass good data (see the box on page 115).

- **Postconditions.** What the routine is guaranteed to do; the state of the world when the routine is done. The fact that the routine has a postcondition implies that it *will* conclude: infinite loops aren't allowed.

- **Class invariants.** A class ensures that this condition is always true from the perspective of a caller. During internal processing of a routine, the invariant may not hold, but by the time the routine exits and control returns to the caller, the invariant must be true. (Note that a class cannot give unrestricted write-access to any data member that participates in the invariant.)

Let's look at the contract for a routine that inserts a data value into a unique, ordered list. In iContract, a preprocessor for Java available from [URL 17], you'd specify it as

```
/**
 * @invariant forall Node n in elements() |
 *     n.prev() != null
 *       implies
 *           n.value().compareTo(n.prev().value()) > 0
 */
public class dbc_list {
  /**
   * @pre contains(aNode) == false
   * @post contains(aNode) == true
   */
  public void insertNode(final Node aNode) {
    // ...
```

Here we are saying that nodes in this list must always be in increasing order. When you insert a new node, it can't exist already, and we guarantee that the node will be found after you have inserted it.

You write these preconditions, postconditions, and invariants in the target programming language, perhaps with some extensions. For example, iContract provides predicate logic operators—forall, exists, and implies—in addition to normal Java constructs. Your assertions can query the state of any object that the method can access, but be sure that the query is free from any side effects (see page 124).

DBC and Constant Parameters

Often, a postcondition will use parameters passed into a method to verify correct behavior. But if the routine is allowed to change the parameter that's passed in, you might be able to circumvent the contract. Eiffel doesn't allow this to happen, but Java does. Here, we use the Java keyword `final` to indicate our intentions that the parameter shouldn't be changed within the method. This isn't foolproof—subclasses are free to redeclare the parameter as non-final. Alternatively, you can use the iContract syntax `variable@pre` to get the original value of the variable as it existed on entry to the method.

The contract between a routine and any potential caller can thus be read as

> *If all the routine's preconditions are met by the caller, the routine shall guarantee that all postconditions and invariants will be true when it completes.*

If either party fails to live up to the terms of the contract, then a remedy (which was previously agreed to) is invoked—an exception is raised, or the program terminates, for instance. Whatever happens, make no mistake that failure to live up to the contract is a bug. It is not something that should ever happen, which is why preconditions should not be used to perform things such as user-input validation.

TIP 31

Design with Contracts

In *Orthogonality*, page 34, we recommended writing "shy" code. Here, the emphasis is on "lazy" code: be strict in what you will accept before you begin, and promise as little as possible in return. Remember, if your contract indicates that you'll accept anything and promise the world in return, then you've got a lot of code to write!

Inheritance and polymorphism are the cornerstones of object-oriented languages and an area where contracts can really shine. Suppose you are using inheritance to create an "is-a-kind-of" relationship, where one class "is-a-kind-of" another class. You probably want to adhere to the *Liskov Substitution Principle* [Lis88]:

> *Subclasses must be usable through the base class interface without the need for the user to know the difference.*

In other words, you want to make sure that the new subtype you have created really "is-a-kind-of" the base type—that it supports the same methods, and that the methods have the same meaning. We can do this with contracts. We need to specify a contract only once, in the base class, to have it applied to every future subclass automatically. A subclass may, optionally, accept a wider range of input, or make stronger guarantees. But it must accept at least as much, and guarantee as much, as its parent.

For example, consider the Java base class `java.awt.Component`. You can treat any visual component in AWT or Swing as a `Component`, without knowing that the actual subclass is a button, a canvas, a menu, or whatever. Each individual component can provide additional, specific functionality, but it has to provide at least the basic capabilities defined by `Component`. But there's nothing to prevent you from creating a subtype of `Component` that provides correctly named methods that do the wrong thing. You can easily create a `paint` method that doesn't paint, or a `setFont` method that doesn't set the font. AWT doesn't have contracts to catch the fact that you didn't live up to the agreement.

Without a contract, all the compiler can do is ensure that a subclass conforms to a particular method signature. But if we put a base class contract in place, we can now ensure that any future subclass can't alter the *meanings* of our methods. For instance, you might want to establish a contract for `setFont` such as the following, which ensures that the font you set is the font you get:

```
/**
 * @pre   f != null
 * @post getFont() == f
 */
public void setFont(final Font f) {
    // ...
```

Implementing DBC

The greatest benefit of using DBC may be that it forces the issue of requirements and guarantees to the forefront. Simply enumerating at design time what the input domain range is, what the boundary conditions are, and what the routine promises to deliver—or, more importantly, what it *doesn't* promise to deliver—is a huge leap forward in writing better software. By not stating these things, you are back to *programming by coincidence* (see page 172), which is where many projects start, finish, and fail.

In languages that do not support DBC in the code, this might be as far as you can go—and that's not too bad. DBC is, after all, a *design* technique. Even without automatic checking, you can put the contract in the code as comments and still get a very real benefit. If nothing else, the commented contracts give you a place to start looking when trouble strikes.

Assertions

While documenting these assumptions is a great start, you can get much greater benefit by having the compiler check your contract for you. You can partially emulate this in some languages by using *assertions* (see *Assertive Programming*, page 122). Why only partially? Can't you use assertions to do everything DBC can do?

Unfortunately, the answer is no. To begin with, there is no support for propagating assertions down an inheritance hierarchy. This means that if you override a base class method that has a contract, the assertions that implement that contract will not be called correctly (unless you duplicate them manually in the new code). You must remember to call the class invariant (and all base class invariants) manually before you exit every method. The basic problem is that the contract is not automatically enforced.

Also, there is no built-in concept of "old" values; that is, values as they existed at the entry to a method. If you're using assertions to enforce contracts, you must add code to the precondition to save any information you'll want to use in the postcondition. Compare this with iContract, where the postcondition can just reference "*variable*@pre," or with Eiffel, which supports "old *expression*."

Finally, the runtime system and libraries are not designed to support contracts, so these calls are not checked. This is a big loss, because it is often at the boundary between your code and the libraries it uses that the most problems are detected (see *Dead Programs Tell No Lies*, page 120 for a more detailed discussion).

Language Support

Languages that feature built-in support of DBC (such as Eiffel and Sather [URL 12]) check pre- and postconditions automatically in the compiler and runtime system. You get the greatest benefit in this case because *all* of the code base (libraries, too) must honor their contracts.

But what about more popular languages such as C, C++, and Java? For these languages, there are preprocessors that process contracts embedded in the original source code as special comments. The preprocessor expands these comments to code that verifies the assertions.

For C and C++, you may want to investigate Nana [URL 18]. Nana doesn't handle inheritance, but it does use the debugger at runtime to monitor assertions in a novel way.

For Java, there is iContract [URL 17]. It takes comments (in JavaDoc form) and generates a new source file with the assertion logic included.

Preprocessors aren't as good as a built-in facility. They can be messy to integrate into your project, and other libraries you use won't have contracts. But they can still be very helpful; when a problem is discovered this way—especially one that you would *never* have found—it's almost like magic.

DBC and Crashing Early

DBC fits in nicely with our concept of crashing early (see *Dead Programs Tell No Lies*, page 120). Suppose you have a method that calculates square roots (such as in the Eiffel class DOUBLE). It needs a precondition that restricts the domain to positive numbers. An Eiffel precondition is declared with the keyword require, and a postcondition is declared with ensure, so you could write

```
sqrt: DOUBLE is
    -- Square root routine
require
    sqrt_arg_must_be_positive: Current >= 0;
--- ...
--- calculate square root here
--- ...
ensure
    ((Result*Result) - Current).abs <= epsilon*Current.abs;
    -- Result should be within error tolerance
end;
```

Who's Responsible?

Who is responsible for checking the precondition, the caller or the routine being called? When implemented as part of the language, the answer is neither: the precondition is tested behind the scenes after the caller invokes the routine but before the routine itself is entered. Thus if there is any explicit checking of parameters to be done, it must be performed by the *caller*, because the routine itself will never see parameters that violate its precondition. (For languages without built-in support, you would need to bracket the *called* routine with a preamble and/or postamble that checks these assertions.)

Consider a program that reads a number from the console, calculates its square root (by calling `sqrt`), and prints the result. The `sqrt` function has a precondition—its argument must not be negative. If the user enters a negative number at the console, it is up to the calling code to ensure that it never gets passed to `sqrt`. This calling code has many options: it could terminate, it could issue a warning and read another number, or it could make the number positive and append an "i" to the result returned by `sqrt`. Whatever its choice, this is definitely not `sqrt`'s problem.

By expressing the domain of the square root function in the precondition of the `sqrt` routine, you shift the burden of correctness to the caller—where it belongs. You can then design the `sqrt` routine secure in the knowledge that its input *will* be in range.

If your algorithm for calculating the square root fails (or isn't within the specified error tolerance), you get an error message and a stack trace to show you the call chain.

If you pass `sqrt` a negative parameter, the Eiffel runtime prints the error "`sqrt_arg_must_be_positive`," along with a stack trace. This is better than the alternative in languages such as Java, C, and C++, where passing a negative number to `sqrt` returns the special value NaN (Not a Number). It may be some time later in the program that you attempt to do some math on NaN, with surprising results.

It's much easier to find and diagnose the problem by crashing early, at the site of the problem.

Other Uses of Invariants

So far we have discussed pre- and postconditions that apply to individual methods and invariants that apply to all methods within a class, but there are other useful ways to use invariants.

Loop Invariants

Getting the boundary conditions right on a nontrivial loop can be problematic. Loops are subject to the banana problem (I know how to spell "banana," but I don't know when to stop), fencepost errors (not knowing whether to count the fenceposts or the spaces between them), and the ubiquitous "off by one" error [URL 52].

Invariants can help in these situations: a *loop invariant* is a statement of the eventual goal of a loop, but is generalized so that it is also valid before the loop executes and on each iteration through the loop. You can think of it as a kind of miniature contract. The classic example is a routine that finds the maximum value in an array.

```
int m = arr[0];    // example assumes arr.length > 0
int i = 1;
// Loop invariant: m = max(arr[0:i-1])
while (i < arr.length) {
  m = Math.max(m, arr[i]);
  i = i + 1;
}
```

(*arr[m:n]* is a notational convenience meaning a slice of the array from index *m* to *n*.) The invariant must be true before the loop runs, and the body of the loop must ensure that it remains true as the loop executes. In this way we know that the invariant also holds when the loop terminates, and therefore that our result is valid. Loop invariants can be coded explicitly as assertions, but they are also useful as design and documentation tools.

Semantic Invariants

You can use *semantic invariants* to express inviolate requirements, a kind of "philosophical contract."

We once wrote a debit card transaction switch. A major requirement was that the user of a debit card should never have the same transaction applied to their account twice. In other words, no matter what sort of failure mode might happen, the error should be on the side of *not* processing a transaction rather than processing a duplicate transaction.

This simple law, driven directly from the requirements, proved to be very helpful in sorting out complex error recovery scenarios, and guided the detailed design and implementation in many areas.

Be sure not to confuse requirements that are fixed, inviolate laws with those that are merely policies that might change with a new management regime. That's why we use the term *semantic* invariants—it must be central to the very *meaning* of a thing, and not subject to the whims of policy (which is what more dynamic business rules are for).

When you find a requirement that qualifies, make sure it becomes a well-known part of whatever documentation you are producing— whether it is a bulleted list in the requirements document that gets signed in triplicate or just a big note on the common whiteboard that everyone sees. Try to state it clearly and unambiguously. For example, in the debit card example, we might write

> ERR IN FAVOR OF THE CONSUMER.

This is a clear, concise, unambiguous statement that's applicable in many different areas of the system. It is our contract with all users of the system, our guarantee of behavior.

Dynamic Contracts and Agents

Until now, we have talked about contracts as fixed, immutable specifications. But in the landscape of autonomous agents, this doesn't need to be the case. By the definition of "autonomous," agents are free to *reject* requests that they do not want to honor. They are free to renegotiate the contract—"I can't provide that, but if you give me this, then I might provide something else."

Certainly any system that relies on agent technology has a *critical* dependence on contractual arrangements—even if they are dynamically generated.

Imagine: with enough components and agents that can negotiate their own contracts among themselves to achieve a goal, we might just solve the software productivity crisis by letting software solve it for us.

But if we can't use contracts by hand, we won't be able to use them automatically. So next time you design a piece of software, design its contract as well.

Related sections include:

- *Orthogonality*, page 34
- *Dead Programs Tell No Lies*, page 120
- *Assertive Programming*, page 122
- *How to Balance Resources*, page 129
- *Decoupling and the Law of Demeter*, page 138
- *Temporal Coupling*, page 150
- *Programming by Coincidence*, page 172
- *Code That's Easy to Test*, page 189
- *Pragmatic Teams*, page 224

Challenges

- Points to ponder: If DBC is so powerful, why isn't it used more widely? Is it hard to come up with the contract? Does it make you think about issues you'd rather ignore for now? Does it force you to THINK!? Clearly, this is a dangerous tool!

Exercises

Answer on p. 288

14. What makes a good contract? Anyone can add preconditions and postconditions, but will they do you any good? Worse yet, will they actually do more harm than good? For the example below and for those in Exercises 15 and 16, decide whether the specified contract is good, bad, or ugly, and explain why.

    First, let's look at an Eiffel example. Here we have a routine for adding a STRING to a doubly linked, circular list (remember that preconditions are labeled with require, and postconditions with ensure).

```
-- Add a unique item to a doubly linked list,
-- and return the newly created NODE.
add_item (item : STRING) : NODE is
    require
        item /= Void                    -- '/=' is 'not equal'.
        find_item(item) = Void          -- Must be unique
    deferred                            -- Abstract base class.
    ensure
        result.next.previous = result   -- Check the newly
        result.previous.next = result   -- added node's links.
        find_item(item) = result        -- Should find it.
    end
```

15. Next, let's try an example in Java—somewhat similar to the example in Exercise 14. insertNumber inserts an integer into an ordered list. Pre- and postconditions are labeled as in iContract (see [URL 17]).

Answer on p. 288

```
private int data[];
/**
 * @post data[index-1] < data[index] &&
 *       data[index] == aValue
 */
public Node insertNumber (final int aValue)
{
  int index = findPlaceToInsert(aValue);
  ...
```

16. Here's a fragment from a stack class in Java. Is this a good contract?

Answer on p. 289

```
/**
 * @pre anItem != null    // Require real data
 * @post pop() == anItem // Verify that it's
 *                       // on the stack
 */
public void push(final String anItem)
```

17. The classic examples of DBC (as in Exercises 14–16) show an implementation of an ADT (Abstract Data Type)—typically a stack or queue. But not many people really write these kinds of low-level classes.

Answer on p. 289

So, for this exercise, design an interface to a kitchen blender. It will eventually be a Web-based, Internet-enabled, CORBA-fied blender, but for now we just need the interface to control it. It has ten speed settings (0 means off). You can't operate it empty, and you can change the speed only one unit at a time (that is, from 0 to 1, and from 1 to 2, not from 0 to 2).

Here are the methods. Add appropriate pre- and postconditions and an invariant.

```
int getSpeed()
void setSpeed(int x)
boolean isFull()
void fill()
void empty()
```

18. How many numbers are in the series $0, 5, 10, 15, \ldots, 100$?

Answer on p. 290

► Dead Programs Tell No Lies

Have you noticed that sometimes other people can detect that things aren't well with you before you're aware of the problem yourself? It's the same with other people's code. If something is starting to go awry with one of our programs, sometimes it is a library routine that catches it first. Maybe a stray pointer has caused us to overwrite a file handle with something meaningless. The next call to `read` will catch it. Perhaps a buffer overrun has trashed a counter we're about to use to determine how much memory to allocate. Maybe we'll get a failure from `malloc`. A logic error a couple of million instructions ago means that the selector for a case statement is no longer the expected 1, 2, or 3. We'll hit the `default` case (which is one reason why each and every case/switch statement needs to have a default clause—we want to know when the "impossible" has happened).

It's easy to fall into the "it can't happen" mentality. Most of us have written code that didn't check that a file closed successfully, or that a trace statement got written as we expected. And all things being equal, it's likely that we didn't need to—the code in question wouldn't fail under any normal conditions. But we're coding defensively. We're looking for rogue pointers in other parts of our program trashing the stack. We're checking that the correct versions of shared libraries were actually loaded.

All errors give you information. You could convince yourself that the error can't happen, and choose to ignore it. Instead, Pragmatic Programmers tell themselves that if there is an error, something very, very bad has happened.

> **TIP 32**
>
> Crash Early

Crash, Don't Trash

One of the benefits of detecting problems as soon as you can is that you can crash earlier. And many times, crashing your program is the best thing you can do. The alternative may be to continue, writing corrupted data to some vital database or commanding the washing machine into its twentieth consecutive spin cycle.

The Java language and libraries have embraced this philosophy. When something unexpected happens within the runtime system, it throws a `RuntimeException`. If not caught, this will percolate up to the top level of the program and cause it to halt, displaying a stack trace.

You can do the same in other languages. If you don't have an exception mechanism, or if your libraries don't throw exceptions, then make sure you handle the errors yourself. In C, macros can be very useful for this:

```
#define CHECK(LINE, EXPECTED)                         \
  { int rc = LINE;                                    \
    if (rc != EXPECTED)                               \
        ut_abort(__FILE__, __LINE__, #LINE,  rc, EXPECTED); }
void ut_abort(char *file, int ln, char *line, int rc, int exp) {
  fprintf(stderr, "%s line %d\n'%s': expected %d, got %d\n",
                  file, ln, line, exp, rc);
  exit(1);
}
```

Then you can wrap calls that should never fail using

```
CHECK(stat("/tmp", &stat_buff), 0);
```

If it should fail, you'd get a message written to `stderr`:

```
source.c line 19
'stat("/tmp", &stat_buff)': expected 0, got -1
```

Clearly it is sometimes inappropriate simply to exit a running program. You may have claimed resources that might not get released, or you may need to write log messages, tidy up open transactions, or interact with other processes. The techniques we discuss in *When to Use Exceptions*, page 125, will help here. However, the basic principle stays the same—when your code discovers that something that was supposed to be impossible just happened, your program is no longer viable. Anything it does from this point forward becomes suspect, so terminate it as soon as possible. A dead program normally does a lot less damage than a crippled one.

Related sections include:
- *Design by Contract*, page 109
- *When to Use Exceptions*, page 125

Assertive Programming

There is a luxury in self-reproach. When we blame ourselves we feel no one else has a right to blame us.
▶ **Oscar Wilde, *The Picture of Dorian Gray***

It seems that there's a mantra that every programmer must memorize early in his or her career. It is a fundamental tenet of computing, a core belief that we learn to apply to requirements, designs, code, comments, just about everything we do. It goes

THIS CAN NEVER HAPPEN...

"This code won't be used 30 years from now, so two-digit dates are fine." "This application will never be used abroad, so why internationalize it?" "`count` can't be negative." "This `printf` can't fail."

Let's not practice this kind of self-deception, particularly when coding.

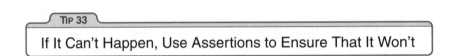

TIP 33

If It Can't Happen, Use Assertions to Ensure That It Won't

Whenever you find yourself thinking "but of course that could never happen," add code to check it. The easiest way to do this is with assertions. In most C and C++ implementations, you'll find some form of `assert` or `_assert` macro that checks a Boolean condition. These macros can be invaluable. If a pointer passed in to your procedure should never be NULL, then check for it:

```
void writeString(char *string) {
    assert(string != NULL);
    ...
```

Assertions are also useful checks on an algorithm's operation. Maybe you've written a clever sort algorithm. Check that it works:

```
for (int i = 0; i < num_entries-1; i++) {
    assert(sorted[i] <= sorted[i+1]);
}
```

Of course, the condition passed to an assertion should not have a side effect (see the box on page 124). Also remember that assertions may be turned off at compile time—never put code that *must* be executed into an `assert`.

Don't use assertions in place of real error handling. Assertions check for things that should never happen: you don't want to be writing code such as

```
printf("Enter 'Y' or 'N': ");
ch = getchar();
assert((ch == 'Y') || (ch == 'N'));    /* bad idea! */
```

And just because the supplied assert macros call exit when an assertion fails, there's no reason why versions you write should. If you need to free resources, have an assertion failure generate an exception, longjmp to an exit point, or call an error handler. Just make sure the code you execute in those dying milliseconds doesn't rely on the information that triggered the assertion failure in the first place.

Leave Assertions Turned On

There is a common misunderstanding about assertions, promulgated by the people who write compilers and language environments. It goes something like this:

> Assertions add some overhead to code. Because they check for things that should never happen, they'll get triggered only by a bug in the code. Once the code has been tested and shipped, they are no longer needed, and should be turned off to make the code run faster. Assertions are a debugging facility.

There are two patently wrong assumptions here. First, they assume that testing finds all the bugs. In reality, for any complex program you are unlikely to test even a miniscule percentage of the permutations your code will be put through (see *Ruthless Testing*, page 245). Second, the optimists are forgetting that your program runs in a dangerous world. During testing, rats probably won't gnaw through a communications cable, someone playing a game won't exhaust memory, and log files won't fill the hard drive. These things might happen when your program runs in a production environment. Your first line of defense is checking for any possible error, and your second is using assertions to try to detect those you've missed.

Turning off assertions when you deliver a program to production is like crossing a high wire without a net because you once made it across in practice. There's dramatic value, but it's hard to get life insurance.

Even if you *do* have performance issues, turn off only those assertions that really hit you. The sort example above may be a critical part of

Assertions and Side Effects

It is embarrassing when the code we add to detect errors actually ends up creating new errors. This can happen with assertions if evaluating the condition has side effects. For example, in Java it would be a bad idea to code something such as

```
while (iter.hasMoreElements()) {
    Test.ASSERT(iter.nextElement() != null);
    Object obj = iter.nextElement();
    // ....
}
```

The `.nextElement()` call in the `ASSERT` has the side effect of moving the iterator past the element being fetched, and so the loop will process only half the elements in the collection. It would be better to write

```
while (iter.hasMoreElements()) {
    Object obj = iter.nextElement();
    Test.ASSERT(obj != null);
    // ....
}
```

This problem is a kind of "Heisenbug"—debugging that changes the behavior of the system being debugged (see [URL 52]).

your application, and may need to be fast. Adding the check means another pass through the data, which might be unacceptable. Make that particular check optional,[2] but leave the rest in.

Related sections include:

- *Debugging*, page 90
- *Design by Contract*, page 109
- *How to Balance Resources*, page 129
- *Programming by Coincidence*, page 172

---

2.   In C-based languages, you can either use the preprocessor or use `if` statements to make assertions optional. Many implementations turn off code generation for the `assert` macro if a compile-time flag is set (or not set). Otherwise, you can place the code within an `if` statement with a constant condition, which many compilers (including most common Java systems) will optimize away.

Exercises

19. A quick reality check. Which of these "impossible" things can happen?

Answer on p. 290

1. A month with fewer than 28 days
2. `stat(".",&sb) == -1` (that is, can't access the current directory)
3. In C++: `a = 2; b = 3;` **if** `(a + b != 5) exit(1);`
4. A triangle with an interior angle sum $\neq 180°$
5. A minute that doesn't have 60 seconds
6. In Java: `(a + 1) <= a`

20. Develop a simple assertion checking class for Java.

Answer on p. 291

When to Use Exceptions

In *Dead Programs Tell No Lies*, page 120, we suggested that it is good practice to check for every possible error—particularly the unexpected ones. However, in practice this can lead to some pretty ugly code; the normal logic of your program can end up being totally obscured by error handling, particularly if you subscribe to the "a routine must have a single return statement" school of programming (we don't). We've seen code that looks something like the following:

```
retcode = OK;
if (socket.read(name) != OK) {
  retcode = BAD_READ;
}
else {
  processName(name);
  if (socket.read(address) != OK) {
    retcode = BAD_READ;
  }
  else {
    processAddress(address);
    if (socket.read(telNo) != OK) {
      retcode = BAD_READ;
    }
    else {
      // etc, etc...
    }
  }
}
return retcode;
```

Fortunately, if the programming language supports exceptions, you can rewrite this code in a far neater way:

```
    retcode = OK;
    try {
      socket.read(name);
      process(name);

      socket.read(address);
      processAddress(address);

      socket.read(telNo);
      // etc, etc...
    }
    catch (IOException e) {
      retcode = BAD_READ;
      Logger.log("Error reading individual: " + e.getMessage());
    }

    return retcode;
```

The normal flow of control is now clear, with all the error handling moved off to a single place.

What *Is* Exceptional?

One of the problems with exceptions is knowing when to use them. We believe that exceptions should rarely be used as part of a program's normal flow; exceptions should be reserved for unexpected events. Assume that an uncaught exception will terminate your program and ask yourself, "Will this code still run if I remove all the exception handlers?" If the answer is "no," then maybe exceptions are being used in nonexceptional circumstances.

For example, if your code tries to open a file for reading and that file does not exist, should an exception be raised?

Our answer is, "It depends." If the file *should* have been there, then an exception is warranted. Something unexpected happened—a file you were expecting to exist seems to have disappeared. On the other hand, if you have no idea whether the file should exist or not, then it doesn't seem exceptional if you can't find it, and an error return is appropriate.

Let's look at an example of the first case. The following code opens the file /etc/passwd, which should exist on all Unix systems. If it fails, it passes on the FileNotFoundException to its caller.

```
    public void open_passwd() throws FileNotFoundException {
      // This may throw FileNotFoundException...
      ipstream = new FileInputStream("/etc/passwd");
      // ...
    }
```

However, the second case may involve opening a file specified by the user on the command line. Here an exception isn't warranted, and the code looks different:

```
public boolean open_user_file(String name)
  throws FileNotFoundException {
  File f = new File(name);
  if (!f.exists()) {
    return false;
  }
  ipstream = new FileInputStream(f);
  return true;
}
```

Note that the `FileInputStream` call can still generate an exception, which the routine passes on. However, the exception will be generated under only truly exceptional circumstances; simply trying to open a file that does not exist will generate a conventional error return.

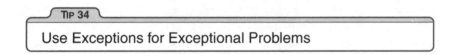

Tip 34

Use Exceptions for Exceptional Problems

Why do we suggest this approach to exceptions? Well, an exception represents an immediate, nonlocal transfer of control—it's a kind of cascading `goto`. Programs that use exceptions as part of their normal processing suffer from all the readability and maintainability problems of classic spaghetti code. These programs break encapsulation: routines and their callers are more tightly coupled via exception handling.

Error Handlers Are an Alternative

An error handler is a routine that is called when an error is detected. You can register a routine to handle a specific category of errors. When one of these errors occurs, the handler will be called.

There are times when you may want to use error handlers, either instead of or alongside exceptions. Clearly, if you are using a language such as C, which does not support exceptions, this is one of your few other options (see the challenge on the next page). However, sometimes error handlers can be used even in languages (such as Java) that have a good exception handling scheme built in.

Consider the implementation of a client-server application, using Java's Remote Method Invocation (RMI) facility. Because of the way RMI is implemented, every call to a remote routine must be prepared to handle a RemoteException. Adding code to handle these exceptions can become tedious, and means that it is difficult to write code that works with both local and remote routines. A possible work-around is to wrap your remote objects in a class that is not remote. This class then implements an error handler interface, allowing the client code to register a routine to be called when a remote exception is detected.

Related sections include:
- *Dead Programs Tell No Lies*, page 120

Challenges
- Languages that do not support exceptions often have some other nonlocal transfer of control mechanism (C has longjmp/setjmp, for example). Consider how you could implement some kind of ersatz exception mechanism using these facilities. What are the benefits and dangers? What special steps do you need to take to ensure that resources are not orphaned? Does it make sense to use this kind of solution whenever you code in C?

Exercises

Answer on p. 292

21. While designing a new container class, you identify the following possible error conditions:

   1. No memory available for a new element in the add routine

   2. Requested entry not found in the fetch routine

   3. null pointer passed to the add routine

   How should each be handled? Should an error be generated, should an exception be raised, or should the condition be ignored?

▶ 25 How to Balance Resources

"I brought you into this world," my father would say, *"and I can take you out. It don't make no difference to me. I'll just make another one like you."*
> ► **Bill Cosby, *Fatherhood***

We all manage resources whenever we code: memory, transactions, threads, files, timers—all kinds of things with limited availability. Most of the time, resource usage follows a predictable pattern: you allocate the resource, use it, and then deallocate it.

However, many developers have no consistent plan for dealing with resource allocation and deallocation. So let us suggest a simple tip:

> **TIP 35**
>
> Finish What You Start

This tip is easy to apply in most circumstances. It simply means that the routine or object that allocates a resource should be responsible for deallocating it. Let's see how it applies by looking at an example of some bad code—an application that opens a file, reads customer information from it, updates a field, and writes the result back. We've eliminated error handling to make the example clearer.

```
void readCustomer(const char *fName, Customer *cRec) {
  cFile = fopen(fName, "r+");
  fread(cRec, sizeof(*cRec), 1, cFile);
}
void writeCustomer(Customer *cRec) {
  rewind(cFile);
  fwrite(cRec, sizeof(*cRec), 1, cFile);
  fclose(cFile);
}
void updateCustomer(const char *fName, double newBalance) {
  Customer cRec;
  readCustomer(fName, &cRec);
  cRec.balance = newBalance;
  writeCustomer(&cRec);
}
```

At first sight, the routine updateCustomer looks pretty good. It seems to implement the logic we require—reading a record, updating the balance, and writing the record back out. However, this tidiness hides a major problem. The routines readCustomer and writeCustomer are tightly coupled[3]—they share the global variable cFile. readCustomer opens the file and stores the file pointer in cFile, and writeCustomer uses that stored pointer to close the file when it finishes. This global variable doesn't even appear in the updateCustomer routine.

Why is this bad? Let's consider the unfortunate maintenance programmer who is told that the specification has changed—the balance should be updated only if the new value is not negative. She goes into the source and changes updateCustomer:

```
void updateCustomer(const char *fName, double newBalance) {
  Customer cRec;
  readCustomer(fName, &cRec);
  if (newBalance >= 0.0) {
    cRec.balance = newBalance;
    writeCustomer(&cRec);
  }
}
```

All seems fine during testing. However, when the code goes into production, it collapses after several hours, complaining of *too many open files*. Because writeCustomer is not getting called in some circumstances, the file is not getting closed.

A very bad solution to this problem would be to deal with the special case in updateCustomer:

```
void updateCustomer(const char *fName, double newBalance) {
  Customer cRec;
  readCustomer(fName, &cRec);
  if (newBalance >= 0.0) {
    cRec.balance = newBalance;
    writeCustomer(&cRec);
  }
  else
    fclose(cFile);
}
```

This will fix the problem—the file will now get closed regardless of the new balance—but the fix now means that *three* routines are coupled through the global cFile. We're falling into a trap, and things are going to start going downhill rapidly if we continue on this course.

---

3.   For a discussion of the dangers of coupled code, see *Decoupling and the Law of Demeter*, page 138.

The *finish what you start* tip tells us that, ideally, the routine that allocates a resource should also free it. We can apply it here by refactoring the code slightly:

```
void readCustomer(FILE *cFile, Customer *cRec) {
  fread(cRec, sizeof(*cRec), 1, cFile);
}
void writeCustomer(FILE *cFile, Customer *cRec) {
  rewind(cFile);
  fwrite(cRec, sizeof(*cRec), 1, cFile);
}
void updateCustomer(const char *fName, double newBalance) {
  FILE *cFile;
  Customer cRec;
  cFile = fopen(fName, "r+");        // >---
  readCustomer(cFile, &cRec);        //    |
  if (newBalance >= 0.0) {           //    |
    cRec.balance = newBalance;       //    |
    writeCustomer(cFile, &cRec);     //    |
  }                                  //    |
  fclose(cFile);                     // <---
}
```

Now all the responsibility for the file is in the updateCustomer routine. It opens the file and (finishing what it starts) closes it before exiting. The routine balances the use of the file: the open and close are in the same place, and it is apparent that for every open there will be a corresponding close. The refactoring also removes an ugly global variable.

Nest Allocations

The basic pattern for resource allocation can be extended for routines that need more than one resource at a time. There are just two more suggestions:

1. Deallocate resources in the opposite order to that in which you allocate them. That way you won't orphan resources if one resource contains references to another.

2. When allocating the same set of resources in different places in your code, always allocate them in the same order. This will reduce the possibility of deadlock. (If process A claims resource1 and is about to claim resource2, while process B has claimed resource2 and is trying to get resource1, the two processes will wait forever.)

It doesn't matter what kind of resources we're using—transactions, memory, files, threads, windows—the basic pattern applies: whoever allocates a resource should be responsible for deallocating it. However, in some languages we can develop the concept further.

Objects and Exceptions

The equilibrium between allocations and deallocations is reminiscent of a class's constructor and destructor. The class represents a resource, the constructor gives you a particular object of that resource type, and the destructor removes it from your scope.

If you are programming in an object-oriented language, you may find it useful to encapsulate resources in classes. Each time you need a particular resource type, you instantiate an object of that class. When the object goes out of scope, or is reclaimed by the garbage collector, the object's destructor then deallocates the wrapped resource.

This approach has particular benefits when you're working with languages such as C++, where exceptions can interfere with resource deallocation.

Balancing and Exceptions

Languages that support exceptions can make resource deallocation tricky. If an exception is thrown, how do you guarantee that everything allocated prior to the exception is tidied up? The answer depends to some extent on the language.

Balancing Resources with C++ Exceptions

C++ supports a try...catch exception mechanism. Unfortunately, this means that there are always at least two possible paths when exiting a routine that catches and then rethrows an exception:

```
void doSomething(void) {
  Node *n = new Node;
  try {
    // do something
  }
  catch (...) {
    delete n;
    throw;
  }
  delete n;
}
```

Notice that the node we create is freed in two places—once in the routine's normal exit path, and once in the exception handler. This is an obvious violation of the *DRY* principle and a maintenance problem waiting to happen.

However, we can use the semantics of C++ to our advantage. Local objects are automatically destroyed on exiting from their enclosing block. This gives us a couple of options. If the circumstances permit, we can change "n" from a pointer to an actual Node object on the stack:

```
void doSomething1(void) {
  Node n;
  try {
    // do something
  }
  catch (...) {
    throw;
  }
}
```

Here we rely on C++ to handle the destruction of the Node object automatically, whether an exception is thrown or not.

If the switch from a pointer is not possible, the same effect can be achieved by wrapping the resource (in this case, a Node pointer) within another class.

```
// Wrapper class for Node resources
class NodeResource {
  Node *n;
 public:
  NodeResource() { n = new Node; }
  ~NodeResource() { delete n; }
  Node *operator->() { return n; }
};
void doSomething2(void) {
  NodeResource n;
  try {
    // do something
  }
  catch (...) {
    throw;
  }
}
```

Now the wrapper class, NodeResource, ensures that when its objects are destroyed the corresponding nodes are also destroyed. For convenience, the wrapper provides a dereferencing operator ->, so that its users can access the fields in the contained Node object directly.

Because this technique is so useful, the standard C++ library provides the template class `auto_ptr`, which gives you automatic wrappers for dynamically allocated objects.

```
void doSomething3(void) {
  auto_ptr<Node> p (new Node);
  // Access the Node as p->...
  // Node automatically deleted at end
}
```

Balancing Resources in Java

Unlike C++, Java implements a lazy form of automatic object destruction. Unreferenced objects are considered to be candidates for garbage collection, and their `finalize` method will get called should garbage collection ever claim them. While a convenience for developers, who no longer get the blame for most memory leaks, it makes it difficult to implement resource clean-up using the C++ scheme. Fortunately, the designers of the Java language thoughtfully added a language feature to compensate, the `finally` clause. When a `try` block contains a `finally` clause, code in that clause is guaranteed to be executed if any statement in the `try` block is executed. It doesn't matter whether an exception is thrown (or even if the code in the `try` block executes a `return`)—the code in the `finally` clause will get run. This means we can balance our resource usage with code such as

```
public void doSomething() throws IOException {
  File tmpFile = new File(tmpFileName);
  FileWriter tmp = new FileWriter(tmpFile);
  try {
    // do some work
  }
  finally {
    tmpFile.delete();
  }
}
```

The routine uses a temporary file, which we want to delete, regardless of how the routine exits. The `finally` block allows us to express this concisely.

When You Can't Balance Resources

There are times when the basic resource allocation pattern just isn't appropriate. Commonly this is found in programs that use dynamic data structures. One routine will allocate an area of memory and link it into some larger structure, where it may stay for some time.

The trick here is to establish a semantic invariant for memory allocation. You need to decide who is responsible for data in an aggregate data structure. What happens when you deallocate the top-level structure? You have three main options:

1. The top-level structure is also responsible for freeing any substructures that it contains. These structures then recursively delete data they contain, and so on.

2. The top-level structure is simply deallocated. Any structures that it pointed to (that are not referenced elsewhere) are orphaned.

3. The top-level structure refuses to deallocate itself if it contains any substructures.

The choice here depends on the circumstances of each individual data structure. However, you need to make it explicit for each, and implement your decision consistently. Implementing any of these options in a procedural language such as C can be a problem: data structures themselves are not active. Our preference in these circumstances is to write a module for each major structure that provides standard allocation and deallocation facilities for that structure. (This module can also provide facilities such as debug printing, serialization, deserialization, and traversal hooks.)

Finally, if keeping track of resources gets tricky, you can write your own form of limited automatic garbage collection by implementing a reference counting scheme on your dynamically allocated objects. The book *More Effective C++* [Mey96] dedicates a section to this topic.

Checking the Balance

Because Pragmatic Programmers trust no one, including ourselves, we feel that it is always a good idea to build code that actually checks that resources are indeed freed appropriately. For most applications, this normally means producing wrappers for each type of resource, and using these wrappers to keep track of all allocations and deallocations. At certain points in your code, the program logic will dictate that the resources will be in a certain state: use the wrappers to check this.

For example, a long-running program that services requests will probably have a single point at the top of its main processing loop where it waits for the next request to arrive. This is a good place to ensure that resource usage has not increased since the last execution of the loop.

At a lower, but no less useful level, you can invest in tools that (among other things) check your running programs for memory leaks. Purify (www.rational.com) and Insure++ (www.parasoft.com) are popular choices.

Related sections include:
- *Design by Contract*, page 109
- *Assertive Programming*, page 122
- *Decoupling and the Law of Demeter*, page 138

Challenges
- Although there are no guaranteed ways of ensuring that you always free resources, certain design techniques, when applied consistently, will help. In the text we discussed how establishing a semantic invariant for major data structures could direct memory deallocation decisions. Consider how *Design by Contract*, page 109, could help refine this idea.

Exercises

Answer on p. 292
22. Some C and C++ developers make a point of setting a pointer to NULL after they deallocate the memory it references. Why is this a good idea?

Answer on p. 292
23. Some Java developers make a point of setting an object variable to NULL after they have finished using the object. Why is this a good idea?

Chapter 5

Bend, or Break

Life doesn't stand still.

Neither can the code that we write. In order to keep up with today's near-frantic pace of change, we need to make every effort to write code that's as loose—as flexible—as possible. Otherwise we may find our code quickly becoming outdated, or too brittle to fix, and may ultimately be left behind in the mad dash toward the future.

In *Reversibility*, on page 44, we talked about the perils of irreversible decisions. In this chapter, we'll tell you how to make *reversible* decisions, so your code can stay flexible and adaptable in the face of an uncertain world.

First we need to look at *coupling*—the dependencies among modules of code. In *Decoupling and the Law of Demeter* we'll show how to keep separate concepts separate, and decrease coupling.

A good way to stay flexible is to write *less* code. Changing code leaves you open to the possibility of introducing new bugs. *Metaprogramming* will explain how to move details out of the code completely, where they can be changed more safely and easily.

In *Temporal Coupling*, we'll look at two aspects of time as they relate to coupling. Do you depend on the "tick" coming before the "tock"? Not if you want to stay flexible.

A key concept in creating flexible code is the separation of a data *model* from a *view*, or presentation, of that model. We'll decouple models from views in *It's Just a View*.

Finally, there's a technique for decoupling modules even further by providing a meeting place where modules can exchange data anonymously and asynchronously. This is the topic of *Blackboards*.

Armed with these techniques, you can write code that will "roll with the punches."

26 ▶ Decoupling and the Law of Demeter

Good fences make good neighbors.
> ▶ **Robert Frost, "Mending Wall"**

In *Orthogonality*, page 34, and *Design by Contract*, page 109, we suggested that writing "shy" code is beneficial. But "shy" works two ways: don't reveal yourself to others, and don't interact with too many people.

Spies, dissidents, revolutionaries, and such are often organized into small groups of people called *cells*. Although individuals in each cell may know each other, they have no knowledge of those in other cells. If one cell is discovered, no amount of truth serum will reveal the names of others outside the cell. Eliminating interactions between cells protects everyone.

We feel that this is a good principle to apply to coding as well. Organize your code into cells (modules) and limit the interaction between them. If one module then gets compromised and has to be replaced, the other modules should be able to carry on.

Minimize Coupling

What's wrong with having modules that know about each other? Nothing in principle—we don't need to be as paranoid as spies or dissidents. However, you do need to be careful about *how many* other modules you interact with and, more importantly, *how* you came to interact with them.

Suppose you are remodeling your house, or building a house from scratch. A typical arrangement involves a "general contractor." You hire the contractor to get the work done, but the contractor may or may not do the construction personally; the work may be offered to various subcontractors. But as the client, you are not involved in dealing with the subcontractors directly—the general contractor assumes that set of headaches on your behalf.

We'd like to follow this same model in software. When we ask an object for a particular service, we'd like the service to be performed on our behalf. We *do not* want the object to give us a third-party object that we have to deal with to get the required service.

For example, suppose you are writing a class that generates a graph of scientific recorder data. You have data recorders spread around the world; each recorder object contains a location object giving its position and time zone. You want to let your users select a recorder and plot its data, labeled with the correct time zone. You might write

```
public void plotDate(Date aDate, Selection aSelection) {
  TimeZone tz =
    aSelection.getRecorder().getLocation().getTimeZone();
  ...
}
```

But now the plotting routine is unnecessarily coupled to *three* classes— Selection, Recorder, and Location. This style of coding dramatically increases the number of classes on which our class depends. Why is this a bad thing? It increases the risk that an unrelated change somewhere else in the system will affect *your* code. For instance, if Fred makes a change to Location such that it no longer directly contains a TimeZone, you have to change your code as well.

Rather than digging though a hierarchy yourself, just ask for what you need directly:

```
public void plotDate(Date aDate, TimeZone aTz) {
  ...
}
plotDate(someDate, someSelection.getTimeZone());
```

We added a method to Selection to get the time zone on our behalf: the plotting routine doesn't care whether the time zone comes from the Recorder directly, from some contained object within Recorder, or whether Selection makes up a different time zone entirely. The selection routine, in turn, should probably just ask the recorder for its time zone, leaving it up to the recorder to get it from its contained Location object.

Traversing relationships between objects directly can quickly lead to a combinatorial explosion[1] of dependency relationships. You can see symptoms of this phenomenon in a number of ways:

1. Large C or C++ projects where the command to link a unit test is longer than the test program itself

2. "Simple" changes to one module that propagate through unrelated modules in the system

3. Developers who are afraid to change code because they aren't sure what might be affected

Systems with many unnecessary dependencies are very hard (and expensive) to maintain, and tend to be highly unstable. In order to keep the dependencies to a minimum, we'll use the *Law of Demeter* to design our methods and functions.

The Law of Demeter for Functions

The Law of Demeter for functions [LH89] attempts to minimize coupling between modules in any given program. It tries to prevent you from reaching into an object to gain access to a third object's methods. The law is summarized in Figure 5.1 on the next page.

By writing "shy" code that honors the Law of Demeter as much as possible, we can achieve our objective:

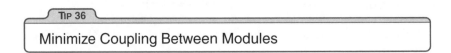

TIP 36

Minimize Coupling Between Modules

Does It Really Make a Difference?

While it sounds good in theory, does following the Law of Demeter really help to create more maintainable code?

Studies have shown [BBM96] that classes in C++ with larger *response sets* are more prone to error than classes with smaller response sets (a

---

1. If n objects all know about each other, then a change to just one object can result in the other $n - 1$ objects needing changes.

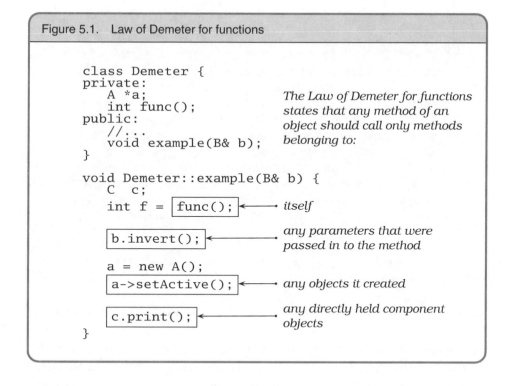

Figure 5.1. Law of Demeter for functions

```
class Demeter {
private:
    A *a;
    int func();
public:
    //...
    void example(B& b);
}

void Demeter::example(B& b) {
    C   c;
    int f = func();

    b.invert();

    a = new A();
    a->setActive();

    c.print();
}
```

The Law of Demeter for functions states that any method of an object should call only methods belonging to:

itself

any parameters that were passed in to the method

any objects it created

any directly held component objects

response set is defined to be the number of functions directly invoked by methods of the class).

Because following the Law of Demeter reduces the size of the response set in the calling class, it follows that classes designed in this way will also tend to have fewer errors (see [URL 56] for more papers and information on the Demeter project).

Using The Law of Demeter will make your code more adaptable and robust, but at a cost: as a "general contractor," your module must delegate and manage any and all subcontractors directly, without involving clients of your module. In practice, this means that you will be writing a large number of wrapper methods that simply forward the request on to a delegate. These wrapper methods will impose both a runtime cost and a space overhead, which may be significant—even prohibitive—in some applications.

As with any technique, you must balance the pros and cons for *your* particular application. In database schema design it is common practice to "denormalize" the schema for a performance improvement: to

<u>**Physical Decoupling**</u>

In this section we're concerned largely with designing to keep things logically decoupled within systems. However, there is another kind of interdependence that becomes highly significant as systems grow larger. In his book *Large-Scale C++ Software Design* [Lak96], John Lakos addresses the issues surrounding the relationships among the files, directories, and libraries that make up a system. Large projects that ignore these *physical design* problems wind up with build cycles that are measured in days and unit tests that may drag in the entire system as support code, among other problems. Mr. Lakos argues convincingly that logical and physical design must proceed in tandem—that undoing the damage done to a large body of code by cyclic dependencies is extremely difficult. We recommend this book if you are involved in large-scale developments, even if C++ isn't your implementation language.

violate the rules of normalization in exchange for speed. A similar trade-off can be made here as well. In fact, by reversing the Law of Demeter and *tightly* coupling several modules, you may realize an important performance gain. As long as it is well known and acceptable for those modules to be coupled, your design is fine.

Otherwise, you may find yourself on the road to a brittle, inflexible future. Or no future at all.

Related sections include:
- *Orthogonality*, page 34
- *Reversibility*, page 44
- *Design by Contract*, page 109
- *How to Balance Resources*, page 129
- *It's Just a View*, page 157
- *Pragmatic Teams*, page 224
- *Ruthless Testing*, page 237

Challenges
- We've discussed how using delegation makes it easier to obey the Law of Demeter and hence reduce coupling. However, writing all of the methods

needed to forward calls to delegated classes is boring and error prone. What are the advantages and disadvantages of writing a preprocessor that generates these calls automatically? Should this preprocessor be run only once, or should it be used as part of the build?

Exercises

24. We discussed the concept of physical decoupling in the box on on the facing page. Which of the following C++ header files is more tightly coupled to the rest of the system?

Answer on p. 293

person1.h:
```
#include "date.h"
class  Person1 {
private:
  Date myBirthdate;
public:
  Person1(Date &birthDate);
  // ...
```

person2.h:
```
class Date;
class  Person2 {
private:
  Date *myBirthdate;
public:
  Person2(Date &birthDate);
  // ...
```

25. For the example below and for those in Exercises 26 and 27, determine if the method calls shown are allowed according to the Law of Demeter. This first one is in Java.

Answer on p. 293

```java
public void showBalance(BankAccount acct) {
  Money amt = acct.getBalance();
  printToScreen(amt.printFormat());
}
```

26. This example is also in Java.

Answer on p. 294

```java
public class Colada {
  private Blender myBlender;
  private Vector myStuff;
  public Colada() {
    myBlender = new Blender();
    myStuff = new Vector();
  }
  private void doSomething() {
    myBlender.addIngredients(myStuff.elements());
  }
}
```

27. This example is in C++.

Answer on p. 294

```cpp
void processTransaction(BankAccount acct, int) {
  Person *who;
  Money amt;

  amt.setValue(123.45);
  acct.setBalance(amt);
  who = acct.getOwner();
  markWorkflow(who->name(), SET_BALANCE);
}
```

Metaprogramming

No amount of genius can overcome a preoccupation with detail.
▶ **Levy's Eighth Law**

Details mess up our pristine code—especially if they change frequently. Every time we have to go in and change the code to accommodate some change in business logic, or in the law, or in management's personal tastes of the day, we run the risk of breaking the system—of introducing a new bug.

So we say "out with the details!" Get them out of the code. While we're at it, we can make our code highly configurable and "soft"—that is, easily adaptable to changes.

Dynamic Configuration

First, we want to make our systems highly configurable. Not just things such as screen colors and prompt text, but deeply ingrained items such as the choice of algorithms, database products, middleware technology, and user-interface style. These items should be implemented as configuration options, not through integration or engineering.

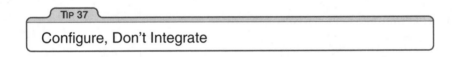

TIP 37

Configure, Don't Integrate

Use *metadata* to describe configuration options for an application: tuning parameters, user preferences, the installation directory, and so on.

What exactly is metadata? Strictly speaking, metadata is data about data. The most common example is probably a database schema or data dictionary. A schema contains data that describes fields (columns) in terms of names, storage lengths, and other attributes. You should be able to access and manipulate this information just as you would any other data in the database.

We use the term in its broadest sense. Metadata is any data that describes the application—how it should run, what resources it should use, and so on. Typically, metadata is accessed and used at runtime, not at compile time. You use metadata all the time—at least your programs do. Suppose you click on an option to hide the toolbar on your

Web browser. The browser will store that preference, as metadata, in some sort of internal database.

This database might be in a proprietary format, or it might use a standard mechanism. Under Windows, either an initialization file (using the suffix .ini) or entries in the system Registry are typical. Under Unix, the X Window System provides similar functionality using Application Default files. Java uses Property files. In all of these environments, you specify a key to retrieve a value. Alternatively, more powerful and flexible implementations of metadata use an embedded scripting language (see *Domain Languages*, page 57, for details).

The Netscape browser has actually implemented preferences using both of these techniques. In Version 3, preferences were saved as simple key/value pairs:

```
SHOW_TOOLBAR: False
```

Later, Version 4 preferences looked more like JavaScript:

```
user_pref("custtoolbar.Browser.Navigation_Toolbar.open", false);
```

Metadata-Driven Applications

But we want to go beyond using metadata for simple preferences. We want to configure and drive the application via metadata as much as possible. Our goal is to think declaratively (specifying *what* is to be done, not *how*) and create highly dynamic and adaptable programs. We do this by adopting a general rule: program for the general case, and put the specifics somewhere else—outside the compiled code base.

> **TIP 38**
>
> Put Abstractions in Code, Details in Metadata

There are several benefits to this approach:

- It forces you to decouple your design, which results in a more flexible and adaptable program.

- It forces you to create a more robust, abstract design by deferring details—deferring them all the way out of the program.

- You can customize the application without recompiling it. You can also use this level of customization to provide easy work-arounds for critical bugs in live production systems.

- Metadata can be expressed in a manner that's much closer to the problem domain than a general-purpose programming language might be (see *Domain Languages*, page 57).

- You may even be able to implement several different projects using the same application engine, but with different metadata.

We want to defer definition of most details until the last moment, and leave the details as soft—as easy to change—as we can. By crafting a solution that allows us to make changes quickly, we stand a better chance of coping with the flood of directional shifts that swamp many projects (see *Reversibility*, page 44).

Business Logic

So you've made the choice of database engine a configuration option, and provided metadata to determine the user-interface style. Can we do more? Definitely.

Because business policy and rules are more likely to change than any other aspect of the project, it makes sense to maintain them in a very flexible format.

For example, your purchasing application may include various corporate policies. Maybe you pay small suppliers in 45 days and large ones in 90 days. Make the definitions of the supplier types, as well as the time periods themselves, configurable. Take the opportunity to generalize.

Maybe you are writing a system with horrendous workflow requirements. Actions start and stop according to complex (and changing) business rules. Consider encoding them in some kind of rule-based (or expert) system, embedded within your application. That way, you'll configure it by writing rules, not cutting code.

Less complex logic can be expressed using a mini-language, removing the need to recompile and redeploy when the environment changes. Have a look at page 58 for an example.

<u>**When to Configure**</u>

As mentioned in *The Power of Plain Text*, page 73, we recommend representing configuration metadata in plain text—it makes life that much easier.

But when should a program read this configuration? Many programs will scan such things only at startup, which is unfortunate. If you need to change the configuration, this forces you to restart the application. A more flexible approach is to write programs that can reload their configuration while they're running. This flexibility comes at a cost: it is more complex to implement.

So consider how your application will be used: if it is a long-running server process, you will want to provide some way to reread and apply metadata while the program is running. For a small client GUI application that restarts quickly, you may not need to.

This phenomenon is not limited to application code. We've all been annoyed at operating systems that force us to reboot when we install some simple application or change an innocuous parameter.

An Example: Enterprise Java Beans

Enterprise Java Beans (EJB) is a framework for simplifying programming in a distributed, transaction-based environment. We mention it here because EJB illustrates how metadata can be used both to configure applications *and* to reduce the complexity of writing code.

Suppose you want to create some Java software that will participate in transactions across different machines, between different database vendors, and with different thread and load-balancing models.

The good news is, you don't have to worry about all that. You write a *bean*—a self-contained object that follows certain conventions—and place it in a *bean container* that manages much of the low-level detail on your behalf. You can write the code for a bean without including any transaction operations or thread management; EJB uses metadata to specify how transactions should be handled.

Thread allocation and load balancing are specified as metadata to the underlying transaction service that the container uses. This separation allows us great flexibility to configure the environment dynamically, at runtime.

The bean's container can manage transactions on the bean's behalf in one of several different styles (including an option where you control your own commits and rollbacks). All of the parameters that affect the bean's behavior are specified in the bean's *deployment descriptor*—a serialized object that contains the metadata we need.

Distributed systems such as EJB are leading the way into a new world of configurable, dynamic systems.

Cooperative Configuration

We've talked about users and developers configuring dynamic applications. But what happens if you let applications configure each other—software that adapts itself to its environment? Unplanned, spur-of-the-moment configuration of existing software is a powerful concept.

Operating systems already configure themselves to hardware as they boot, and Web browsers update themselves with new components automatically.

Your larger applications probably already have issues with handling different versions of data and different releases of libraries and operating systems. Perhaps a more dynamic approach will help.

Don't Write Dodo-Code

Without metadata, your code is not as adaptable or flexible as it could be. Is this a bad thing? Well, out here in the real world, species that don't adapt die.

The dodo didn't adapt to the presence of humans and their livestock on the island of Mauritius, and quickly became extinct.[2] It was the first documented extinction of a species at the hand of man.

Don't let your project (or your career) go the way of the dodo.

---

2. It didn't help that the settlers beat the placid (read *stupid*) birds to death with clubs for sport.

Related sections include:

- *Orthogonality*, page 34
- *Reversibility*, page 44
- *Domain Languages*, page 57
- *The Power of Plain Text*, page 73

Challenges

- For your current project, consider how much of the application might be moved out of the program itself to metadata. What would the resultant "engine" look like? Would you be able to reuse that engine in the context of a different application?

Exercises

28. Which of the following things would be better represented as code within a program, and which externally as metadata?

Answer on p. 295

1. Communication port assignments
2. An editor's support for highlighting the syntax of various languages
3. An editor's support for different graphic devices
4. A state machine for a parser or scanner
5. Sample values and results for use in unit testing

Temporal Coupling

What is *temporal coupling* all about, you may ask. It's about time.

Time is an often ignored aspect of software architectures. The only time that preoccupies us is the time on the schedule, the time left until we ship—but this is not what we're talking about here. Instead, we are talking about the role of time as a design element of the software itself. There are two aspects of time that are important to us: concurrency (things happening at the same time) and ordering (the relative positions of things in time).

We don't usually approach programming with either of these aspects in mind. When people first sit down to design an architecture or write a program, things tend to be linear. That's the way most people think— *do this* and then always *do that*. But thinking this way leads to *temporal coupling*: coupling in time. Method A must always be called before method B; only one report can be run at a time; you must wait for the screen to redraw before the button click is received. Tick must happen before tock.

This approach is not very flexible, and not very realistic.

We need to allow for concurrency[3] and to think about decoupling any time or order dependencies. In doing so, we can gain flexibility and reduce any time-based dependencies in many areas of development: workflow analysis, architecture, design, and deployment.

Workflow

On many projects, we need to model and analyze the users' workflows as part of requirements analysis. We'd like to find out what *can* happen at the same time, and what must happen in a strict order. One way to do this is to capture their description of workflow using a notation such as the *UML activity diagram.*[4]

---

3. We won't go into the details of concurrent or parallel programming here; a good computer science textbook should cover the basics, including scheduling, deadlock, starvation, mutual exclusion/semaphores, and so on.

4. For more information on all of the UML diagram types, see [FS97].

An activity diagram consists of a set of actions drawn as rounded boxes. The arrow leaving an action leads to either another action (which can start once the first action completes) or to a thick line called a *synchronization bar*. Once *all* the actions leading into a synchronization bar are complete, you can then proceed along any arrows leaving the bar. An action with no arrows leading into it can be started at any time.

You can use activity diagrams to maximize parallelism by identifying activities that *could be* performed in parallel, but aren't.

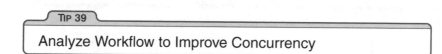

TIP 39

Analyze Workflow to Improve Concurrency

For instance, in our blender project (Exercise 17, page 119), users may initially describe their current workflow as follows.

1. Open blender
2. Open piña colada mix
3. Put mix in blender
4. Measure 1/2 cup white rum
5. Pour in rum
6. Add 2 cups of ice
7. Close blender
8. Liquefy for 2 minutes
9. Open blender
10. Get glasses
11. Get pink umbrellas
12. Serve

Even though they describe these actions serially, and may even perform them serially, we notice that many of them could be performed in parallel, as we show in the activity diagram in Figure 5.2 on the next page.

It can be eye-opening to see where the dependencies really exist. In this instance, the top-level tasks (1, 2, 4, 10, and 11) can all happen concurrently, up front. Tasks 3, 5, and 6 can happen in parallel later.

If you were in a piña colada-making contest, these optimizations may make all the difference.

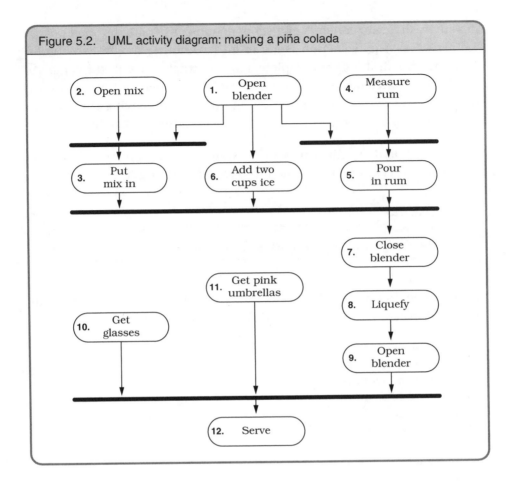

Figure 5.2. UML activity diagram: making a piña colada

Architecture

We wrote an On-Line Transaction Processing (OLTP) system a few years ago. At its simplest, all the system had to do was read a request and process the transaction against the database. But we wrote a three-tier, multiprocessing distributed application: each component was an independent entity that ran concurrently with all other components. While this sounds like more work, it wasn't: taking advantage of temporal decoupling made it *easier* to write. Let's take a closer look at this project.

The system takes in requests from a large number of data communication lines and processes transactions against a back-end database.

The design addresses the following constraints:

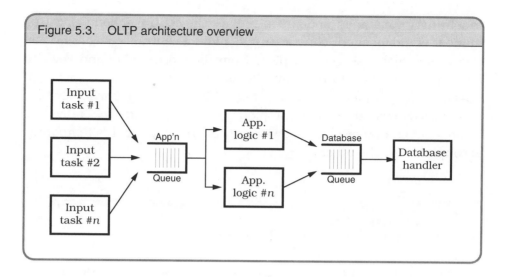

Figure 5.3. OLTP architecture overview

- Database operations take a relatively long time to complete.
- For each transaction, we must not block communication services while a database transaction is being processed.
- Database performance suffers with too many concurrent sessions.
- Multiple transactions are in progress concurrently on each data line.

The solution that gave us the best performance and cleanest architecture looked something like Figure 5.3.

Each box represents a separate process; processes communicate via work queues. Each input process monitors one incoming communication line, and makes requests to the application server. All requests are asynchronous: as soon as the input process makes its current request, it goes back to monitoring the line for more traffic. Similarly, the application server makes requests of the database process,[5] and is notified when the individual transaction is complete.

This example also shows a way to get quick and dirty load balancing among multiple consumer processes: the *hungry consumer* model.

---

5. Even though we show the database as a single, monolithic entity, it is not. The database software is partitioned into several processes and client threads, but this is handled internally by the database software and isn't part of our example.

In a hungry consumer model, you replace the central scheduler with a number of independent consumer tasks and a centralized work queue. Each consumer task grabs a piece from the work queue and goes on about the business of processing it. As each task finishes its work, it goes back to the queue for some more. This way, if any particular task gets bogged down, the others can pick up the slack, and each individual component can proceed at its own pace. Each component is temporally decoupled from the others.

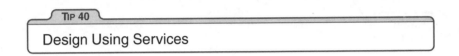

Tip 40

Design Using Services

Instead of components, we have really created *services*—independent, concurrent objects behind well-defined, consistent interfaces.

Design for Concurrency

The rising acceptance of Java as a platform has exposed more developers to multithreaded programming. But programming with threads imposes some design constraints—and that's a good thing. Those constraints are actually so helpful that we want to abide by them whenever we program. It will help us decouple our code and fight *programming by coincidence* (see page 172).

With linear code, it's easy to make assumptions that lead to sloppy programming. But concurrency forces you to think through things a bit more carefully—you're not alone at the party anymore. Because things can now happen at the "same time," you may suddenly see some time-based dependencies.

To begin with, any global or static variables must be protected from concurrent access. Now may be a good time to ask yourself *why* you need a global variable in the first place. In addition, you need to make sure that you present consistent state information, regardless of the order of calls. For example, when is it valid to query the state of your object? If your object is in an invalid state between certain calls, you may be relying on a coincidence that no one can call your object at that point in time.

Suppose you have a windowing subsystem where the widgets are first created and then shown on the display in two separate steps. You aren't allowed to set state in the widget until it is shown. Depending on how the code is set up, you may be relying on the fact that no other object can use the created widget until you've shown it on the screen.

But this may not be true in a concurrent system. Objects must always be in a valid state when called, and they can be called at the most awkward times. You must ensure that an object is in a valid state *any* time it could possibly be called. Often this problem shows up with classes that define separate constructor and initialization routines (where the constructor doesn't leave the object in an initialized state). Using class invariants, discussed in *Design by Contract*, page 109, will help you avoid this trap.

Cleaner Interfaces

Thinking about concurrency and time-ordered dependencies can lead you to design cleaner interfaces as well. Consider the C library routine strtok, which breaks a string into tokens.

The design of strtok isn't thread safe,[6] but that isn't the worst part: look at the time dependency. You must make the first call to strtok with the variable you want to parse, and all successive calls with a NULL instead. If you pass in a non-NULL value, it restarts the parse on that buffer instead. Without even considering threads, suppose you wanted to use strtok to parse two separate strings at the same time:

```
char buf1[BUFSIZ];
char buf2[BUFSIZ];
char *p, *q;
strcpy(buf1, "this is a test");
strcpy(buf2, "this ain't gonna work");
p = strtok(buf1, " ");
q = strtok(buf2, " ");
while (p && q) {
  printf("%s %s\n", p, q);
  p = strtok(NULL, " ");
  q = strtok(NULL, " ");
}
```

---

6. It uses static data to maintain the current position in the buffer. The static data isn't protected against concurrent access, so it isn't thread safe. In addition, it clobbers the first argument you pass in, which can lead to some nasty surprises.

The code as shown will not work: there is implicit state retained in `strtok` between calls. You have to use `strtok` on just one buffer at a time.

Now in Java, the design of a string parser has to be different. It must be thread safe and present a consistent state.

```
StringTokenizer st1 = new StringTokenizer("this is a test");
StringTokenizer st2 = new StringTokenizer("this test will work");

while (st1.hasMoreTokens() && st2.hasMoreTokens()) {
  System.out.println(st1.nextToken());
  System.out.println(st2.nextToken());
}
```

`StringTokenizer` is a much cleaner, more maintainable, interface. It contains no surprises, and won't cause mysterious bugs in the future, as `strtok` might.

TIP 41

Always Design for Concurrency

Deployment

Once you've designed an architecture with an element of concurrency, it becomes easier to think about handling *many* concurrent services: the model becomes pervasive.

Now you can be flexible as to how the application is deployed: stand-alone, client-server, or *n*-tier. By architecting your system as independent services, you can make the configuration dynamic as well. By planning for concurrency, and decoupling operations in time, you have all these options—including the stand-alone option, where you can choose *not* to be concurrent.

Going the other way (trying to add concurrency to a nonconcurrent application) is *much* harder. If we design to allow for concurrency, we can more easily meet scalability or performance requirements when the time comes—and if the time never comes, we still have the benefit of a cleaner design.

Isn't it about time?

Related sections include:
- *Design by Contract*, page 109
- *Programming by Coincidence*, page 172

Challenges
- How many tasks do you perform in parallel when you get ready for work in the morning? Could you express this in a UML activity diagram? Can you find some way to get ready more quickly by increasing concurrency?

It's Just a View

Still, a man hears
What he wants to hear
And disregards the rest
La la la...
   ▶ **Simon and Garfunkel, "The Boxer"**

Early on we are taught not to write a program as a single big chunk, but that we should "divide and conquer" and separate a program into modules. Each module has its own responsibilities; in fact, a good definition of a module (or class) is that it has a single, well-defined responsibility.

But once you separate a program into different modules based on responsibility, you have a new problem. At runtime, how do the objects talk to each other? How do you manage the logical dependencies between them? That is, how do you synchronize changes in state (or updates to data values) in these different objects? It needs to be done in a clean, flexible manner—we don't want them to know too much about each other. We want each module to be like the man in the song and just hear what it wants to hear.

We'll start off with the concept of an *event*. An event is simply a special message that says "something interesting just happened" (interesting, of course, lies in the eye of the beholder). We can use events to signal changes in one object that some other object may be interested in.

Using events in this way minimizes coupling between those objects—the sender of the event doesn't need to have any explicit knowledge of the receiver. In fact, there could be multiple receivers, each one focused on its own agenda (of which the sender is blissfully unaware).

We need to exercise some care in using events, however. In an early version of Java, for example, one routine received *all* the events destined for a particular application. Not exactly the road to easy maintenance or evolution.

Publish/Subscribe

Why is it bad to push all the events through a single routine? It violates object encapsulation—that one routine now has to have intimate knowledge of the interactions among many objects. It also increases the coupling—and we're trying to *decrease* coupling. Because the objects themselves have to have knowledge of these events as well, you are probably going to violate the *DRY* principle, orthogonality, and perhaps even sections of the Geneva Convention. You may have seen this kind of code—it is usually dominated by a huge `case` statement or multiway `if-then`. We can do better.

Objects should be able to register to receive only the events they need, and should never be sent events they don't need. We don't want to spam our objects! Instead, we can use a *publish/subscribe* protocol, illustrated using the *UML sequence diagram* in Figure 5.4 on the next page.[7]

A sequence diagram shows the flow of messages among several objects, with objects arranged in columns. Each message is shown as a labeled arrow from the sender's column to the receiver's column. An asterisk in the label means that more than one message of this type can be sent.

If we are interested in certain events generated by a `Publisher`, all we have to do is register ourselves. The `Publisher` keeps track of all interested `Subscriber` objects; when the `Publisher` generates an event of interest, it will call each `Subscriber` in turn and notify them that the event has occurred.

---

7. See also the Observer pattern in [GHJV95] for more information.

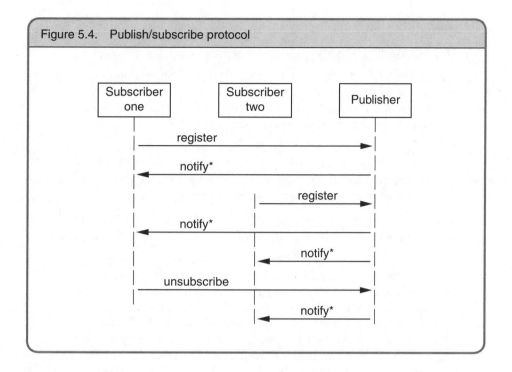

Figure 5.4.   Publish/subscribe protocol

There are several variations on this theme—mirroring other communication styles. Objects may use publish/subscribe on a peer-to-peer basis (as we saw above); they may use a "software bus" where a centralized object maintains the database of listeners and dispatches messages appropriately. You might even have a scheme where critical events get broadcast to all listeners—registered or not. One possible implementation of events in a distributed environment is illustrated by the CORBA Event Service, described in the box on the following page.

We can use this publish/subscribe mechanism to implement a very important design concept: the separation of a model from views of the model. Let's start with a GUI-based example, using the Smalltalk design in which this concept was born.

Model-View-Controller

Suppose you have a spreadsheet application. In addition to the numbers in the spreadsheet itself, you also have a graph that displays the

The CORBA Event Service

The CORBA Event Service allows participating objects to send and receive event notifications via a common bus, the *event channel*. The event channel arbitrates event handling, and also decouples event producers from event consumers. It works in two basic ways: *push* and *pull*.

In push mode, event suppliers inform the event channel that an event has occurred. The channel then automatically distributes that event to all client objects that have registered interest.

In pull mode, clients periodically poll the event channel, which in turn polls the supplier that offers event data corresponding to the request.

Although the CORBA Event Service can be used to implement all of the event models discussed in this section, you can also view it as a different animal. CORBA facilitates communication among objects written in different programming languages running on geographically dispersed machines with different architectures. Sitting on top of CORBA, the event service gives you a decoupled way of interacting with applications around the world, written by people you've never met, using programming languages you'd rather not know about.

numbers as a bar chart and a running total dialog box that shows the sum of a column in the spreadsheet.

Obviously, we don't want to have three separate copies of the data. So we create a *model*—the data itself, with common operations to manipulate it. Then we can create separate *views* that display the data in different ways: as a spreadsheet, as a graph, or in a totals box. Each of these views may have its own *controller*. The graph view may have a controller that allows you to zoom in or out, or pan around the data, for example. None of this affects the data itself, just that view.

This is the key concept behind the Model-View-Controller (MVC) idiom: separating the model from both the GUI that represents it *and* the controls that manage the view.[8]

---

8. The view and controller are tightly coupled, and in some implementations of MVC the view and controller are a single component.

By doing so, you can take advantage of some interesting possibilities. You can support multiple views of the same data model. You can use common viewers on many different data models. You can even support multiple controllers to provide nontraditional input mechanisms.

> **Tip 42**
>
> Separate Views from Models

By loosening the coupling between the model and the view/controller, you buy yourself a lot of flexibility at low cost. In fact, this technique is one of the most important ways of maintaining reversibility (see *Reversibility*, page 44).

Java Tree View

A good example of an MVC design can be found in the Java tree widget. The tree widget (which displays a clickable, traversable tree) is actually a set of several different classes organized in an MVC pattern.

To produce a fully functional tree widget, all you need to do is provide a data source that conforms to the `TreeModel` interface. Your code now becomes the model for the tree.

The view is created by the `TreeCellRenderer` and `TreeCellEditor` classes, which can be inherited from and customized to provide different colors, fonts, and icons in the widget. `JTree` acts as the controller for the tree widget and provides some general viewing functionality.

Because we have decoupled the model from the view, we simplify the programming a great deal. You don't have to think about programming a tree widget anymore. Instead, you just provide a data source.

Suppose the vice president comes up to you and wants a quick application that lets her navigate the company's organizational chart, which is held in a legacy database on the mainframe. Just write a wrapper that takes the mainframe data, presents it as a `TreeModel`, and *voilà*: you have a fully navigable tree widget.

Now you can get fancy and start using the viewer classes; you can change how nodes are rendered, and use special icons, fonts, or colors. When the VP comes back and says the new corporate standards dictate the use of a Skull and Crossbones icon for certain employees, you can make the changes to TreeCellRenderer without touching any other code.

Beyond GUIs

While MVC is typically taught in the context of GUI development, it is really a general-purpose programming technique. The view is an interpretation of the model (perhaps a subset)—it doesn't need to be graphical. The controller is more of a coordination mechanism, and doesn't have to be related to any sort of input device.

- **Model.** The abstract data model representing the target object. The model has no direct knowledge of any views or controllers.
- **View.** A way to interpret the model. It subscribes to changes in the model and logical events from the controller.
- **Controller.** A way to control the view and provide the model with new data. It publishes events to both the model and the view.

Let's look at a nongraphical example.

Baseball is a unique institution. Where else can you learn such gems of trivia as "this has become the highest-scoring game played on a Tuesday, in the rain, under artificial lights, between teams whose names start with a vowel?" Suppose we were charged with developing software to support those intrepid announcers who must dutifully report on the scores, the statistics, and the trivia.

Clearly we need information on the game in progress—the teams playing, the conditions, the player at bat, the score, and so on. These facts form our models; they will be updated as new information arrives (a pitcher is changed, a player strikes out, it starts raining...).

We'll then have a number of view objects that use these models. One view might look for runs so it can update the current score. Another may receive notifications of new batters, and retrieve a brief summary of their year-to-date statistics. A third viewer may look at the data and check for new world records. We might even have a trivia viewer, responsible for coming up with those weird and useless facts that thrill the viewing public.

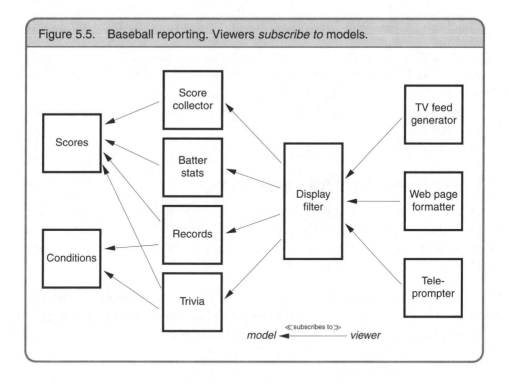

Figure 5.5.   Baseball reporting. Viewers *subscribe to* models.

But we don't want to flood the poor announcer with all of these views directly. Instead, we'll have each view generate notifications of "interesting" events, and let some higher-level object schedule what gets shown.[9]

These viewer objects have suddenly become models for the higher-level object, which itself might then be a model for different formatting viewers. One formatting viewer might create the teleprompter script for the announcer, another might generate video captions directly on the satellite uplink, another might update the network's or team's Web pages (see Figure 5.5).

This kind of model-viewer network is a common (and valuable) design technique. Each link decouples raw data from the events that created it—each new viewer is an abstraction. And because the relationships are a network (not just a linear chain), we have a lot of flexibility. Each

---

9.   The fact that a plane flies overhead probably isn't interesting unless it's the 100th plane to fly overhead that night.

model may have *many* viewers, and one viewer may work with multiple models.

In advanced systems such as this one, it can be handy to have *debugging views*—specialized views that show you in-depth details of the model. Adding a facility to trace individual events can be a great time saver as well.

Still Coupled (After All These Years)

Despite the decrease in coupling we have achieved, listeners and event generators (subscribers and publishers) still have *some* knowledge of each other. In Java, for instance, they must agree on common interface definitions and calling conventions.

In the next section, we'll look at ways of reducing coupling even further by using a form of publish and subscribe where *none* of the participants need know about each other, or call each other directly.

Related sections include:
- *Orthogonality*, page 34
- *Reversibility*, page 44
- *Decoupling and the Law of Demeter*, page 138
- *Blackboards*, page 165
- *It's All Writing*, page 248

Exercises

Answer on p. 296

29. Suppose you have an airline reservation system that includes the concept of a flight:

```
public interface Flight {
  // Return false if flight full.
  public boolean addPassenger(Passenger p);
  public void addToWaitList(Passenger p);
  public int getFlightCapacity();
  public int getNumPassengers();
}
```

If you add a passenger to the wait list, they'll be put on the flight automatically when an opening becomes available.

There's a massive reporting job that goes through looking for overbooked or full flights to suggest when additional flights might be scheduled. It works fine, but it takes hours to run.

We'd like to have a little more flexibility in processing wait-list passengers, and we've got to do something about that big report—it takes too long to run. Use the ideas from this section to redesign this interface.

▶ Blackboards

30

The writing is on the wall...

You may not usually associate *elegance* with police detectives, picturing instead some sort of doughnut and coffee cliché. But consider how detectives might use a *blackboard* to coordinate and solve a murder investigation.

Suppose the chief inspector starts off by setting up a large blackboard in the conference room. On it, he writes a single question:

H. DUMPTY (MALE, EGG): ACCIDENT OR MURDER?

Did Humpty really fall, or was he pushed? Each detective may make contributions to this potential murder mystery by adding facts, statements from witnesses, any forensic evidence that might arise, and so on. As the data accumulates, a detective might notice a connection and post that observation or speculation as well. This process continues, across all shifts, with many different people and agents, until the case is closed. A sample blackboard is shown in Figure 5.6 on the next page.

Some key features of the blackboard approach are:

- None of the detectives needs to know of the existence of any other detective—they watch the board for new information, and add their findings.

- The detectives may be trained in different disciplines, may have different levels of education and expertise, and may not even work in the same precinct. They share a desire to solve the case, but that's all.

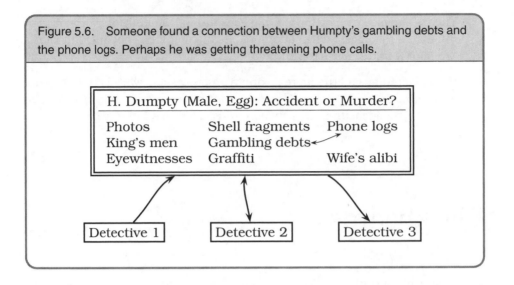

Figure 5.6.   Someone found a connection between Humpty's gambling debts and the phone logs. Perhaps he was getting threatening phone calls.

- Different detectives may come and go during the course of the process, and may work different shifts.

- There are no restrictions on what may be placed on the blackboard. It may be pictures, sentences, physical evidence, and so on.

We've worked on a number of projects that involved a workflow or distributed data gathering process. With each, designing a solution around a simple blackboard model gave us a solid metaphor to work with: all of the features listed above using detectives are just as applicable to objects and code modules.

A blackboard system lets us decouple our objects from each other completely, providing a forum where knowledge consumers and producers can exchange data anonymously and asynchronously. As you might guess, it also cuts down on the amount of code we have to write.

Blackboard Implementations

Computer-based blackboard systems were originally invented for use in artificial intelligence applications where the problems to be solved were large and complex—speech recognition, knowledge-based reasoning systems, and so on.

Modern distributed blackboard-like systems such as JavaSpaces and T Spaces [URL 50, URL 25] are based on a model of key/value pairs first popularized in Linda [CG90], where the concept was known as *tuple space.*

With these systems, you can store active Java objects—not just data—on the blackboard, and retrieve them by partial matching of fields (via templates and wildcards) or by subtypes. For example, suppose you had a type `Author`, which is a subtype of `Person`. You could search a blackboard containing `Person` objects by using an `Author` template with a `lastName` value of "Shakespeare." You'd get Bill Shakespeare the author, but not Fred Shakespeare the gardener.

The main operations in JavaSpaces are:

Name	Function
read	Search for and retrieve data from the space.
write	Put an item into the space.
take	Similar to read, but removes the item from the space as well.
notify	Set up a notification to occur whenever an object is written that matches the template.

T Spaces supports a similar set of operations, but with different names and slightly different semantics. Both systems are built like a database product; they provide atomic operations and distributed transactions to ensure data integrity.

Since we can store objects, we can use a blackboard to design algorithms based on a *flow of objects*, not just data. It's as if our detectives could pin people to the blackboard—witnesses themselves, not just their statements. Anyone can ask a witness questions in the pursuit of the case, post the transcript, and move that witness to another area of the blackboard, where he might respond differently (if you allow the witness to read the blackboard too).

A big advantage of systems such as these is that you have a single, consistent interface to the blackboard. When building a conventional distributed application, you can spend a great deal of time crafting unique API calls for every distributed transaction and interaction in the system. With the combinatorial explosion of interfaces and interactions, the project can quickly become a nightmare.

Organizing Your Blackboard

When the detectives work on large cases, the blackboard may become cluttered, and it may become difficult to locate data on the board. The solution is to *partition* the blackboard and start to organize the data on the blackboard somehow.

Different software systems handle this partitioning in different ways; some use fairly flat *zones* or *interest groups*, while others adopt a more hierarchical treelike structure.

The blackboard style of programming removes the need for so many interfaces, making for a more elegant and consistent system.

Application Example

Suppose we are writing a program to accept and process mortgage or loan applications. The laws that govern this area are odiously complex, with federal, state, and local governments all having their say. The lender must prove they have disclosed certain things, and must ask for certain information—but must *not* ask certain other questions, and so on, and so on.

Beyond the miasma of applicable law, we also have the following problems to contend with.

- There is no guarantee on the order in which data arrives. For instance, queries for a credit check or title search may take a substantial amount of time, while items such as name and address may be available immediately.

- Data gathering may be done by different people, distributed across different offices, in different time zones.

- Some data gathering may be done automatically by other systems. This data may arrive asynchronously as well.

- Nonetheless, certain data may still be dependent on other data. For instance, you may not be able to start the title search for a car until you get proof of ownership or insurance.

- Arrival of new data may raise new questions and policies. Suppose the credit check comes back with a less than glowing report; now you need these five extra forms and perhaps a blood sample.

You can try to handle every possible combination and circumstance using a workflow system. Many such systems exist, but they can be complex and programmer intensive. As regulations change, the workflow must be reorganized: people may have to change their procedures and hard-wired code may have to be rewritten.

A blackboard, in combination with a rules engine that encapsulates the legal requirements, is an elegant solution to the difficulties found here. Order of data arrival is irrelevant: when a fact is posted it can trigger the appropriate rules. Feedback is easily handled as well: the output of any set of rules can post to the blackboard and cause the triggering of yet more applicable rules.

> **TIP 43**
>
> ## Use Blackboards to Coordinate Workflow

We can use the blackboard to coordinate disparate facts and agents, while still maintaining independence and even isolation among participants.

You can accomplish the same results with more brute-force methods, of course, but you'll have a more brittle system. When it breaks, all the king's horses and all the king's men might not get your program working again.

Related sections include:
- *The Power of Plain Text*, page 73
- *It's Just a View*, page 157

Challenges
- Do you use blackboard systems in the real world—the message board by the refrigerator, or the big whiteboard at work? What makes them effective? Are messages ever posted with a consistent format? Does it matter?

Exercises

*Answer
on p. 297*

30. For each of the following applications, would a blackboard system be appropriate or not? Why?

1. **Image processing.** You'd like to have a number of parallel processes grab chunks of an image, process them, and put the completed chunk back.

2. **Group calendaring.** You've got people scattered across the globe, in different time zones, and speaking different languages, trying to schedule a meeting.

3. **Network monitoring tool.** The system gathers performance statistics and collects trouble reports. You'd like to implement some agents to use this information to look for trouble in the system.

Chapter 6

While You Are Coding

Conventional wisdom says that once a project is in the coding phase, the work is mostly mechanical, transcribing the design into executable statements. We think that this attitude is the single biggest reason that many programs are ugly, inefficient, poorly structured, unmaintainable, and just plain wrong.

Coding is not mechanical. If it were, all the CASE tools that people pinned their hopes on in the early 1980s would have replaced programmers long ago. There are decisions to be made every minute—decisions that require careful thought and judgment if the resulting program is to enjoy a long, accurate, and productive life.

Developers who don't actively think about their code are programming by coincidence—the code might work, but there's no particular reason why. In *Programming by Coincidence*, we advocate a more positive involvement with the coding process.

While most of the code we write executes quickly, we occasionally develop algorithms that have the potential to bog down even the fastest processors. In *Algorithm Speed*, we discuss ways to estimate the speed of code, and we give some tips on how to spot potential problems before they happen.

Pragmatic Programmers think critically about all code, including our own. We constantly see room for improvement in our programs and our designs. In *Refactoring*, we look at techniques that help us fix up existing code even while we're in the midst of a project.

Something that should be in the back of your mind whenever you're producing code is that you'll someday have to test it. Make code easy to test, and you'll increase the likelihood that it will actually get tested, a thought we develop in *Code That's Easy to Test*.

Finally, in *Evil Wizards*, we suggest that you should be careful of tools that write reams of code on your behalf unless you understand what they're doing.

Most of us can drive a car largely on autopilot—we don't explicitly command our foot to press a pedal, or our arm to turn the wheel—we just think "slow down and turn right." However, good, safe drivers are constantly reviewing the situation, checking for potential problems, and putting themselves into good positions in case the unexpected happens. The same is true of coding—it may be largely routine, but keeping your wits about you could well prevent a disaster.

Programming by Coincidence

Do you ever watch old black-and-white war movies? The weary soldier advances cautiously out of the brush. There's a clearing ahead: are there any land mines, or is it safe to cross? There aren't any indications that it's a minefield—no signs, barbed wire, or craters. The soldier pokes the ground ahead of him with his bayonet and winces, expecting an explosion. There isn't one. So he proceeds painstakingly through the field for a while, prodding and poking as he goes. Eventually, convinced that the field is safe, he straightens up and marches proudly forward, only to be blown to pieces.

The soldier's initial probes for mines revealed nothing, but this was merely lucky. He was led to a false conclusion—with disastrous results.

As developers, we also work in minefields. There are hundreds of traps just waiting to catch us each day. Remembering the soldier's tale, we should be wary of drawing false conclusions. We should avoid programming by coincidence—relying on luck and accidental successes—in favor of *programming deliberately*.

How to Program by Coincidence

Suppose Fred is given a programming assignment. Fred types in some code, tries it, and it seems to work. Fred types in some more code, tries it, and it still seems to work. After several weeks of coding this way, the program suddenly stops working, and after hours of trying to fix it, he still doesn't know why. Fred may well spend a significant amount of time chasing this piece of code around without ever being able to fix it. No matter what he does, it just doesn't ever seem to work right.

Fred doesn't know why the code is failing because *he didn't know why it worked in the first place*. It seemed to work, given the limited "testing" that Fred did, but that was just a coincidence. Buoyed by false confidence, Fred charged ahead into oblivion. Now, most intelligent people may know someone like Fred, but *we* know better. We don't rely on coincidences—do we?

Sometimes we might. Sometimes it can be pretty easy to confuse a happy coincidence with a purposeful plan. Let's look at a few examples.

Accidents of Implementation

Accidents of implementation are things that happen simply because that's the way the code is currently written. You end up relying on undocumented error or boundary conditions.

Suppose you call a routine with bad data. The routine responds in a particular way, and you code based on that response. But the author didn't intend for the routine to work that way—it was never even considered. When the routine gets "fixed," your code may break. In the most extreme case, the routine you called may not even be designed to do what you want, but it *seems* to work okay. Calling things in the wrong order, or in the wrong context, is a related problem.

```
paint(g);
invalidate();
validate();
revalidate();
repaint();
paintImmediately(r);
```

Here it looks like Fred is desperately trying to get something out on the screen. But these routines were never designed to be called this way; although they seem to work, that's really just a coincidence.

To add insult to injury, when the component finally does get drawn, Fred won't try to go back and take out the spurious calls. "It works now, better leave well enough alone...."

It's easy to be fooled by this line of thought. Why should you take the risk of messing with something that's working? Well, we can think of several reasons:

- It may not really be working—it might just look like it is.

- The boundary condition you rely on may be just an accident. In different circumstances (a different screen resolution, perhaps), it might behave differently.

- Undocumented behavior may change with the next release of the library.

- Additional and unnecessary calls make your code slower.

- Additional calls also increase the risk of introducing new bugs of their own.

For code you write that others will call, the basic principles of good modularization and of hiding implementation behind small, well-documented interfaces can all help. A well-specified contract (see *Design by Contract*, page 109) can help eliminate misunderstandings.

For routines you call, rely only on documented behavior. If you can't, for whatever reason, then document your assumption well.

Accidents of Context

You can have "accidents of context" as well. Suppose you are writing a utility module. Just because you are currently coding for a GUI environment, does the module have to rely on a GUI being present? Are you relying on English-speaking users? Literate users? What else are you relying on that isn't guaranteed?

Implicit Assumptions

Coincidences can mislead at all levels—from generating requirements through to testing. Testing is particularly fraught with false causalities and coincidental outcomes. It's easy to assume that *X* causes *Y*, but as we said in *Debugging*, page 90: don't assume it, prove it.

At all levels, people operate with many assumptions in mind—but these assumptions are rarely documented and are often in conflict between different developers. Assumptions that aren't based on well-established facts are the bane of all projects.

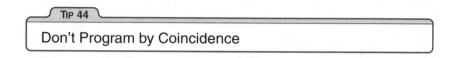

TIP 44

Don't Program by Coincidence

How to Program Deliberately

We want to spend less time churning out code, catch and fix errors as early in the development cycle as possible, and create fewer errors to begin with. It helps if we can program deliberately:

- Always be aware of what you are doing. Fred let things get slowly out of hand, until he ended up boiled, like the frog in *Stone Soup and Boiled Frogs*, page 7.

- Don't code blindfolded. Attempting to build an application you don't fully understand, or to use a technology you aren't familiar with, is an invitation to be misled by coincidences.

- Proceed from a plan, whether that plan is in your head, on the back of a cocktail napkin, or on a wall-sized printout from a CASE tool.

- Rely only on reliable things. Don't depend on accidents or assumptions. If you can't tell the difference in particular circumstances, assume the worst.

- Document your assumptions. *Design by Contract*, page 109, can help clarify your assumptions in your own mind, as well as help communicate them to others.

- Don't just test your code, but test your assumptions as well. Don't guess; actually try it. Write an assertion to test your assumptions (see *Assertive Programming*, page 122). If your assertion is right, you have improved the documentation in your code. If you discover your assumption is wrong, then count yourself lucky.

- Prioritize your effort. Spend time on the important aspects; more than likely, these are the hard parts. If you don't have fundamentals or infrastructure correct, brilliant bells and whistles will be irrelevant.

- Don't be a slave to history. Don't let existing code dictate future code. All code can be replaced if it is no longer appropriate. Even within one program, don't let what you've already done constrain what you do next—be ready to refactor (see *Refactoring*, page 184). This decision may impact the project schedule. The assumption is that the impact will be less than the cost of *not* making the change.[1]

So next time something seems to work, but you don't know why, make sure it isn't just a coincidence.

Related sections include:
- *Stone Soup and Boiled Frogs*, page 7
- *Debugging*, page 90
- *Design by Contract*, page 109
- *Assertive Programming*, page 122
- *Temporal Coupling*, page 150
- *Refactoring*, page 184
- *It's All Writing*, page 248

Exercises

Answer on p. 298

31. Can you identify some coincidences in the following C code fragment? Assume that this code is buried deep in a library routine.

```
fprintf(stderr, "Error, continue?");
gets(buf);
```

Answer on p. 298

32. This piece of C code might work some of the time, on some machines. Then again, it might not. What's wrong?

```
/* Truncate string to its last maxlen chars */
void string_tail(char *string, int maxlen) {
  int len = strlen(string);
  if (len > maxlen) {
    strcpy(string, string + (len - maxlen));
  }
}
```

---

1. You can also go too far here. We once knew a developer who rewrote all source he was given because he had his own naming conventions.

33. This code comes from a general-purpose Java tracing suite. The function writes a string to a log file. It passes its unit test, but fails when one of the Web developers uses it. What coincidence does it rely on?

Answer on p. 299

```
public static void debug(String s) throws IOException {
  FileWriter fw = new FileWriter("debug.log", true);
  fw.write(s);
  fw.flush();
  fw.close();
}
```

Algorithm Speed

In *Estimating*, page 64, we talked about estimating things such as how long it takes to walk across town, or how long a project will take to finish. However, there is another kind of estimating that Pragmatic Programmers use almost daily: estimating the resources that algorithms use—time, processor, memory, and so on.

This kind of estimating is often crucial. Given a choice between two ways of doing something, which do you pick? You know how long your program runs with 1,000 records, but how will it scale to 1,000,000? What parts of the code need optimizing?

It turns out that these questions can often be answered using common sense, some analysis, and a way of writing approximations called the "big O" notation.

What Do We Mean by Estimating Algorithms?

Most nontrivial algorithms handle some kind of variable input—sorting n strings, inverting an $m \times n$ matrix, or decrypting a message with an n-bit key. Normally, the size of this input will affect the algorithm: the larger the input, the longer the running time or the more memory used.

If the relationship were always linear (so that the time increased in direct proportion to the value of n), this section wouldn't be important. However, most significant algorithms are not linear. The good news is that many are sublinear. A binary search, for example, doesn't need to look at every candidate when finding a match. The bad news is that other algorithms are considerably worse than linear; runtimes or memory requirements increase far faster than n. An algorithm that takes a minute to process ten items may take a lifetime to process 100.

We find that whenever we write anything containing loops or recursive calls, we subconsciously check the runtime and memory requirements. This is rarely a formal process, but rather a quick confirmation that what we're doing is sensible in the circumstances. However, we sometimes *do* find ourselves performing a more detailed analysis. That's when the $O()$ notation comes in useful.

The $O()$ Notation

The $O()$ notation is a mathematical way of dealing with approximations. When we write that a particular sort routine sorts n records in $O(n^2)$ time, we are simply saying that the worst-case time taken will vary as the square of n. Double the number of records, and the time will increase roughly fourfold. Think of the O as meaning *on the order of.* The $O()$ notation puts an upper bound on the value of the thing we're measuring (time, memory, and so on). If we say a function takes $O(n^2)$ time, then we know that the upper bound of the time it takes will not grow faster than n^2. Sometimes we come up with fairly complex $O()$ functions, but because the highest-order term will dominate the value as n increases, the convention is to remove all low-order terms, and not to bother showing any constant multiplying factors. $O(\frac{n^2}{2} + 3n)$ is the same as $O(\frac{n^2}{2})$, which is equivalent to $O(n^2)$. This is actually a weakness of the $O()$ notation—one $O(n^2)$ algorithm may be 1,000 times faster than another $O(n^2)$ algorithm, but you won't know it from the notation.

Figure 6.1 shows several common $O()$ notations you'll come across, along with a graph comparing running times of algorithms in each category. Clearly, things quickly start getting out of hand once we get over $O(n^2)$.

For example, suppose you've got a routine that takes 1 s to process 100 records. How long will it take to process 1,000? If your code is $O(1)$, then it will still take 1 s. If it's $O(\lg(n))$, then you'll probably be waiting about 3 s. $O(n)$ will show a linear increase to 10 s, while an $O(n \lg(n))$ will take some 33 s. If you're unlucky enough to have an $O(n^2)$ routine, then sit back for 100 s while it does its stuff. And if you're using an exponential

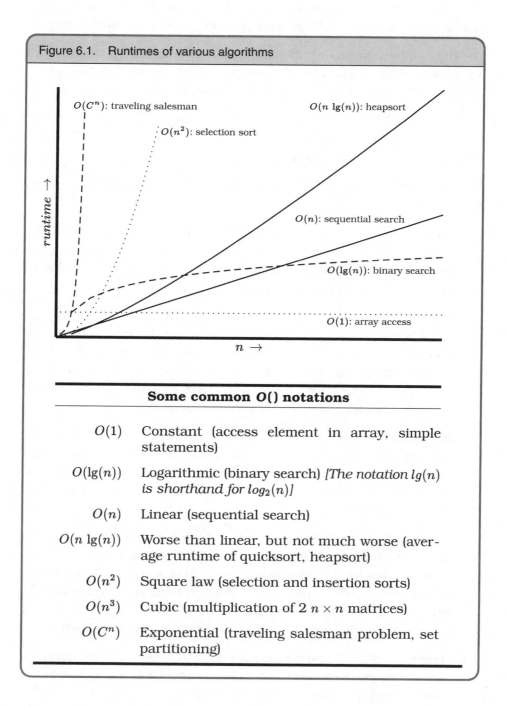

Figure 6.1.   Runtimes of various algorithms

Some common $O()$ notations

$O(1)$	Constant (access element in array, simple statements)
$O(\lg(n))$	Logarithmic (binary search) *[The notation $\lg(n)$ is shorthand for $\log_2(n)$]*
$O(n)$	Linear (sequential search)
$O(n\lg(n))$	Worse than linear, but not much worse (average runtime of quicksort, heapsort)
$O(n^2)$	Square law (selection and insertion sorts)
$O(n^3)$	Cubic (multiplication of 2 $n \times n$ matrices)
$O(C^n)$	Exponential (traveling salesman problem, set partitioning)

algorithm $O(2^n)$, you might want to make a cup of coffee—your routine should finish in about 10^{263} years. Let us know how the universe ends.

The $O()$ notation doesn't apply just to time; you can use it to represent any other resources used by an algorithm. For example, it is often useful to be able to model memory consumption (see Exercise 35 on page 183).

Common Sense Estimation

You can estimate the order of many basic algorithms using common sense.

- **Simple loops.** If a simple loop runs from 1 to n, then the algorithm is likely to be $O(n)$—time increases linearly with n. Examples include exhaustive searches, finding the maximum value in an array, and generating checksums.

- **Nested loops.** If you nest a loop inside another, then your algorithm becomes $O(m \times n)$, where m and n are the two loops' limits. This commonly occurs in simple sorting algorithms, such as bubble sort, where the outer loop scans each element in the array in turn, and the inner loop works out where to place that element in the sorted result. Such sorting algorithms tend to be $O(n^2)$.

- **Binary chop.** If your algorithm halves the set of things it considers each time around the loop, then it is likely to be logarithmic, $O(\lg(n))$ (see Exercise 37, page 183). A binary search of a sorted list, traversing a binary tree, and finding the first set bit in a machine word can all be $O(\lg(n))$.

- **Divide and conquer.** Algorithms that partition their input, work on the two halves independently, and then combine the result can be $O(n \lg(n))$. The classic example is quicksort, which works by partitioning the data into two halves and recursively sorting each. Although technically $O(n^2)$, because its behavior degrades when it is fed sorted input, the average runtime of quicksort is $O(n \lg(n))$.

- **Combinatoric.** Whenever algorithms start looking at the permutations of things, their running times may get out of hand. This is because permutations involve factorials (there are $5! = 5 \times 4 \times 3 \times 2 \times 1 = 120$ permutations of the digits from 1 to 5). Time a combinatoric algorithm for five elements: it will take six times longer to run it for six, and 42 times longer for seven. Examples include algorithms for many of the acknowledged *hard* problems—the traveling salesman problem, optimally packing things into a container, partitioning a set of numbers so that each set has the same total, and so on. Often, heuristics are used to reduce the running times of these types of algorithms in particular problem domains.

Algorithm Speed in Practice

It's unlikely that you'll spend much time during your career writing sort routines. The ones in the libraries available to you will probably outperform anything you may write without substantial effort. However, the basic kinds of algorithms we've described earlier pop up time and time again. Whenever you find yourself writing a simple loop, you know that you have an $O(n)$ algorithm. If that loop contains an inner loop, then you're looking at $O(m \times n)$. You should be asking yourself how large these values can get. If the numbers are bounded, then you'll know how long the code will take to run. If the numbers depend on external factors (such as the number of records in an overnight batch run, or the number of names in a list of people), then you might want to stop and consider the effect that large values may have on your running time or memory consumption.

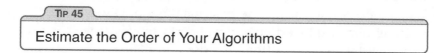

TIP 45

Estimate the Order of Your Algorithms

There are some approaches you can take to address potential problems. If you have an algorithm that is $O(n^2)$, try to find a divide and conquer approach that will take you down to $O(n \lg(n))$.

If you're not sure how long your code will take, or how much memory it will use, try running it, varying the input record count or whatever is likely to impact the runtime. Then plot the results. You should soon get a good idea of the shape of the curve. Is it curving upward, a straight line, or flattening off as the input size increases? Three or four points should give you an idea.

Also consider just what you're doing in the code itself. A simple $O(n^2)$ loop may well perform better than a complex, $O(n \lg(n))$ one for smaller values of n, particularly if the $O(n \lg(n))$ algorithm has an expensive inner loop.

In the middle of all this theory, don't forget that there are practical considerations as well. Runtime may look like it increases linearly for small input sets. But feed the code millions of records and suddenly the time degrades as the system starts to thrash. If you test a sort routine with random input keys, you may be surprised the first time it encounters ordered input. Pragmatic Programmers try to cover both the theoretical and practical bases. After all this estimating, the only timing that counts is the speed of your code, running in the production environment, with real data.[2] This leads to our next tip.

TIP 46

Test Your Estimates

If it's tricky getting accurate timings, use *code profilers* to count the number of times the different steps in your algorithm get executed, and plot these figures against the size of the input.

Best Isn't Always Best

You also need to be pragmatic about choosing appropriate algorithms—the fastest one is not always the best for the job. Given a small input set, a straightforward insertion sort will perform just as well as a quick-sort, and will take you less time to write and debug. You also need to be careful if the algorithm you choose has a high setup cost. For small input sets, this setup may dwarf the running time and make the algorithm inappropriate.

Also be wary of *premature optimization*. It's always a good idea to make sure an algorithm really is a bottleneck before investing your precious time trying to improve it.

---

2.   In fact, while testing the sort algorithms used as an exercise for this section on a 64MB Pentium, the authors ran out of real memory while running the radix sort with more than seven million numbers. The sort started using swap space, and times degraded dramatically.

Related sections include:

- *Estimating*, page 64

Challenges

- Every developer should have a feel for how algorithms are designed and analyzed. Robert Sedgewick has written a series of accessible books on the subject ([Sed83, SF96, Sed92] and others). We recommend adding one of his books to your collection, and making a point of reading it.

- For those who like more detail than Sedgewick provides, read Donald Knuth's definitive *Art of Computer Programming* books, which analyze a wide range of algorithms [Knu97a, Knu97b, Knu98].

- In Exercise 34, we look at sorting arrays of long integers. What is the impact if the keys are more complex, and the overhead of key comparison is high? Does the key structure affect the efficiency of the sort algorithms, or is the fastest sort always fastest?

Exercises

34. We have coded a set of simple sort routines, which can be downloaded from our Web site (www.pragmaticprogrammer.com). Run them on various machines available to you. Do your figures follow the expected curves? What can you deduce about the relative speeds of your machines? What are the effects of various compiler optimization settings? Is the radix sort indeed linear?

Answer on p. 299

35. The routine below prints out the contents of a binary tree. Assuming the tree is balanced, roughly how much stack space will the routine use while printing a tree of 1,000,000 elements? (Assume that subroutine calls impose no significant stack overhead.)

Answer on p. 300

```
void printTree(const Node *node) {
  char buffer[1000];
  if (node) {
    printTree(node->left);
    getNodeAsString(node, buffer);
    puts(buffer);
    printTree(node->right);
  }
}
```

36. Can you see any way to reduce the stack requirements of the routine in Exercise 35 (apart from reducing the size of the buffer)?

Answer on p. 300

37. On page 180, we claimed that a binary chop is $O(lg(n))$. Can you prove this?

Answer on p. 301

Refactoring

Change and decay in all around I see . . .
> ▶ **H. F. Lyte, "Abide With Me"**

As a program evolves, it will become necessary to rethink earlier decisions and rework portions of the code. This process is perfectly natural.
Code needs to evolve; it's not a static thing.

Unfortunately, the most common metaphor for software development
is building construction (Bertrand Meyer [Mey97b] uses the term "Software Construction"). But using construction as the guiding metaphor
implies these steps:

1. An architect draws up blueprints.

2. Contractors dig the foundation, build the superstructure, wire and
   plumb, and apply finishing touches.

3. The tenants move in and live happily ever after, calling building
   maintenance to fix any problems.

Well, software doesn't quite work that way. Rather than construction,
software is more like *gardening*—it is more organic than concrete. You
plant many things in a garden according to an initial plan and conditions. Some thrive, others are destined to end up as compost. You may
move plantings relative to each other to take advantage of the inter-
play of light and shadow, wind and rain. Overgrown plants get split
or pruned, and colors that clash may get moved to more aesthetically
pleasing locations. You pull weeds, and you fertilize plantings that are
in need of some extra help. You constantly monitor the health of the
garden, and make adjustments (to the soil, the plants, the layout) as
needed.

Business people are comfortable with the metaphor of building construction: it is more scientific than gardening, it's repeatable, there's
a rigid reporting hierarchy for management, and so on. But we're not
building skyscrapers—we aren't as constrained by the boundaries of
physics and the real world.

The gardening metaphor is much closer to the realities of software
development. Perhaps a certain routine has grown too large, or is trying

to accomplish too much—it needs to be split into two. Things that don't work out as planned need to be weeded or pruned.

Rewriting, reworking, and re-architecting code is collectively known as *refactoring*.

When Should You Refactor?

When you come across a stumbling block because the code doesn't quite fit anymore, or you notice two things that should really be merged, or anything else at all strikes you as being "wrong," *don't hesitate to change it*. There's no time like the present. Any number of things may cause code to qualify for refactoring:

- **Duplication.** You've discovered a violation of the *DRY* principle (*The Evils of Duplication*, page 26).

- **Nonorthogonal design.** You've discovered some code or design that could be made more orthogonal (*Orthogonality*, page 34).

- **Outdated knowledge.** Things change, requirements drift, and your knowledge of the problem increases. Code needs to keep up.

- **Performance.** You need to move functionality from one area of the system to another to improve performance.

Refactoring your code—moving functionality around and updating earlier decisions—is really an exercise in *pain management*. Let's face it, changing source code around can be pretty painful: it was almost working, and now it's *really* torn up. Many developers are reluctant to start ripping up code just because it isn't quite right.

Real-World Complications

So you go to your boss or client and say, "This code works, but I need another week to refactor it."

We can't print their reply.

Time pressure is often used as an excuse for not refactoring. But this excuse just doesn't hold up: fail to refactor now, and there'll be a far greater time investment to fix the problem down the road—when there are more dependencies to reckon with. Will there be more time available then? Not in our experience.

You might want to explain this principle to the boss by using a medical analogy: think of the code that needs refactoring as a "growth." Removing it requires invasive surgery. You can go in now, and take it out while it is still small. Or, you could wait while it grows and spreads—but removing it then will be both more expensive and more dangerous. Wait even longer, and you may lose the patient entirely.

> ### TIP 47
>
> ### Refactor Early, Refactor Often

Keep track of the things that need to be refactored. If you can't refactor something immediately, make sure that it gets placed on the schedule. Make sure that users of the affected code *know* that it is scheduled to be refactored and how this might affect them.

How Do You Refactor?

Refactoring started out in the Smalltalk community, and, along with other trends (such as design patterns), has started to gain a wider audience. But as a topic it is still fairly new; there isn't much published on it. The first major book on refactoring ([FBB+99], and also [URL 47]) is being published around the same time as this book.

At its heart, refactoring is redesign. Anything that you or others on your team designed can be redesigned in light of new facts, deeper understandings, changing requirements, and so on. But if you proceed to rip up vast quantities of code with wild abandon, you may find yourself in a worse position than when you started.

Clearly, refactoring is an activity that needs to be undertaken slowly, deliberately, and carefully. Martin Fowler offers the following simple tips on how to refactor without doing more harm than good (see the box on page 30 in [FS97]):

1. Don't try to refactor and add functionality at the same time.

2. Make sure you have good tests before you begin refactoring. Run the tests as often as possible. That way you will know quickly if your changes have broken anything.

Automatic Refactoring

Historically, Smalltalk users have always enjoyed a *class browser* as part of the IDE. Not to be confused with Web browsers, class browsers let users navigate through and examine class hierarchies and methods.

Typically, class browsers allow you to edit code, create new methods and classes, and so on. The next variation on this idea is the *refactoring browser*.

A refactoring browser can semiautomatically perform common refactoring operations for you: splitting up a long routine into smaller ones, automatically propagating changes to method and variable names, drag and drop to assist you in moving code, and so on.

As we write this book, this technology has yet to appear outside of the Smalltalk world, but this is likely to change at the same speed that Java changes—rapidly. In the meantime, the pioneering Smalltalk refactoring browser can be found online at [URL 20].

3. Take short, deliberate steps: move a field from one class to another, fuse two similar methods into a superclass. Refactoring often involves making many localized changes that result in a larger-scale change. If you keep your steps small, and test after each step, you will avoid prolonged debugging.

We'll talk more about testing at this level in *Code That's Easy to Test*, page 189, and larger-scale testing in *Ruthless Testing*, page 237, but Mr. Fowler's point of maintaining good regression tests is the key to refactoring with confidence.

It can also be helpful to make sure that drastic changes to a module—such as altering its interface or its functionality in an incompatible manner—break the build. That is, old clients of this code should fail to compile. You can then quickly find the old clients and make the necessary changes to bring them up to date.

So next time you see a piece of code that isn't quite as it should be, fix both it and everything that depends on it. Manage the pain: if it hurts now, but is going to hurt even more later, you might as well get it over with. Remember the lessons of *Software Entropy*, page 4: don't live with broken windows.

Related sections include:

- *The Cat Ate My Source Code*, page 2
- *Software Entropy*, page 4
- *Stone Soup and Boiled Frogs*, page 7
- *The Evils of Duplication*, page 26
- *Orthogonality*, page 34
- *Programming by Coincidence*, page 172
- *Code That's Easy to Test*, page 189
- *Ruthless Testing*, page 237

Exercises

Answer on p. 302

38. The following code has obviously been updated several times over the years, but the changes haven't improved its structure. Refactor it.

```
if (state == TEXAS) {
  rate = TX_RATE;
  amt  = base * TX_RATE;
  calc = 2*basis(amt) + extra(amt)*1.05;
}
else if ((state == OHIO) || (state == MAINE)) {
  rate = (state == OHIO) ? OH_RATE : ME_RATE;
  amt  = base * rate;
  calc = 2*basis(amt) + extra(amt)*1.05;
  if (state == OHIO)
    points = 2;
}
else {
  rate = 1;
  amt  = base;
  calc = 2*basis(amt) + extra(amt)*1.05;
}
```

Answer on p. 303

39. The following Java class needs to support a few more shapes. Refactor the class to prepare it for the additions.

```
public class Shape {
  public static final int SQUARE     = 1;
  public static final int CIRCLE     = 2;
  public static final int RIGHT_TRIANGLE = 3;

  private int    shapeType;
  private double size;

  public Shape(int shapeType, double size) {
    this.shapeType = shapeType;
    this.size      = size;
  }
  // ... other methods ...
```

```
      public double area() {
        switch (shapeType) {
        case SQUARE:     return size*size;
        case CIRCLE:     return Math.PI*size*size/4.0;
        case RIGHT_TRIANGLE: return size*size/2.0;
        }
        return 0;
      }
    }
```

40. This Java code is part of a framework that will be used throughout your project. Refactor it to be more general and easier to extend in the future.

Answer on p. 303

```
    public class Window {
      public Window(int width, int height) { ... }
      public void setSize(int width, int height) { ... }
      public boolean overlaps(Window w) { ... }
      public int getArea() { ... }
    }
```

Code That's Easy to Test

The *Software IC* is a metaphor that people like to toss around when discussing reusability and component-based development.[3] The idea is that software components should be combined just as integrated circuit chips are combined. This works only if the components you are using are known to be reliable.

Chips are designed to be tested—not just at the factory, not just when they are installed, but also in the field when they are deployed. More complex chips and systems may have a full Built-In Self Test (BIST) feature that runs some base-level diagnostics internally, or a Test Access Mechanism (TAM) that provides a test harness that allows the external environment to provide stimuli and collect responses from the chip.

We can do the same thing in software. Like our hardware colleagues, we need to build testability into the software from the very beginning, and test each piece thoroughly before trying to wire them together.

---

3. The term "Software IC" (Integrated Circuit) seems to have been invented in 1986 by Cox and Novobilski in their Objective-C book *Object-Oriented Programming* [CN91].

Unit Testing

Chip-level testing for hardware is roughly equivalent to *unit testing* in software—testing done on each module, in isolation, to verify its behavior. We can get a better feeling for how a module will react in the big wide world once we have tested it throughly under controlled (even contrived) conditions.

A software unit test is code that exercises a module. Typically, the unit test will establish some kind of artificial environment, then invoke routines in the module being tested. It then checks the results that are returned, either against known values or against the results from previous runs of the same test (regression testing).

Later, when we assemble our "software IC's" into a complete system, we'll have confidence that the individual parts work as expected, and then we can use the same unit test facilities to test the system as a whole. We talk about this large-scale checking of the system in *Ruthless Testing*, page 237.

Before we get that far, however, we need to decide what to test at the unit level. Typically, programmers throw a few random bits of data at the code and call it tested. We can do much better, using the ideas behind *design by contract*.

Testing Against Contract

We like to think of unit testing as *testing against contract* (see *Design by Contract*, page 109). We want to write test cases that ensure that a given unit honors its contract. This will tell us two things: whether the code meets the contract, and whether the contract means what we think it means. We want to test that the module delivers the functionality it promises, over a wide range of test cases and boundary conditions.

What does this mean in practice? Let's look at the square root routine we first encountered on page 114. Its contract is simple:

```
require
  argument >= 0;
ensure
  ((Result * Result) - argument).abs <= epsilon*argument;
```

This tells us what to test:

- Pass in a negative argument and ensure that it is rejected.

- Pass in an argument of zero to ensure that it is accepted (this is the boundary value).

- Pass in values between zero and the maximum expressible argument and verify that the difference between the square of the result and the original argument is less than some small fraction of the argument.

Armed with this contract, and assuming that our routine does its own pre- and postcondition checking, we can write a basic test script to exercise the square root function.

```
public void testValue(double num, double expected) {
  double result = 0.0;
  try {                        // We may throw a
    result = mySqrt(num);      // precondition exception
  }
  catch (Throwable e) {
    if (num < 0.0)             // If input is < 0, then
      return;                  // we're expecting the
    else                       // exception, otherwise
      assert(false);           // force a test failure
  }
  assert(Math.abs(expected-result) < epsilon*expected);
}
```

Then we can call this routine to test our square root function:

```
testValue(-4.0,  0.0);
testValue( 0.0,  0.0);
testValue( 2.0,  1.4142135624);
testValue(64.0,  8.0);
testValue(1.0e7, 3162.2776602);
```

This is a pretty simple test; in the real world, any nontrivial module is likely to be dependent on a number of other modules, so how do we go about testing the combination?

Suppose we have a module A that uses a LinkedList and a Sort. In order, we would test:

1. LinkedList's contract, in full

2. Sort's contract, in full

3. A's contract, which relies on the other contracts but does not directly expose them

This style of testing requires you to test subcomponents of a module first. Once the subcomponents have been verified, then the module itself can be tested.

If `LinkedList` and `Sort`'s tests passed, but A's test failed, we can be pretty sure that the problem is in A, or in A's *use* of one of those subcomponents. This technique is a great way to reduce debugging effort: we can quickly concentrate on the likely source of the problem within module A, and not waste time reexamining its subcomponents.

Why do we go to all this trouble? Above all, we want to avoid creating a "time bomb"—something that sits around unnoticed and blows up at an awkward moment later in the project. By emphasizing testing against contract, we can try to avoid as many of those downstream disasters as possible.

TIP 48

Design to Test

When you design a module, or even a single routine, you should design both its contract and the code to test that contract. By designing code to pass a test and fulfill its contract, you may well consider boundary conditions and other issues that wouldn't occur to you otherwise. There's no better way to fix errors than by avoiding them in the first place. In fact, by building the tests *before* you implement the code, you get to try out the interface before you commit to it.

Writing Unit Tests

The unit tests for a module shouldn't be shoved in some far-away corner of the source tree. They need to be conveniently located. For small projects, you can embed the unit test for a module in the module itself. For larger projects, we suggest moving each test into a subdirectory. Either way, remember that if it isn't easy to find, it won't be used.

By making the test code readily accessible, you are providing developers who may use your code with two invaluable resources:

1. Examples of how to use all the functionality of your module

2. A means to build regression tests to validate any future changes to the code

It's convenient, but not always practical, for each class or module to contain its own unit test. In Java, for example, every class can have its own `main`. In all but the application's main class file, the `main` routine can be used to run unit tests; it will be ignored when the application itself is run. This has the benefit that the code you ship still contains the tests, which can be used to diagnose problems in the field.

In C++ you can achieve the same effect (at compile time) by using `#ifdef` to compile unit test code selectively. For example, here's a very simple unit test in C++, embedded in our module, that checks our square root function using a `testValue` routine similar to the Java one defined previously:

```
#ifdef __TEST__
int main(int argc, char **argv)
{
  argc--; argv++;          // skip program name
  if (argc < 2) {          // do standard tests if no args
    testValue(-4.0,  0.0);
    testValue( 0.0,  0.0);
    testValue( 2.0,  1.4142135624);
    testValue(64.0,  8.0);
    testValue(1.0e7, 3162.2776602);
  }
  else {                   // else use args
    double num, expected;
    while (argc >= 2) {
      num = atof(argv[0]);
      expected = atof(argv[1]);
      testValue(num,expected);
      argc -= 2;
      argv += 2;
    }
  }
  return 0;
}
#endif
```

This unit test will either run a minimal set of tests or, if given arguments, allow you to pass data in from the outside world. A shell script could use this ability to run a much more complete set of tests.

What do you do if the correct response for a unit test is to exit, or abort the program? In that case, you need to be able to select the test to run, perhaps by specifying an argument on the command line. You'll also need to pass in parameters if you need to specify different starting conditions for your tests.

But providing unit tests isn't enough. You must run them, and run them often. It also helps if the class *passes* its tests once in a while.

Using Test Harnesses

Because we usually write *a lot* of test code, and do a lot of testing, we'll make life easier on ourselves and develop a standard testing harness for the project. The main shown in the previous section is a very simple test harness, but usually we'll need more functionality than that.

A test harness can handle common operations such as logging status, analyzing output for expected results, and selecting and running the tests. Harnesses may be GUI driven, may be written in the same target language as the rest of the project, or may be implemented as a combination of makefiles and Perl scripts. A simple test harness is shown in the answer to Exercise 41 on page 305.

In object-oriented languages and environments, you might create a base class that provides these common operations. Individual tests can subclass from that and add specific test code. You could use a standard naming convention and reflection in Java to build a list of tests dynamically. This technique is a nice way of honoring the *DRY* principle—you don't have to maintain a list of available tests. But before you go off and start writing your own harness, you may want to investigate Kent Beck and Erich Gamma's xUnit at [URL 22]. You might also want to look at our book *Pragmatic Unit Testing* [HT03] for an introduction to JUnit.

Regardless of the technology you decide to use, test harnesses should include the following capabilities:

- A standard way to specify setup and cleanup
- A method for selecting individual tests or all available tests
- A means of analyzing output for expected (or unexpected) results
- A standardized form of failure reporting

Tests should be composable; that is, a test can be composed of subtests of subcomponents to any depth. We can use this feature to test selected parts of the system or the entire system just as easily, using the same tools.

> ### Ad Hoc Testing
>
> During debugging, we may end up creating some particular tests on-the-fly. These may be as simple as a `print` statement, or a piece of code entered interactively in a debugger or IDE environment.
>
> At the end of the debugging session, you need to formalize the ad hoc test. If the code broke once, it is likely to break again. Don't just throw away the test you created; add it to the existing unit test.

For example, using JUnit (the Java member of the xUnit family), we might write our square root test as follows:

```java
public class JUnitExample extends TestCase {
  public JUnitExample(final String name) {
    super(name);
  }
  protected void setUp() {
    // Load up test data...
    testData.addElement(new DblPair(-4.0,0.0));
    testData.addElement(new DblPair(0.0,0.0));
    testData.addElement(new DblPair(64.0,8.0));
    testData.addElement(new DblPair(Double.MAX_VALUE,
                                   1.3407807929942597E154));
  }
  public void testMySqrt() {
    double num, expected, result = 0.0;
    Enumeration enum = testData.elements();
    while (enum.hasMoreElements()) {
      DblPair p = (DblPair)enum.nextElement();
      num      = p.getNum();
      expected = p.getExpected();
      testValue(num, expected);
    }
  }
  public static Test suite() {
    TestSuite suite= new TestSuite();
    suite.addTest(new JUnitExample("testMySqrt"));
    return suite;
  }
}
```

JUnit is designed to be composable: we could add as many tests as we wanted to this suite, and each of those tests could in turn be a suite. In addition, you have your choice of a graphical or batch interface to drive the tests.

Build a Test Window

Even the best sets of tests are unlikely to find all the bugs; there's something about the damp, warm conditions of a production environment that seems to bring them out of the woodwork.

This means you'll often need to test a piece of software once it has been deployed—with real-world data flowing though its veins. Unlike a circuit board or chip, we don't have *test pins* in software, but we *can* provide various views into the internal state of a module, without using the debugger (which may be inconvenient or impossible in a production application).

Log files containing trace messages are one such mechanism. Log messages should be in a regular, consistent format; you may want to parse them automatically to deduce processing time or logic paths that the program took. Poorly or inconsistently formatted diagnostics are just so much "spew"—they are difficult to read and impractical to parse.

Another mechanism for getting inside running code is the "hot-key" sequence. When this particular combination of keys is pressed, a diagnostic control window pops up with status messages and so on. This isn't something you normally would reveal to end users, but it can be very handy for the help desk.

For larger, more complex server code, a nifty technique for providing a view into its operation is to include a built-in Web server. Anyone can point a Web browser to the application's HTTP port (which is usually on a nonstandard number, such as 8080) and see internal status, log entries, and possibly even some sort of a debug control panel. This may sound difficult to implement, but it's not. Freely available and embeddable HTTP Web servers are available in a variety of modern languages. A good place to start looking is [URL 58].

A Culture of Testing

All software you write *will* be tested—if not by you and your team, then by the eventual users—so you might as well plan on testing it thoroughly. A little forethought can go a long way toward minimizing maintenance costs and help-desk calls.

Despite its hacker reputation, the Perl community has a very strong commitment to unit and regression testing. The Perl standard module installation procedure supports a regression test by invoking

```
% make test
```

There's nothing magic about Perl itself in this regard. Perl makes it easier to collate and analyze test results to ensure compliance, but the big advantage is simply that it's a standard—tests go in a particular place, and have a certain expected output. *Testing is more cultural than technical;* we can instill this testing culture in a project regardless of the language being used.

> TIP 49
> ### Test Your Software, or Your Users Will

Related sections include:
- *The Cat Ate My Source Code*, page 2
- *Orthogonality*, page 34
- *Design by Contract*, page 109
- *Refactoring*, page 184
- *Ruthless Testing*, page 237

Exercises

41. Design a test jig for the blender interface described in the answer to Exercise 17 on page 289. Write a shell script that will perform a regression test for the blender. You need to test basic functionality, error and boundary conditions, and any contractual obligations. What restrictions are placed on changing the speed? Are they being honored?

Answer on p. 305

Evil Wizards

There's no denying it—applications are getting harder and harder to write. User interfaces in particular are becoming increasingly sophisticated. Twenty years ago, the average application would have a glass teletype interface (if it had an interface at all). Asynchronous terminals would typically provide a character interactive display, while pollable devices (such as the ubiquitous IBM 3270) would let you fill in an entire screen before hitting SEND. Now, users expect graphical user interfaces, with context-sensitive help, cut and paste, drag and drop, OLE integration, and MDI or SDI. Users are looking for Web-browser integration and thin-client support.

All the time the applications themselves are getting more complex. Most developments now use a multitier model, possibly with some middleware layer or a transaction monitor. These programs are expected to be dynamic and flexible, and to interoperate with applications written by third parties.

Oh, and did we mention that we needed it all next week?

Developers are struggling to keep up. If we were using the same kind of tools that produced the basic dumb-terminal applications 20 years ago, we'd never get anything done.

So the tool makers and infrastructure vendors have come up with a magic bullet, the *wizard*. Wizards are great. Do you need an MDI application with OLE container support? Just click a single button, answer a couple of simple questions, and the wizard will automatically generate skeleton code for you. The Microsoft Visual C++ environment creates over 1,200 lines of code for this scenario, automatically. Wizards are hard at work in other contexts, too. You can use wizards to create server components, implement Java beans, and handle network interfaces— all complex areas where it's nice to have expert help.

But using a wizard designed by a guru does not automatically make Joe developer equally expert. Joe can feel pretty good—he's just produced a mass of code and a pretty spiffy-looking program. He just adds in the specific application functionality and it's ready to ship. But unless Joe actually understands the code that has been produced on his behalf, he's fooling himself. He's programming by coincidence. Wizards are a one-way street—they cut the code for you, and then move on. If the code they produce isn't quite right, or if circumstances change and you need to adapt the code, you're on your own.

We are not against wizards. On the contrary, we dedicate an entire section (*Code Generators*, page 102) to writing your own. But if you *do* use a wizard, and you don't understand all the code that it produces, you won't be in control of your own application. You won't be able to maintain it, and you'll be struggling when it comes time to debug.

> **TIP 50**
>
> **Don't Use Wizard Code You Don't Understand**

Some people feel that this is an extreme position. They say that developers routinely rely on things they don't fully understand—the quantum mechanics of integrated circuits, the interrupt structure of the processor, the algorithms used to schedule processes, the code in the supplied libraries, and so on. We agree. And we'd feel the same about wizards if they were simply a set of library calls or standard operating system services that developers could rely on. But they're not. Wizards generate code that becomes an integral part of Joe's application. The wizard code is not factored out behind a tidy interface—it is interwoven line by line with functionality that Joe writes.[4] Eventually, it stops being the wizard's code and starts being Joe's. And no one should be producing code they don't fully understand.

Related sections include:
- *Orthogonality*, page 34
- *Code Generators*, page 102

Challenges
- If you have a GUI-building wizard available, use it to generate a skeleton application. Go through every line of code it produces. Do you understand it all? Could you have produced it yourself? Would you have produced it yourself, or is it doing things you don't need?

---

4.   However, there are other techniques that help manage complexity. We discuss two, beans and AOP, in *Orthogonality*, page 34.

Chapter 7

Before the Project

Do you ever get the feeling that your project is doomed, even before it starts? Sometimes it might be, unless you establish some basic ground rules first. Otherwise, you might as well suggest that it be shut down now, and save the sponsor some money.

At the very beginning of a project, you'll need to determine the requirements. Simply listening to users is not enough: read *The Requirements Pit* to find out more.

Conventional wisdom and constraint management are the topics of *Solving Impossible Puzzles*. Whether you are performing requirements, analysis, coding, or testing, difficult problems will crop up. Most of the time, they won't be as difficult as they first appear to be.

When you think you've got the problems solved, you may still not feel comfortable with jumping in and starting. Is it simple procrastination, or is it something more? *Not Until You're Ready* offers advice on when it may be prudent to listen to that cautionary voice inside your head.

Starting too soon is one problem, but waiting too long may be even worse. In *The Specification Trap*, we'll discuss the advantages of specification by example.

Finally, we'll look at some of the pitfalls of formal development processes and methodologies in *Circles and Arrows*. No matter how well thought out it is, and regardless of which "best practices" it includes, no method can replace *thinking*.

With these critical issues sorted out *before* the project gets under way, you can be better positioned to avoid "analysis paralysis" and actually begin your successful project.

The Requirements Pit

Perfection is achieved, not when there is nothing left to add, but when there is nothing left to take away....

▶ **Antoine de St. Exupery, *Wind, Sand, and Stars*, 1939**

Many books and tutorials refer to *requirements gathering* as an early phase of the project. The word "gathering" seems to imply a tribe of happy analysts, foraging for nuggets of wisdom that are lying on the ground all around them while the Pastoral Symphony plays gently in the background. "Gathering" implies that the requirements are already there—you need merely find them, place them in your basket, and be merrily on your way.

It doesn't quite work that way. Requirements rarely lie on the surface. Normally, they're buried deep beneath layers of assumptions, misconceptions, and politics.

TIP 51

Don't Gather Requirements—Dig for Them

Digging for Requirements

How can you recognize a true requirement while you're digging through all the surrounding dirt? The answer is both simple and complex.

The simple answer is that a requirement is a statement of something that needs to be accomplished. Good requirements might include the following:

- An employee record may be viewed only by a nominated group of people.

- The cylinder-head temperature must not exceed the critical value, which varies by engine.

- The editor will highlight keywords, which will be selected depending on the type of file being edited.

However, very few requirements are as clear-cut, and that's what makes requirements analysis complex.

The first statement in the list above may have been stated by the users as "Only an employee's supervisors and the personnel department may view that employee's records." Is this statement truly a requirement? Perhaps today, but it embeds business policy in an absolute statement. Policies change regularly, so we probably don't want to hardwire them into our requirements. Our recommendation is to document these policies separately from the requirement, and hyperlink the two. Make the requirement the general statement, and give the developers the policy information as an example of the type of thing they'll need to support in the implementation. Eventually, policy may end up as metadata in the application.

This is a relatively subtle distinction, but it's one that will have profound implications for the developers. If the requirement is stated as "Only personnel can view an employee record," the developer may end up coding an explicit test every time the application accesses these files. However, if the statement is "Only authorized users may access an employee record," the developer will probably design and implement some kind of access control system. When policy changes (and it will), only the metadata for that system will need to be updated. In fact, gathering requirements in this way naturally leads you to a system that is well factored to support metadata.

The distinctions among requirements, policy, and implementation can get very blurred when user interfaces are discussed. "The system must let you choose a loan term" is a statement of requirement. "We need a list box to select the loan term" may or may not be. If the users absolutely must have a list box, then it is a requirement. If instead they are describing the ability to choose, but are using *listbox* as an example, then it may not be. The box on page 205 discusses a project that went horribly wrong because the users' interface needs were ignored.

It's important to discover the underlying reason *why* users do a particular thing, rather than just *the way* they currently do it. At the end of the day, your development has to solve their *business problem*, not just meet their stated requirements. Documenting the reasons behind requirements will give your team invaluable information when making daily implementation decisions.

There's a simple technique for getting inside your users' requirements that isn't used often enough: become a user. Are you writing a system for the help desk? Spend a couple of days monitoring the phones with an experienced support person. Are you automating a manual stock control system? Work in the warehouse for a week.[1] As well as giving you insight into how the system will *really* be used, you'd be amazed at how the request "May I sit in for a week while you do your job?" helps build trust and establishes a basis for communication with your users. Just remember not to get in the way!

> TIP 52
>
> ### Work with a User to Think Like a User

The requirements mining process is also the time to start to build a rapport with your user base, learning their expectations and hopes for the system you are building. See *Great Expectations*, page 255, for more.

Documenting Requirements

So you are sitting down with the users and prying genuine requirements from them. You come across a few likely scenarios that describe what the application needs to do. Ever the professional, you want to write these down and publish a document that everyone can use as a basis for discussions—the developers, the end users, and the project sponsors.

That's a pretty wide audience.

Ivar Jacobson [Jac94] proposed the concept of *use cases* to capture requirements. They let you describe a particular *use* of the system— not in terms of user interface, but in a more abstract fashion. Unfortunately, Jacobson's book was a little vague on details, so there are now many different opinions on what a use case should be. Is it formal or informal, simple prose or a structured document (like a form)? What level of detail is appropriate (remember we have a wide audience)?

---

1. Does a week sound like a long time? It really isn't, particularly when you're looking at processes in which management and workers occupy different worlds. Management will give you one view of how things operate, but when you get down on the floor, you'll find a very different reality—one that will take time to assimilate.

Sometimes the Interface *Is* the System

In an article in *Wired* magazine (January 1999, page 176), producer and musician Brian Eno described an incredible piece of technology—the ultimate mixing board. It does anything to sound that can be done. And yet, instead of letting musicians make better music, or produce a recording faster or less expensively, it gets in the way; it disrupts the creative process.

To see why, you have to look at how recording engineers work. They balance sounds intuitively. Over the years, they develop an innate feedback loop between their ears and their fingertips—sliding faders, rotating knobs, and so on. However, the interface to the new mixer didn't leverage off those abilities. Instead, it forced its users to type on a keyboard or click a mouse. The functions it provided were comprehensive, but they were packaged in unfamiliar and exotic ways. The functions the engineers needed were sometimes hidden behind obscure names, or were achieved with nonintuitive combinations of basic facilities.

That environment has a requirement to leverage existing skill sets. While slavishly duplicating what already exists doesn't allow for progress, we must be able to provide a *transition* to the future.

For example, the recording engineers may have been better served by some sort of touchscreen interface—still tactile, still mounted as a traditional mixing board might be, yet allowing the software to go beyond the realm of fixed knobs and switches. Providing a comfortable transition through familiar metaphors is one way to help get buy-in.

This example also illustrates our belief that successful tools adapt to the hands that use them. In this case, it is the tools that you build for others that must be adaptable.

One way of looking at use cases is to emphasize their goal-driven nature. Alistair Cockburn has a paper that describes this approach, as well as templates that can be used (strictly or not) as a starting place ([Coc97a], also online at [URL 46]). Figure 7.1 on the following page shows an abbreviated example of his template, while Figure 7.2 shows his sample use case.

By using a formal template as an *aide-mémoire*, you can be sure that you include all the information you need in a use case: performance

Figure 7.1. Cockburn's use case template

A. CHARACTERISTIC INFORMATION
  – Goal in context
  – Scope
  – Level
  – Preconditions
  – Success end condition
  – Failed end condition
  – Primary actor
  – Trigger
B. MAIN SUCCESS SCENARIO
C. EXTENSIONS
D. VARIATIONS
E. RELATED INFORMATION
  – Priority
  – Performance target
  – Frequency
  – Superordinate use case
  – Subordinate use cases
  – Channel to primary actor
  – Secondary actors
  – Channel to secondary actors
F. SCHEDULE
G. OPEN ISSUES

characteristics, other involved parties, priority, frequency, and various errors and exceptions that can crop up ("nonfunctional requirements"). This is also a great place to record user comments such as "oh, except if we get a *xxx* condition, then we have to do *yyy* instead." The template also serves as a ready-made agenda for meetings with your users.

This sort of organization supports the hierarchical structuring of use cases—nesting more detailed use cases inside higher-level ones. For example, *post debit* and *post credit* both elaborate on *post transaction*.

Use Case Diagrams

Workflow can be captured with UML activity diagrams, and conceptual-level class diagrams can sometimes be useful for modeling the business

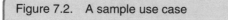

Figure 7.2. A sample use case

USE CASE 5: BUY GOODS

A. **CHARACTERISTIC INFORMATION**
- **Goal in context:** Buyer issues request directly to our company, expects goods shipped and to be billed.
- **Scope:** Company
- **Level:** Summary
- **Preconditions:** We know buyer, their address, etc.
- **Success end condition:** Buyer has goods, we have money for the goods.
- **Failed end condition:** We have not sent the goods, buyer has not sent the money.
- **Primary actor:** Buyer, any agent (or computer) acting for the customer
- **Trigger:** Purchase request comes in.

B. **MAIN SUCCESS SCENARIO**
1. Buyer calls in with a purchase request.
2. Company captures buyer's name, address, requested goods, etc.
3. Company gives buyer information on goods, prices, delivery dates, etc.
4. Buyer signs for order.
5. Company creates order, ships order to buyer.
6. Company ships invoice to buyer.
7. Buyer pays invoice.

C. **EXTENSIONS**
3a. Company is out of one of the ordered items: Renegotiate order.
4a. Buyer pays directly with credit card: Take payment by credit card (use case 44).
7a. Buyer returns goods: Handle returned goods (use case 105).

D. **VARIATIONS**
1. Buyer may use phone in, fax in, Web order form, electronic interchange.
7. Buyer may pay by cash, money order, check, or credit card.

E. **RELATED INFORMATION**
- **Priority:** Top
- **Performance target:** 5 minutes for order, 45 days until paid
- **Frequency:** 200/day
- **Superordinate use case:** Manage customer relationship (use case 2).
- **Subordinate use cases:** Create order (15). Take payment by credit card (44). Handle returned goods (105).
- **Channel to primary actor:** May be phone, file, or interactive
- **Secondary actors:** Credit card company, bank, shipping service

F. **SCHEDULE**
- **Due date:** Release 1.0

G. **OPEN ISSUES**
- What happens if we have part of the order?
- What happens if credit card is stolen?

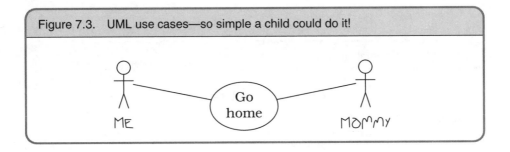

Figure 7.3.   UML use cases—so simple a child could do it!

at hand. But true use cases are textual descriptions, with a hierarchy and cross-links. Use cases can contain hyperlinks to other use cases, and they can be nested within each other.

It seems incredible to us that anyone would seriously consider documenting information this dense using only simplistic stick people such as Figure 7.3. Don't be a slave to any notation; use whatever method best communicates the requirements with your audience.

Overspecifying

A big danger in producing a requirements document is being too specific. Good requirements documents remain abstract. Where requirements are concerned, the simplest statement that accurately reflects the business need is best. This doesn't mean you can be vague—you must capture the underlying semantic invariants as requirements, and document the specific or current work practices as policy.

Requirements are not architecture. Requirements are not design, nor are they the user interface. Requirements are *need*.

Seeing Further

The Year 2000 problem is often blamed on short-sighted programmers, desperate to save a few bytes in the days when mainframes had less memory than a modern TV remote control.

But it wasn't the programmers' doing, and it wasn't really a memory usage issue. If anything, it was the system analysts' and designers' fault. The Y2K problem came about from two main causes: a failure to see beyond current business practice, and a violation of the *DRY* principle.

Businesses were using the two-digit shortcut long before computers came on the scene. It was common practice. The earliest data processing applications merely automated existing business processes, and simply repeated the mistake. Even if the architecture required two-digit years for data input, reporting, and storage, there should have been an abstraction of a DATE that "knew" the two digits were an abbreviated form of the real date.

> TIP 53
>
> **Abstractions Live Longer than Details**

Does "seeing further" require you to predict the future? No. It means generating statements such as

> *The system makes active use of an abstraction of DATEs. The system will implement DATE services, such as formatting, storage, and math operations, consistently and universally.*

The requirements will specify only that dates are used. It may hint that some math may be done on dates. It may tell you that dates will be stored on various forms of secondary storage. These are genuine requirements for a DATE module or class.

Just One More Wafer-Thin Mint...

Many projects failures are blamed on an increase in scope—also known as feature bloat, creeping featurism, or requirements creep. This is an aspect of the boiled-frog syndrome from *Stone Soup and Boiled Frogs*, page 7. What can we do to prevent requirements from creeping up on us?

In the literature, you will find descriptions of many metrics, such as bugs reported and fixed, defect density, cohesion, coupling, function points, lines of code, and so on. These metrics may be tracked by hand or with software.

Unfortunately, not many projects seem to track requirements actively. This means that they have no way to report on changes of scope—who requested a feature, who approved it, total number of requests approved, and so on.

The key to managing growth of requirements is to point out each new feature's impact on the schedule to the project sponsors. When the project is a year late from initial estimates and accusations start flying, it can be helpful to have an accurate, complete picture of how, and when, requirements growth occurred.

It's easy to get sucked into the "just one more feature" maelstrom, but by tracking requirements you can get a clearer picture that "just one more feature" is really the fifteenth new feature added this month.

Maintain a Glossary

As soon as you start discussing requirements, users and domain experts will use certain terms that have specific meaning to them. They may differentiate between a "client" and a "customer," for example. It would then be inappropriate to use either word casually in the system.

Create and maintain a *project glossary*—one place that defines all the specific terms and vocabulary used in a project. All participants in the project, from end users to support staff, should use the glossary to ensure consistency. This implies that the glossary needs to be widely accessible—a good argument for Web-based documentation (more on that in a moment).

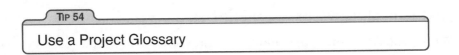

TIP 54

Use a Project Glossary

It's very hard to succeed on a project where the users and developers refer to the same thing by different names or, even worse, refer to different things by the same name.

Get the Word Out

In *It's All Writing*, page 248, we discuss publishing of project documents to internal Web sites for easy access by all participants. This method of distribution is particularly useful for requirements documents.

By presenting requirements as a hypertext document, we can better address the needs of a diverse audience—we can give each reader what they want. Project sponsors can cruise along at a high level of abstraction to ensure that business objectives are met. Programmers can use hyperlinks to "drill down" to increasing levels of detail (even referencing appropriate definitions or engineering specifications).

Web-based distribution also avoids the typical two-inch-thick binder entitled *Requirements Analysis* that no one ever reads and that becomes outdated the instant ink hits paper.

If it's on the Web, the programmers may even read it.

Related sections include:
- *Stone Soup and Boiled Frogs*, page 7
- *Good-Enough Software*, page 9
- *Circles and Arrows*, page 220
- *It's All Writing*, page 248
- *Great Expectations*, page 255

Challenges
- Can you use the software you are writing? Is it possible to have a good feel for requirements *without* being able to use the software yourself?

- Pick a non-computer-related problem you currently need to solve. Generate requirements for a noncomputer solution.

Exercises
42. Which of the following are probably genuine requirements? Restate those that are not to make them more useful (if possible). *Answer on p. 307*

    1. The response time must be less than 500 ms.

    2. Dialog boxes will have a gray background.

    3. The application will be organized as a number of front-end processes and a back-end server.

    4. If a user enters non-numeric characters in a numeric field, the system will beep and not accept them.

    5. The application code and data must fit within 256kB.

Solving Impossible Puzzles

Gordius, the King of Phrygia, once tied a knot that no one could untie. It was said that he who solved the riddle of the Gordian Knot would rule all of Asia. So along comes Alexander the Great, who chops the knot to bits with his sword. Just a little different interpretation of the requirements, that's all... and he did end up ruling most of Asia.

Every now and again, you will find yourself embroiled in the middle of a project when a really tough puzzle comes up: some piece of engineering that you just can't get a handle on, or perhaps some bit of code that is turning out to be much harder to write than you thought. Maybe it looks impossible. But is it really as hard as it seems?

Consider real-world puzzles—those devious little bits of wood, wrought iron, or plastic that seem to turn up as Christmas presents or at garage sales. All you have to do is remove the ring, or fit the T-shaped pieces in the box, or whatever.

So you pull on the ring, or try to put the T's in the box, and quickly discover that the obvious solutions just don't work. The puzzle can't be solved that way. But even though it's obvious, that doesn't stop people from trying the same thing—over and over—thinking there must be a way.

Of course, there isn't. The solution lies elsewhere. The secret to solving the puzzle is to identify the real (not imagined) constraints, and find a solution therein. Some constraints are *absolute*; others are merely *preconceived notions*. Absolute constraints *must* be honored, however distasteful or stupid they may appear to be. On the other hand, some apparent constraints may not be real constraints at all. For example, there's that old bar trick where you take a brand new, unopened champagne bottle and bet that you can drink beer out of it. The trick is to turn the bottle upside down, and pour a small quantity of beer in the hollow in the bottom of the bottle. Many software problems can be just as sneaky.

Degrees of Freedom

The popular buzz-phrase "thinking outside the box" encourages us to recognize constraints that might not be applicable and to ignore them.

But this phrase isn't entirely accurate. If the "box" is the boundary of constraints and conditions, then the trick is to *find* the box, which may be considerably larger than you think.

The key to solving puzzles is both to recognize the constraints placed on you and to recognize the degrees of freedom you *do* have, for in those you'll find your solution. This is why some puzzles are so effective; you may dismiss potential solutions too readily.

For example, can you connect all of the dots in the following puzzle and return to the starting point with just three straight lines—without lifting your pen from the paper or retracing your steps [Hol78]?

● ●

● ●

You must challenge any preconceived notions and evaluate whether or not they are real, hard-and-fast constraints.

It's not whether you think inside the box or outside the box. The problem lies in *finding* the box—identifying the real constraints.

TIP 55

Don't Think Outside the Box—*Find* the Box

When faced with an intractable problem, enumerate *all* the possible avenues you have before you. Don't dismiss anything, no matter how unusable or stupid it sounds. Now go through the list and explain why a certain path cannot be taken. Are you sure? Can you *prove* it?

Consider the Trojan horse—a novel solution to an intractable problem. How do you get troops into a walled city without being discovered? You can bet that "through the front door" was initially dismissed as suicide.

Categorize and prioritize your constraints. When woodworkers begin a project, they cut the longest pieces first, then cut the smaller pieces out of the remaining wood. In the same manner, we want to identify the most restrictive constraints first, and fit the remaining constraints within them.

By the way, a solution to the Four Posts puzzle is shown on page 307.

There Must Be an Easier Way!

Sometimes you will find yourself working on a problem that seems much harder than you thought it should be. Maybe it feels like you're going down the wrong path—that there must be an easier way than this! Perhaps you are running late on the schedule now, or even despair of ever getting the system to work because this particular problem is "impossible."

That's when you step back a pace and ask yourself these questions:

- *Is* there an easier way?

- Are you trying to solve the right problem, or have you been distracted by a peripheral technicality?

- *Why* is this thing a problem?

- What is it that's making it so hard to solve?

- Does it have to be done this way?

- Does it have to be done at all?

Many times a surprising revelation will come to you as you try to answer one of these questions. Many times a reinterpretation of the requirements can make a whole set of problems go away—just like the Gordian knot.

All you need are the real constraints, the misleading constraints, and the wisdom to know the difference.

Challenges

- Take a hard look at whatever difficult problem you are embroiled in today. Can you cut the Gordian knot? Ask yourself the key questions we outlined above, especially *"Does it have to be done this way?"*

- Were you handed a set of constraints when you signed on to your current project? Are they all still applicable, and is the interpretation of them still valid?

▶ 38 <u>Not Until You're Ready</u>

He who hesitates is sometimes saved.
> **James Thurber, *The Glass in the Field***

Great performers share a trait: they know when to start and when to wait. The diver stands on the high-board, waiting for the perfect moment to jump. The conductor stands before the orchestra, arms raised, until she senses that the moment is right to start the piece.

You are a great performer. You too need to listen to the voice that whispers "wait." If you sit down to start typing and there's some nagging doubt in your mind, heed it.

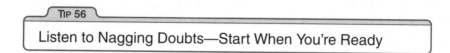

TIP 56

Listen to Nagging Doubts—Start When You're Ready

There used to be a style of tennis coaching called "inner tennis." You'd spend hours hitting balls over the net, not particularly trying for accuracy, but instead verbalizing just where the ball hit relative to some target (often a chair). The idea was that the feedback would train your subconscious and reflexes, so that you improved without consciously knowing how or why.

As a developer, you've been doing the same kind of thing during your entire career. You've been trying things and seeing which worked and which didn't. You've been accumulating experience and wisdom. When you feel a nagging doubt, or experience some reluctance when faced with a task, heed it. You may not be able to put your finger on exactly what's wrong, but give it time and your doubts will probably crystallize into something more solid, something you can address. Software development is still not a science. Let your instincts contribute to your performance.

Good Judgment or Procrastination?

Everyone fears the blank sheet of paper. Starting a new project (or even a new module in an existing project) can be an unnerving experience. Many of us would prefer to put off making the initial commitment of starting. So how can you tell when you're simply procrastinating, rather than responsibly waiting for all the pieces to fall into place?

A technique that has worked for us in these circumstances is to start prototyping. Choose an area that you feel will be difficult and begin producing some kind of proof of concept. One of two things will typically happen. Shortly after starting, you may feel that you're wasting your time. This boredom is probably a good indication that your initial reluctance was just a desire to put off the commitment to start. Give up on the prototype, and hack into the real development.

On the other hand, as the prototype progresses you may have one of those moments of revelation when you suddenly realize that some basic premise was wrong. Not only that, but you'll see clearly how you can put it right. You'll feel comfortable abandoning the prototype and launching into the project proper. Your instincts were right, and you've just saved yourself and your team a considerable amount of wasted effort.

When you make the decision to prototype as a way of investigating your unease, be sure to remember why you're doing it. The last thing you want is to find yourself several weeks into serious development before remembering that you started out writing a prototype.

Somewhat cynically, starting work on a prototype might also be more politically acceptable than simply announcing that "I don't feel right about starting" and firing up `solitaire`.

Challenges

- Discuss the fear-of-starting syndrome with your colleagues. Do others experience the same thing? Do they heed it? What tricks do they use to overcome it? Can a group help overcome an individual's reluctance, or is that just peer pressure?

The Specification Trap

39 ▶

The Landing Pilot is the Non-Handling Pilot until the 'decision altitude' call, when the Handling Non-Landing Pilot hands the handling to the Non-Handling Landing Pilot, unless the latter calls 'go-around,' in which case the Handling Non-Landing Pilot continues handling and the Non-Handling Landing Pilot continues non-handling until the next call of 'land' or 'go-around' as appropriate. In view of recent confusions over these rules, it was deemed necessary to restate them clearly.

> ▶ **British Airways memorandum, quoted in** *Pilot Magazine*,
> **December 1996**

Program specification is the process of taking a requirement and reducing it down to the point where a programmer's skill can take over. It is an act of communication, explaining and clarifying the world in such a way as to remove major ambiguities. As well as talking to the developer who will be performing the initial implementation, the specification is a record for future generations of programmers who will be maintaining and enhancing the code. The specification is also an agreement with the user—a codification of their needs and an implicit contract that the final system will be in line with that requirement.

Writing a specification is quite a responsibility.

The problem is that many designers find it difficult to stop. They feel that unless every little detail is pinned down in excruciating detail they haven't earned their daily dollar.

This is a mistake for several reasons. First, it's naive to assume that a specification will ever capture every detail and nuance of a system or its requirement. In restricted problem domains, there are formal methods that can describe a system, but they still require the designer to explain the meaning of the notation to the end users—there is still a human interpretation going on to mess things up. Even without the problems inherent in this interpretation, it is very unlikely that the average user knows going in to a project exactly what they need. They may say they have an understanding of the requirement, and they may sign off on the 200-page document you produce, but you can guarantee that once they see the running system you'll be inundated with change requests.

Second, there is a problem with the expressive power of language itself. All the diagramming techniques and formal methods still rely on natural language expressions of the operations to be performed.[2] And natural language is really not up to the job. Look at the wording of any contract: in an attempt to be precise, lawyers have to bend the language in the most unnatural ways.

Here's a challenge for you. Write a short description that tells someone how to tie bows in their shoelaces. Go on, try it!

If you are anything like us, you probably gave up somewhere around "now roll your thumb and forefinger so that the free end passes under and inside the left lace. . . ." It is a phenomenally difficult thing to do. And yet most of us can tie our shoes without conscious thought.

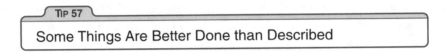

TIP 57

Some Things Are Better Done than Described

Finally, there is the straightjacket effect. A design that leaves the coder no room for interpretation robs the programming effort of any skill and art. Some would say this is for the best, but they're wrong. Often, it is only during coding that certain options become apparent. While coding, you may think *"Look at that. Because of the particular way I coded this routine, I could add this additional functionality with almost no effort"* or *"The specification says to do this, but I could achieve an almost identical result by doing it a different way, and I could do it in half the time."* Clearly, you shouldn't just hack in and make the changes, but you wouldn't even have spotted the opportunity if you were constrained by an overly prescriptive design.

As a Pragmatic Programmer, you should tend to view requirements gathering, design, and implementation as different facets of the same process—the delivery of a quality system. Distrust environments where requirements are gathered, specifications are written, and then coding starts, all in isolation. Instead, try to adopt a seamless approach: specification and implementation are simply different aspects of the same process—an attempt to capture and codify a requirement. Each should

---

2.   There are some formal techniques that attempt to express operations algebraically, but these techniques are rarely used in practice. They still require that the analysts explain the meaning to the end users.

flow directly into the next, with no artificial boundaries. You'll find that a healthy development process encourages feedback from implementation and testing into the specification process.

Just to be clear, we are not against generating specifications. Indeed, we recognize that there are times where incredibly detailed specifications are demanded—for contractual reasons, because of the environment where you work, or because of the nature of the product you are developing.[3] Just be aware that you reach a point of diminishing, or even negative, returns as the specifications get more and more detailed. Also be careful about building specifications layered on top of specifications, without any supporting implementation or prototyping; it's all too easy to specify something that can't be built.

The longer you allow specifications to be security blankets, protecting developers from the scary world of writing code, the harder it will be to move on to hacking out code. Don't fall into this specification spiral: at some point, you need to start coding! If you find your team all wrapped up in warm, comfy specifications, break them out. Look at prototyping, or consider a tracer bullet development.

Related sections include:
- *Tracer Bullets*, page 48

Challenges
- The shoelace example mentioned in the text is an interesting illustration of the problems of written descriptions. Did you consider describing the process using diagrams rather than words? Photographs? Some formal notation from topology? Models with wire laces? How would you teach a toddler?

  Sometimes a picture is worth more than any number of words. Sometimes it is worthless. If you find yourself overspecifying, would pictures or special notations help? How detailed do they have to be? When is a drawing tool better than a whiteboard?

---

3. Detailed specifications are clearly appropriate for life-critical systems. We feel they should also be produced for interfaces and libraries used by others. When your entire output is seen as a set of routine calls, you'd better make sure those calls are well specified.

Circles and Arrows

[photographs] with circles and arrows and a paragraph on the back of each one explaining what each one was, to be used as evidence against us...
   ▶ **Arlo Guthrie, "Alice's Restaurant"**

From structured programming, through chief programmer teams, CASE tools, waterfall development, the spiral model, Jackson, ER diagrams, Booch clouds, OMT, Objectory, and Coad/Yourdon, to today's UML, computing has never been short of methods intended to make programming more like engineering. Each method gathers its disciples, and each enjoys a period of popularity. Then each is replaced by the next. Of all of them, perhaps only the first—structured programming—has enjoyed a long life.

Yet some developers, adrift in a sea of sinking projects, keep clinging to the latest fad just as shipwreck victims latch onto passing driftwood. As each new piece floats by they painfully swim over, hoping it will be better. At the end of the day, though, it doesn't matter how good the flotsam is, the developers are still aimlessly adrift.

Don't get us wrong. We like (some) formal techniques and methods. But we believe that blindly adopting any technique without putting it into the context of your development practices and capabilities is a recipe for disappointment.

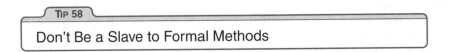

TIP 58

Don't Be a Slave to Formal Methods

Formal methods have some serious shortcomings.

- Most formal methods capture requirements using a combination of diagrams and some supporting words. These pictures represent the designers' understanding of the requirements. However in many cases these diagrams are meaningless to the end users, so the designers have to interpret them. Therefore, there is no real formal checking of the requirements by the actual user of the system— everything is based on the designers' explanations, just as in old-fashioned written requirements. We see some benefit in capturing requirements this way, but we prefer, where possible, to show the user a prototype and let them play with it.

- Formal methods seem to encourage specialization. One group of people works on a data model, another looks at the architecture, while requirements gatherers collect use cases (or their equivalent). We've seen this lead to poor communication and wasted effort. There is also a tendency to fall back into the *us versus them* mentality of designers against coders. We prefer to understand the whole of the system we're working on. It may not be possible to have an in-depth grasp of every aspect of a system, but you should know how the components interact, where the data lives, and what the requirements are.

- We like to write adaptable, dynamic systems, using metadata to allow us to change the character of applications at runtime. Most current formal methods combine a static object or data model with some kind of event- or activity-charting mechanism. We haven't yet come across one that allows us to illustrate the kind of dynamism we feel systems should exhibit. In fact, most formal methods will lead you astray, encouraging you to set up static relationships between objects that really should be knitted together dynamically.

Do Methods Pay Off?

In a 1999 CACM article [Gla99b], Robert Glass reviews the research into the productivity and quality improvements gained using seven different software development technologies (4GLs, structured techniques, CASE tools, formal methods, clean room methodology, process models, and object orientation). He reports that the initial hype surrounding all of these methods was overblown. Although there is an indication that some methods have benefits, these benefits start to manifest themselves only after a significant productivity and quality drop while the technique is adopted and its users train themselves. Never underestimate the cost of adopting new tools and methods. Be prepared to treat the first projects using these techniques as a learning experience.

Should We Use Formal Methods?

Absolutely. But always remember that formal development methods are just one more tool in the toolbox. If, after careful analysis, you feel you need to use a formal method, then embrace it—but remember who is in charge. Never become a slave to a methodology: circles and arrows make poor masters. Pragmatic Programmers look at methodologies critically, then extract the best from each and meld them into a set of working practices that gets better each month. This is crucial. You should work constantly to refine and improve your processes. Never accept the rigid confines of a methodology as the limits of your world.

Don't give in to the false authority of a method. People may walk into meetings with an acre of class diagrams and 150 use cases, but all that paper is still just their fallible interpretation of requirements and design. Try not to think about how much a tool cost when you look at its output.

TIP 59

Expensive Tools Do Not Produce Better Designs

Formal methods certainly have their place in development. However, if you come across a project where the philosophy is "the class diagram *is* the application, the rest is mechanical coding," you know you're looking at a waterlogged project team and a long paddle home.

Related sections include:
- *The Requirements Pit*, page 202

Challenges
- Use case diagrams are part of the UML process for gathering requirements (see *The Requirements Pit*, page 202). Are they an effective way of communicating with your users? If not, why are you using them?

- How can you tell if a formal method is bringing your team benefits? What can you measure? What constitutes an improvement? Can you distinguish between benefits of the tool and increased experience on the part of team members?

- Where is the break-even point for introducing new methods to your team? How do you evaluate the trade-off between future benefits and current losses of productivity as the tool is introduced?

- Are tools that work for large projects good for small ones? How about the other way around?

Chapter 8

Pragmatic Projects

As your project gets under way, we need to move away from issues of individual philosophy and coding to talk about larger, project-sized issues. We aren't going to go into specifics of project management, but we will talk about a handful of critical areas that can make or break any project.

As soon as you have more than one person working on a project, you need to establish some ground rules and delegate parts of the project accordingly. In *Pragmatic Teams*, we'll show how to do this while honoring the pragmatic philosophy.

The single most important factor in making project-level activities work consistently and reliably is to automate your procedures. We'll explain why, and show some real-life examples in *Ubiquitous Automation*.

Earlier, we talked about testing as you code. In *Ruthless Testing*, we go to the next step of project-wide testing philosophy and tools—especially if you don't have a large QA staff at your beck and call.

The only thing that developers dislike more than testing is documentation. Whether you have technical writers helping you or are doing it on your own, we'll show you how to make the chore less painful and more productive in *It's All Writing*.

Success is in the eye of the beholder—the sponsor of the project. The perception of success is what counts, and in *Great Expectations* we'll show you some tricks to delight every project's sponsor.

The last tip in the book is a direct consequence of all the rest. In *Pride and Prejudice*, we encourage you to sign your work, and to take pride in what you do.

Pragmatic Teams

At Group L, Stoffel oversees six first-rate programmers, a managerial challenge roughly comparable to herding cats.
▶ ***The Washington Post Magazine, June 9, 1985***

So far in this book we've looked at pragmatic techniques that help an individual be a better programmer. Can these methods work for teams as well?

The answer is a resounding "yes!" There are advantages to being a pragmatic individual, but these advantages are multiplied manyfold if the individual is working on a pragmatic team.

In this section we'll look briefly at how pragmatic techniques can be applied to teams as a whole. These notes are only a start. Once you've got a group of pragmatic developers working in an enabling environment, they'll quickly develop and refine their own team dynamics that work for them.

Let's recast some of the previous sections in terms of teams.

No Broken Windows

Quality is a team issue. The most diligent developer placed on a team that just doesn't care will find it difficult to maintain the enthusiasm needed to fix niggling problems. The problem is further exacerbated if the team actively discourages the developer from spending time on these fixes.

Teams as a whole should not tolerate broken windows—those small imperfections that no one fixes. The team *must* take responsibility for the quality of the product, supporting developers who understand the *no broken windows* philosophy we describe in *Software Entropy*, page 4, and encouraging those who haven't yet discovered it.

Some team methodologies have a *quality officer*—someone to whom the team delegates the responsibility for the quality of the deliverable. This is clearly ridiculous: quality can come only from the individual contributions of *all* team members.

Boiled Frogs

Remember the poor frog in the pan of water, back in *Stone Soup and Boiled Frogs*, page 7? It doesn't notice the gradual change in its environment, and ends up cooked. The same can happen to individuals who aren't vigilant. It can be difficult to keep an eye on your overall environment in the heat of project development.

It's even easier for teams as a whole to get boiled. People assume that someone else is handling an issue, or that the team leader must have OK'd a change that your user is requesting. Even the best-intentioned teams can be oblivious to significant changes in their projects.

Fight this. Make sure everyone actively monitors the environment for changes. Maybe appoint a *chief water tester*. Have this person check constantly for increased scope, decreased time scales, additional features, new environments—anything that wasn't in the original agreement. Keep metrics on new requirements (see page 209). The team needn't reject changes out of hand—you simply need to be aware that they're happening. Otherwise, it'll be *you* in the hot water.

Communicate

It's obvious that developers in a team must talk to each other. We gave some suggestions to facilitate this in *Communicate!* on page 18. However, it's easy to forget that the team itself has a presence within the organization. The team as an entity needs to communicate clearly with the rest of the world.

To outsiders, the worst project teams are those that appear sullen and reticent. They hold meetings with no structure, where no one wants to talk. Their documents are a mess: no two look the same, and each uses different terminology.

Great project teams have a distinct personality. People look forward to meetings with them, because they know that they'll see a well-prepared performance that makes everyone feel good. The documentation they produce is crisp, accurate, and consistent. The team speaks with one voice.[1] They may even have a sense of humor.

There is a simple marketing trick that helps teams communicate as one: generate a brand. When you start a project, come up with a name for it, ideally something off-the-wall. (In the past, we've named projects after things such as killer parrots that prey on sheep, optical illusions, and mythical cities.) Spend 30 minutes coming up with a zany logo, and use it on your memos and reports. Use your team's name liberally when talking with people. It sounds silly, but it gives your team an identity to build on, and the world something memorable to associate with your work.

Don't Repeat Yourself

In *The Evils of Duplication*, page 26, we talked about the difficulties of eliminating duplicated work between members of a team. This duplication leads to wasted effort, and can result in a maintenance nightmare. Clearly good communication can help here, but sometimes something extra is needed.

Some teams appoint a member as the project librarian, responsible for coordinating documentation and code repositories. Other team members can use this person as the first port of call when they're looking for something. A good librarian will also be able to spot impending duplication by reading the material that they're handling.

When the project's too big for one librarian (or when no one wants to play the role), appoint people as focal points for various functional aspects of the work. If people want to talk over date handling, they should know to talk with Mary. If there's a database schema issue, see Fred.

And don't forget the value of groupware systems and local Usenet newsgroups for communicating and archiving questions and answers.

---

1.   The team speaks with one voice—externally. Internally, we strongly encourage lively, robust debate. Good developers tend to be passionate about their work.

Orthogonality

Traditional team organization is based on the old-fashioned waterfall method of software construction. Individuals are assigned roles based on their job function. You'll find business analysts, architects, designers, programmers, testers, documenters, and the like.[2] There is an implicit hierarchy here—the closer to the user you're allowed, the more senior you are.

Taking things to the extreme, some development cultures dictate strict divisions of responsibility; coders aren't allowed to talk to testers, who in turn aren't allowed to talk to the chief architect, and so on. Some organizations then compound the problem by having different sub-teams report through separate management chains.

It is a mistake to think that the activities of a project—analysis, design, coding, and testing—can happen in isolation. They can't. These are different views of the same problem, and artificially separating them can cause a boatload of trouble. Programmers who are two or three levels removed from the actual users of their code are unlikely to be aware of the context in which their work is used. They will not be able to make informed decisions.

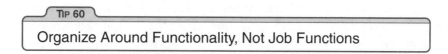

TIP 60

Organize Around Functionality, Not Job Functions

We favor splitting teams functionally. Divide your people into small teams, each responsible for a particular functional aspect of the final system. Let the teams organize themselves internally, building on individual strengths as they can. Each team has responsibilities to others in the project, as defined by their agreed-upon commitments. The exact set of commitments changes with each project, as does the allocation of people into teams.

Functionality here does not necessarily mean end-user use cases. The database access layer counts, as does the help subsystem. We're looking for cohesive, largely self-contained teams of people—exactly the

---

2.   In *The Rational Unified Process: An Introduction*, the author identifies 27 separate roles within a project team! [Kru98]

same criteria we should be using when we modularize code. There are warning signs that the team organization is wrong—a classic example is having two subteams working on the same program module or class.

How does this functional style of organization help? Organize our resources using the same techniques we use to organize code, using techniques such as contracts (*Design by Contract*, page 109), decoupling (*Decoupling and the Law of Demeter*, page 138), and orthogonality (*Orthogonality*, page 34), and we help isolate the team as a whole from the effects of change. If the user suddenly decides to change database vendors, only the database team should be affected. Should marketing suddenly decide to use an off-the-shelf tool for the calendar function, the calendar group takes a hit. Properly executed, this kind of group approach can dramatically reduce the number of interactions between individuals' work, reducing time scales, increasing quality, and cutting down on the number of defects. This approach can also lead to a more committed set of developers. Each team knows that they alone are responsible for a particular function, so they feel more ownership of their output.

However, this approach works only with responsible developers and strong project management. Creating a pool of autonomous teams and letting them loose without leadership is a recipe for disaster. The project needs at least two "heads"—one technical, the other administrative. The technical head sets the development philosophy and style, assigns responsibilities to teams, and arbitrates the inevitable "discussions" between people. The technical head also looks constantly at the big picture, trying to find any unnecessary commonality between teams that could reduce the orthogonality of the overall effort. The administrative head, or project manager, schedules the resources that the teams need, monitors and reports on progress, and helps decide priorities in terms of business needs. The administrative head might also act as the team's ambassador when communicating with the outside world.

Teams on larger projects need additional resources: a librarian who indexes and stores code and documentation, a tool builder who provides common tools and environments, operational support, and so on.

This type of team organization is similar in spirit to the old chief programmer team concept, first documented in 1972 [Bak72].

Automation

A great way to ensure both consistency and accuracy is to automate everything the team does. Why lay code out manually when your editor can do it automatically as you type? Why complete test forms when the overnight build can run tests automatically?

Automation is an essential component of every project team—important enough for us to dedicate an entire section to it, starting on the following page. To ensure that things get automated, appoint one or more team members as *tool builders* to construct and deploy the tools that automate the project drudgery. Have them produce makefiles, shell scripts, editor templates, utility programs, and the like.

Know When to Stop Adding Paint

Remember that teams are made up of individuals. Give each member the ability to shine in his or her own way. Give them just enough structure to support them and to ensure that the project delivers against its requirements. Then, like the painter in *Good-Enough Software,* page 11, resist the temptation to add more paint.

Related sections include:
- *Software Entropy,* page 4
- *Stone Soup and Boiled Frogs,* page 7
- *Good-Enough Software,* page 9
- *Communicate!,* page 18
- *The Evils of Duplication,* page 26
- *Orthogonality,* page 34
- *Design by Contract,* page 109
- *Decoupling and the Law of Demeter,* page 138
- *Ubiquitous Automation,* page 230

Challenges
- Look around for successful teams outside the area of software development. What makes them successful? Do they use any of the processes discussed in this section?

- Next time you start a project, try convincing people to brand it. Give your organization time to become used to the idea, and then do a quick audit to see what difference it made, both within the team and externally.

- Team Algebra: In school, we are given problems such as "If it takes 4 workers 6 hours to dig a ditch, how long would it take 8 workers?" In real life, however, what factors affect the answer to: "If it takes 4 programmers 6 months to develop an application, how long would it take 8 programmers?" In how many scenarios is the time actually reduced?

Ubiquitous Automation

Civilization advances by extending the number of important operations we can perform without thinking.
   ▶ **Alfred North Whitehead**

At the dawn of the age of automobiles, the instructions for starting a Model-T Ford were more than two pages long. With modern cars, you just turn the key—the starting procedure is automatic and foolproof. A person following a list of instructions might flood the engine, but the automatic starter won't.

Although computing is still an industry at the Model-T stage, we can't afford to go through two pages of instructions again and again for some common operation. Whether it is the build and release procedure, code review paperwork, or any other recurring task on the project, it has to be automatic. We may have to build the starter and fuel injector from scratch, but once it's done, we can just turn the key from then on.

In addition, we want to ensure consistency and repeatability on the project. Manual procedures leave consistency up to chance; repeatability isn't guaranteed, especially if aspects of the procedure are open to interpretation by different people.

All on Automatic

We were once at a client site where all the developers were using the same IDE. Their system administrator gave each developer a set of instructions on installing add-on packages to the IDE. These instructions filled many pages—pages full of click here, scroll there, drag this, double-click that, and do it again.

Not surprisingly, every developer's machine was loaded slightly differently. Subtle differences in the application's behavior occurred when different developers ran the same code. Bugs would appear on one machine but not on others. Tracking down version differences of any one component usually revealed a surprise.

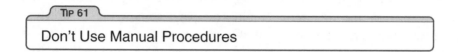

TIP 61

Don't Use Manual Procedures

People just aren't as repeatable as computers are. Nor should we expect them to be. A shell script or batch file will execute the same instructions, in the same order, time after time. It can be put under source control, so you can examine changes to the procedure over time as well ("but it *used* to work. . .").

Another favorite tool of automation is cron (or "at" on Windows NT). It allows us to schedule unattended tasks to run periodically—usually in the middle of the night. For example, the following crontab file specifies that a project's nightly command be run at five minutes past midnight every day, that the backup be run at 3:15 a.m. on weekdays, and that expense_reports be run at midnight on the first of the month.

```
# MIN HOUR DAY MONTH DAYOFWEEK    COMMAND
# ---------------------------------------------------------------
   5    0    *    *      *         /projects/Manhattan/bin/nightly
  15    3    *    *     1-5        /usr/local/bin/backup
   0    0    1    *      *         /home/accounting/expense_reports
```

Using cron, we can schedule backups, the nightly build, Web site maintenance, and anything else that needs to be done—unattended, automatically.

Compiling the Project

Compiling the project is a chore that should be reliable and repeatable. We generally compile projects with makefiles, even when using an IDE environment. There are several advantages in using makefiles. It is a scripted, automatic procedure. We can add in hooks to generate code for us, and run regression tests automatically. IDEs have their advantages, but with IDEs alone it can be hard to achieve the level of automation that we're looking for. We want to check out, build, test, and ship with a single command.

Generating Code

In *The Evils of Duplication*, page 26, we advocated generating code to derive knowledge from common sources. We can exploit make's dependency analysis mechanism to make this process easy. It's a pretty simple matter to add rules to a makefile to generate a file from some other source automatically. For example, suppose we wanted to take an XML file, generate a Java file from it, and compile the result.

```
.SUFFIXES: .java .class .xml
.xml.java:
        perl convert.pl $<  > $@
.java.class:
        $(JAVAC) $(JAVAC_FLAGS) $<
```

Type make test.class, and make will automatically look for a file named test.xml, build a .java file by running a Perl script, and then compile that file to produce test.class.

We can use the same sort of rules to generate source code, header files, or documentation automatically from some other form as well (see *Code Generators*, page 102).

Regression Tests

You can also use the makefile to run regression tests for you, either for an individual module or for an entire subsystem. You can easily test the *entire* project with just one command at the top of the source tree, or you can test an individual module by using the same command in a single directory. See *Ruthless Testing*, page 237, for more on regression testing.

> ### Recursive make
>
> Many projects set up recursive, hierarchical makefiles for project builds and testing. But be aware of some potential problems.
>
> make calculates dependencies between the various targets it has to build. But it can analyze only the dependencies that exist within one single make invocation. In particular, a recursive make has no knowledge of dependencies that other invocations of make may have. If you are careful and precise, you can get the proper results, but it's easy to cause extra work unnecessarily—or miss a dependency and *not* recompile when it's needed.
>
> In addition, build dependencies may not be the same as test dependencies, and you may need separate hierarchies.

Build Automation

A *build* is a procedure that takes an empty directory (and a known compilation environment) and builds the project from scratch, producing whatever you hope to produce as a final deliverable—a CD-ROM master image or a self-extracting archive, for instance. Typically a project build will encompass the following steps.

1. Check out the source code from the repository.

2. Build the project from scratch, typically from a top-level makefile. Each build is marked with some form of release or version number, or perhaps a date stamp.

3. Create a distributable image. This procedure may entail fixing file ownership and permissions, and producing all examples, documentation, README files, and anything else that will ship with the product, in the exact format that will be required when you ship.[3]

4. Run specified tests (make test).

---

3. If you are producing a CD-ROM in ISO9660 format, for example, you would run the program that produces a bit-for-bit image of the 9660 file system. Why wait until the night before you ship to make sure it works?

For most projects, this level of build is run automatically every night. In this nightly build, you will typically run more complete tests than an individual might run while building some specific portion of the project. The important point is to have the full build run *all* available tests. You want to know if a regression test failed because of one of today's code changes. By identifying the problem close to the source, you stand a better chance of finding and fixing it.

When you don't run tests regularly, you may discover that the application broke due to a code change made three months ago. Good luck finding that one.

Final Builds

Final builds, which you intend to ship as products, may have different requirements from the regular nightly build. A final build may require that the repository be locked, or tagged with the release number, that optimization and debug flags be set differently, and so on. We like to use a separate make target (such as make final) that sets all of these parameters at once.

Remember that if the product is compiled differently from earlier versions, then you must test against *this* version all over again.

Automatic Administrivia

Wouldn't it be nice if programmers could actually devote all of their time to programming? Unfortunately, this is rarely the case. There is e-mail to be answered, paperwork to be filled out, documents to be posted to the Web, and so on. You may decide to create a shell script to do some of the dirty work, but you still have to remember to run the script when needed.

Because memory is the second thing you lose as you age,[4] we don't want to rely on it too heavily. We can run scripts to perform procedures for us automatically, based on the *content* of source code and documents. Our goal is to maintain an automatic, unattended, content-driven workflow.

---

4. What's the first? I forget.

Web Site Generation

Many development teams use an internal Web site for project communication, and we think this is a great idea. But we don't want to spend too much time maintaining the Web site, and we don't want to let it get stale or out of date. Misleading information is worse than no information at all.

Documentation that is extracted from code, requirements analyses, design documents, and any drawings, charts, or graphs all need to be published to the Web on a regular basis. We like to publish these documents automatically as part of the nightly build or as a hook into the source code check-in procedure.

However it is done, Web content should be generated automatically from information in the repository and published *without* human intervention. This is really another application of the *DRY* principle: information exists in one form as checked-in code and documents. The view from the Web browser is simply that—just a view. You shouldn't have to maintain that view by hand.

Any information generated by the nightly build should be accessible on the development Web site: results of the build itself (for example, the build results might be presented as a one-page summary that includes compiler warnings, errors, and current status), regression tests, performance statistics, coding metrics and any other static analysis, and so on.

Approval Procedures

Some projects have various administrative workflows that must be followed. For instance, code or design reviews need to be scheduled and followed through, approvals may need to be granted, and so on. We can use automation—and especially the Web site—to help ease the paperwork burden.

Suppose you wanted to automate code review scheduling and approval. You might put a special marker in each source code file:

```
/* Status: needs_review */
```

A simple script could go through all of the source code and look for all files that had a status of needs_review, indicating that they were ready to be reviewed. You could then post a list of those files as a

Web page, automatically send e-mail to the appropriate people, or even schedule a meeting automatically using some calendar software.

You can set up a form on a Web page for the reviewers to register approval or disapproval. After the review, the status can be automatically changed to `reviewed`. Whether you have a code walk-through with all the participants is up to you; you can still do the paperwork automatically. (In an article in the April 1999 CACM, Robert Glass summarizes research that seems to indicate that, while code inspection is effective, conducting reviews in meetings is not [Gla99a].)

The Cobbler's Children

The cobbler's children have no shoes. Often, people who develop software use the poorest tools to do the job.

But we have all the raw materials we need to craft better tools. We have `cron`. We have `make`, Ant, and CruiseControl for automation (see [Cla04]). And we have Ruby, Perl, and other high-level scripting languages for quickly developing custom tools, Web page generators, code generators, test harnesses, and so on.

Let the computer do the repetitious, the mundane—it will do a better job of it than we would. We've got more important and more difficult things to do.

Related sections include:
- *The Cat Ate My Source Code*, page 2
- *The Evils of Duplication*, page 26
- *The Power of Plain Text*, page 73
- *Shell Games*, page 77
- *Debugging*, page 90
- *Code Generators*, page 102
- *Pragmatic Teams*, page 224
- *Ruthless Testing*, page 237
- *It's All Writing*, page 248

Challenges
- Look at your habits throughout the workday. Do you see any repetitive tasks? Do you type the same sequence of commands over and over again?

Try writing a few shell scripts to automate the process. Do you always click on the same sequence of icons repeatedly? Can you create a macro to do all that for you?

- How much of your project paperwork can be automated? Given the high expense of programming staff,[5] determine how much of the project's budget is being wasted on administrative procedures. Can you justify the amount of time it would take to craft an automated solution based on the overall cost savings it would achieve?

Ruthless Testing

Most developers hate testing. They tend to test gently, subconsciously knowing where the code will break and avoiding the weak spots. Pragmatic Programmers are different. We are *driven* to find our bugs *now*, so we don't have to endure the shame of others finding our bugs later.

Finding bugs is somewhat like fishing with a net. We use fine, small nets (unit tests) to catch the minnows, and big, coarse nets (integration tests) to catch the killer sharks. Sometimes the fish manage to escape, so we patch any holes that we find, in hopes of catching more and more slippery defects that are swimming about in our project pool.

> TIP 62
> Test Early. Test Often. Test Automatically.

We want to start testing as soon as we have code. Those tiny minnows have a nasty habit of becoming giant, man-eating sharks pretty fast, and catching a shark is quite a bit harder. But we don't want to have to do all that testing by hand.

---

5. For estimating purposes, you can figure an industry average of about US$100,000 per head—that's salary plus benefits, training, office space and overhead, and so on.

Many teams develop elaborate test plans for their projects. Sometimes they will even use them. But we've found that teams that use automated tests have a much better chance of success. Tests that run with every build are much more effective than test plans that sit on a shelf.

The earlier a bug is found, the cheaper it is to remedy. "Code a little, test a little" is a popular saying in the Smalltalk world,[6] and we can adopt that mantra as our own by writing test code at the same time (or even before) we write the production code.

In fact, a good project may well have *more* test code than production code. The time it takes to produce this test code is worth the effort. It ends up being much cheaper in the long run, and you actually stand a chance of producing a product with close to zero defects.

Additionally, knowing that you've passed the test gives you a high degree of confidence that a piece of code is "done."

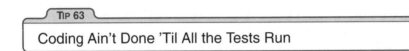

TIP 63

Coding Ain't Done 'Til All the Tests Run

Just because you have finished hacking out a piece of code doesn't mean you can go tell your boss or your client that it's *done*. It's not. First of all, code is never really done. More importantly, you can't claim that it is usable by anyone until it passes all of the available tests.

We need to look at three main aspects of project-wide testing: what to test, how to test, and when to test.

What to Test

There are several major types of software testing that you need to perform:

- Unit testing
- Integration testing
- Validation and verification

---

6.   eXtreme Programming [URL 45] calls this concept "continuous integration, relentless testing."

- Resource exhaustion, errors, and recovery
- Performance testing
- Usability testing

This list is by no means complete, and some specialized projects will require various other types of testing as well. But it gives us a good starting point.

Unit Testing

A *unit test* is code that exercises a module. We covered this topic by itself in *Code That's Easy to Test*, page 189. Unit testing is the foundation of all the other forms of testing that we'll discuss in this section. If the parts don't work by themselves, they probably won't work well together. All of the modules you are using must pass their own unit tests before you can proceed.

Once all of the pertinent modules have passed their individual tests, you're ready for the next stage. You need to test how all the modules use and interact with each other throughout the system.

Integration Testing

Integration testing shows that the major subsystems that make up the project work and play well with each other. With good contracts in place and well tested, any integration issues can be detected easily. Otherwise, integration becomes a fertile breeding ground for bugs. In fact, it is often the single largest source of bugs in the system.

Integration testing is really just an extension of the unit testing we've described—only now you're testing how entire subsystems honor their contracts.

Validation and Verification

As soon as you have an executable user interface or prototype, you need to answer an all-important question: the users told you what they wanted, but is it what they need?

Does it meet the functional requirements of the system? This, too, needs to be tested. A bug-free system that answers the wrong question isn't very useful. Be conscious of end-user access patterns and how they differ from developer test data (for an example, see the story about brush strokes on page 92).

Resource Exhaustion, Errors, and Recovery

Now that you have a pretty good idea that the system will behave correctly under ideal conditions, you need to discover how it will behave under *real-world* conditions. In the real world, your programs don't have limitless resources; they run out of things. A few limits your code may encounter include:

- Memory
- Disk space
- CPU bandwidth
- Wall-clock time
- Disk bandwidth
- Network bandwidth
- Color palette
- Video resolution

You might actually check for disk space or memory allocation failures, but how often do you test for the others? Will your application fit on a 640 × 480 screen with 256 colors? Will it run on a 1600 × 1280 screen with 24-bit color without looking like a postage stamp? Will the batch job finish before the archive starts?

You can detect environmental limitations, such as the video specifications, and adapt as appropriate. Not all failures are recoverable, however. If your code detects that memory has been exhausted, your options are limited: you may not have enough resources left to do anything except fail.

When the system does fail,[7] will it fail gracefully? Will it try, as best it can, to save its state and prevent loss of work? Or will it "GPF" or "core-dump" in the user's face?

---

7. Our copy editor wanted us to change this sentence to "*If* the system does fail...." We resisted.

Performance Testing

Performance testing, stress testing, or testing under load may be an important aspect of the project as well.

Ask yourself if the software meets the performance requirements under real-world conditions—with the expected number of users, or connections, or transactions per second. Is it scalable?

For some applications, you may need specialized testing hardware or software to simulate the load realistically.

Usability Testing

Usability testing is different from the types of testing discussed so far. It is performed with real users, under real environmental conditions.

Look at usability in terms of human factors. Were there any misunderstandings during requirements analysis that need to be addressed? Does the software fit the user like an extension of the hand? (Not only do we want our own tools to fit our hands, but we want the tools we create for users to fit their hands as well.)

As with validation and verification, you need to perform usability testing as early as you can, while there is still time to make corrections. For larger projects, you may want to bring in human factors specialists. (If nothing else, it's fun to play with the one-way mirrors).

Failure to meet usability criteria is just as big a bug as dividing by zero.

How to Test

We've looked at *what* to test. Now we'll turn our attention to *how* to test, including:

- Regression testing
- Test data
- Exercising GUI systems
- Testing the tests
- Testing thoroughly

<u>**Design/Methodology Testing**</u>

Can you test the design of the code itself and the methodology you used to build the software? After a fashion, yes you can. You do this by analyzing *metrics*—measurements of various aspects of the code. The simplest metric (and often the least interesting) is *lines of code*—how big is the code itself?

There are a wide variety of other metrics you can use to examine code, including:

- McCabe Cyclomatic Complexity Metric (measures complexity of decision structures)
- Inheritance fan-in (number of base classes) and fan-out (number of derived modules using this one as a parent)
- Response set (see *Decoupling and the Law of Demeter*, page 138)
- Class coupling ratios (see [URL 48])

Some metrics are designed to give you a "passing grade," while others are useful only by comparison. That is, you calculate these metrics for every module in the system and see how a particular module relates to its brethren. Standard statistical techniques (such as mean and standard deviation) are usually used here.

If you find a module whose metrics are markedly different from all the rest, you need to ask yourself if that is appropriate. For some modules, it may be okay to "blow the curve." But for those that *don't* have a good excuse, it can indicate potential problems.

Regression Testing

A regression test compares the output of the current test with previous (or known) values. We can ensure that bugs we fixed today didn't break things that were working yesterday. This is an important safety net, and it cuts down on unpleasant surprises.

All of the tests we've mentioned so far can be run as regression tests, ensuring that we haven't lost any ground as we develop new code. We can run regressions to verify performance, contracts, validity, and so on.

Test Data

Where do we get the data to run all these tests? There are only two kinds of data: real-world data and synthetic data. We actually need to use both, because the different natures of these kinds of data will expose different bugs in our software.

Real-world data comes from some actual source. Possibly it has been collected from an existing system, a competitor's system, or a prototype of some sort. It represents typical user data. The big surprises come as you discover what *typical* means. This is most likely to reveal defects and misunderstandings in requirements analysis.

Synthetic data is artificially generated, perhaps under certain statistical constraints. You may need to use synthetic data for any of the following reasons.

- You need a lot of data, possibly more than any real-world sample could provide. You might be able to use the real-world data as a seed to generate a larger sample set, and tweak certain fields that need to be unique.

- You need data to stress the boundary conditions. This data may be completely synthetic: date fields containing February 29, 1999, huge record sizes, or addresses with foreign postal codes.

- You need data that exhibits certain statistical properties. Want to see what happens if every third transaction fails? Remember the sort algorithm that slows to a crawl when handed presorted data? You can present data in random or sorted order to expose this kind of weakness.

Exercising GUI Systems

Testing GUI-intensive systems often requires specialized testing tools. These tools may be based on a simple event capture/playback model, or they may require specially written scripts to drive the GUI. Some systems combine elements of both.

Less sophisticated tools enforce a high degree of coupling between the version of software being tested and the test script itself: if you move a dialog box or make a button smaller, the test may not be able to find it, and may fail. Most modern GUI testing tools use a number of different techniques to get around this problem, and try to adjust to minor layout differences.

However, you can't automate everything. Andy worked on a graphics system that allowed the user to create and display nondeterministic visual effects which simulated various natural phenomena. Unfortunately, during testing you couldn't just grab a bitmap and compare the output with a previous run, because it was designed to be different every time. For situations such as this one, you may have no choice but to rely on manual interpretation of test results.

One of the many advantages of writing decoupled code (see *Decoupling and the Law of Demeter*, page 138) is more modular testing. For instance, for data processing applications that have a GUI front end, your design should be decoupled enough so that you can test the application logic *without* having a GUI present. This idea is similar to testing your subcomponents first. Once the application logic has been validated, it becomes easier to locate bugs that show up with the user interface in place (it's likely that the bugs were created by the user-interface code).

Testing the Tests

Because we can't write perfect software, it follows that we can't write perfect test software either. We need to test the tests.

Think of our set of test suites as an elaborate security system, designed to sound the alarm when a bug shows up. How better to test a security system than to try to break in?

After you have written a test to detect a particular bug, *cause* the bug deliberately and make sure the test complains. This ensures that the test will catch the bug if it happens for real.

> TIP 64
> **Use Saboteurs to Test Your Testing**

If you are *really* serious about testing, you might want to appoint a *project saboteur*. The saboteur's role is to take a separate copy of the source tree, introduce bugs on purpose, and verify that the tests will catch them.

When writing tests, make sure that alarms sound when they should.

Testing Thoroughly

Once you are confident that your tests are correct, and are finding bugs you create, how do you know if you have tested the code base thoroughly enough?

The short answer is "you don't," and you never will. But there are products on the market that can help. These *coverage analysis* tools watch your code during testing and keep track of which lines of code have been executed and which haven't. These tools help give you a general feel for how comprehensive your testing is, but don't expect to see 100% coverage.

Even if you do happen to hit every line of code, that's not the whole picture. What *is* important is the number of states that your program may have. States are not equivalent to lines of code. For instance, suppose you have a function that takes two integers, each of which can be a number from 0 to 999.

```
int test(int a, int b) {
  return a / (a + b);
}
```

In theory, this three-line function has 1,000,000 logical states, 999,999 of which will work correctly and one that will not (when a + b equals zero). Simply knowing that you executed this line of code doesn't tell you that—you would need to identify all possible states of the program. Unfortunately, in general this is a *really hard* problem. Hard as in, "The sun will be a cold hard lump before you can solve it."

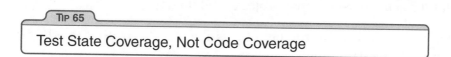

TIP 65

Test State Coverage, Not Code Coverage

Even with good code coverage, the data you use for testing still has a huge impact, and, more importantly, the *order* in which you traverse code may have the largest impact of all.

When to Test

Many projects tend to leave testing to the last minute—right where it will be cut against the sharp edge of a deadline.[8] We need to start much sooner than that. As soon as any production code exists, it needs to be tested.

Most testing should be done automatically. It's important to note that by "automatically" we mean that the test *results* are interpreted automatically as well. See *Ubiquitous Automation*, page 230, for more on this subject.

We like to test as frequently as we can, and always before we check code into the source repository. Some source code control systems, such as Aegis, can do this automatically. Otherwise, we just type

```
% make test
```

Usually, it isn't a problem to run regressions on all of the individual unit tests and integration tests as often as needed.

But some tests may not be easily run on a such a frequent basis. Stress tests, for instance, may require special setup or equipment, and some hand holding. These tests may be run less often—weekly or monthly, perhaps. But it is important that they be run on a regular, scheduled basis. If it can't be done automatically, then make sure it appears on the schedule, with all the necessary resources allocated to the task.

Tightening the Net

Finally, we'd like to reveal the single most important concept in testing. It is an obvious one, and virtually every textbook says to do it this way. But for some reason, most projects still do not.

If a bug slips through the net of existing tests, you need to add a new test to trap it next time.

---

8.   **dead·line** \ded-līn\ *n* (1864) a line drawn within or around a prison that a prisoner passes at the risk of being shot—*Webster's Collegiate Dictionary*.

TIP 66

Find Bugs Once

Once a human tester finds a bug, it should be the *last* time a human tester finds that bug. The automated tests should be modified to check for that particular bug from then on, every time, with no exceptions, no matter how trivial, and no matter how much the developer complains and says, "Oh, that will never happen again."

Because it will happen again. And we just don't have the time to go chasing after bugs that the automated tests could have found for us. We have to spend our time writing new code—and new bugs.

Related sections include:
- *The Cat Ate My Source Code*, page 2
- *Debugging*, page 90
- *Decoupling and the Law of Demeter*, page 138
- *Refactoring*, page 184
- *Code That's Easy to Test*, page 189
- *Ubiquitous Automation*, page 230

Challenges
- Can you automatically test your project? Many teams are forced to answer "no." Why? Is it too hard to define the acceptable results? Won't this make it hard to prove to the sponsors that the project is "done"?

  Is it too hard to test the application logic independent of the GUI? What does this say about the GUI? About coupling?

It's All Writing

The palest ink is better than the best memory.
▶ **Chinese Proverb**

Typically, developers don't give much thought to documentation. At best it is an unfortunate necessity; at worst it is treated as a low-priority task in the hope that management will forget about it at the end of the project.

Pragmatic Programmers embrace documentation as an integral part of the overall development process. Writing documentation can be made easier by not duplicating effort or wasting time, and by keeping documentation close at hand—in the code itself, if possible.

These aren't exactly original or novel thoughts; the idea of wedding code and documentation appears in Donald Knuth's work on literate programming and in Sun's JavaDoc utility, among others. We want to downplay the dichotomy between code and documentation, and instead treat them as two views of the same model (see *It's Just a View*, page 157). In fact, we want to go a little further and apply *all* of our pragmatic principles to documentation as well as to code.

TIP 67
Treat English as Just Another Programming Language

There are basically two kinds of documentation produced for a project: internal and external. Internal documentation includes source code comments, design and test documents, and so on. External documentation is anything shipped or published to the outside world, such as user manuals. But regardless of the intended audience, or the role of the writer (developer or technical writer), all documentation is a mirror of the code. If there's a discrepancy, the code is what matters—for better or worse.

TIP 68
Build Documentation In, Don't Bolt It On

We'll start with internal documentation.

Comments in Code

Producing formatted documents from the comments and declarations in source code is fairly straightforward, but first we have to ensure that we actually *have* comments in the code. Code should have comments, but too many comments can be just as bad as too few.

In general, comments should discuss *why* something is done, its purpose and its goal. The code already shows *how* it is done, so commenting on this is redundant—and is a violation of the *DRY* principle.

Commenting source code gives you the perfect opportunity to document those elusive bits of a project that can't be documented anywhere else: engineering trade-offs, why decisions were made, what other alternatives were discarded, and so on.

We like to see a *simple* module-level header comment, comments for significant data and type declarations, and a brief per-class and per-method header, describing how the function is used and anything that it does that is not obvious.

Variable names, of course, should be well chosen and meaningful. `foo`, for instance, is meaningless, as is `doit` or `manager` or `stuff`. Hungarian notation (where you encode the variable's type information in the name itself) is utterly inappropriate in object-oriented systems. Remember that you (and others after you) will be *reading* the code many hundreds of times, but only *writing* it a few times. Take the time to spell out `connectionPool` instead of `cp`.

Even worse than meaningless names are *misleading* names. Have you ever had someone explain inconsistencies in legacy code such as, "The routine called `getData` really writes data to disk"? The human brain will repeatedly foul this up—it's called the *Stroop Effect* [Str35]. You can try the following experiment yourself to see the effects of such interference. Get some colored pens, and use them to write down the names of colors. However, never write a color name using that color pen. You could write the word "blue" in green, the word "brown" in red, and so on. (Alternatively, we have a sample set of colors already drawn on our Web site at `www.pragmaticprogrammer.com`.) Once you have the color names drawn, try to say aloud the color with which each word is drawn, as fast as you can. At some point you'll trip up and start reading the names of the colors, and not the colors themselves. Names are deeply meaningful to your brain, and misleading names add chaos to your code.

You can document parameters, but ask yourself if it is really necessary in all cases. The level of comment suggested by the JavaDoc tool seems appropriate:

```
/**
 * Find the peak (highest) value within a specified date
 * range of samples.
 *
 * @param   aRange Range of dates to search for data.
 * @param   aThreshold Minimum value to consider.
 * @return the value, or <code>null</code> if no value found
 *         greater than or equal to the threshold.
 */
public Sample findPeak(DateRange aRange, double aThreshold);
```

Here's a list of things that should *not* appear in source comments.

- **A list of the functions exported by code in the file.** There are programs that analyze source for you. Use them, and the list is guaranteed to be up to date.

- **Revision history.** This is what source code control systems are for (see *Source Code Control*, page 86). However, it can be useful to include information on the date of last change and the person who made it.[9]

- **A list of other files this file uses.** This can be determined more accurately using automatic tools.

- **The name of the file.** If it must appear in the file, don't maintain it by hand. RCS and similar systems can keep this information up to date automatically. If you move or rename the file, you don't want to have to remember to edit the header.

One of the most important pieces of information that *should* appear in the source file is the author's name—not necessarily who edited the file last, but the owner. Attaching responsibility and accountability to source code does wonders in keeping people honest (see *Pride and Prejudice*, page 258).

---

9. This kind of information, as well as the filename, is provided by the RCS Id tag.

The project may also require certain copyright notices or other legal boilerplate to appear in each source file. Get your editor to insert these for you automatically.

With meaningful comments in place, tools such as JavaDoc [URL 7] and DOC++ [URL 21] can extract and format them to automatically produce API-level documentation. This is one specific example of a more general technique we use—*executable documents*.

Executable Documents

Suppose we have a specification that lists the columns in a database table. We'll then have a separate set of SQL commands to create the actual table in the database, and probably some kind of programming language record structure to hold the contents of a row in the table. The same information is repeated three times. Change any one of these three sources, and the other two are immediately out of date. This is a clear violation of the *DRY* principle.

To correct this problem, we need to choose the authoritative source of information. This may be the specification, it may be a database schema tool, or it may be some third source altogether. Let's choose the specification document as the source. It's now our *model* for this process. We then need to find a way to export the information it contains as different *views*—a database schema and a high-level language record, for example.[10]

If your document is stored as plain text with markup commands (using HTML, LaTeX, or troff, for example), then you can use tools such as Perl to extract the schema and reformat it automatically. If your document is in a word processor's binary format, then see the box on the following page for some options.

Your document is now an integral part of the project development. The only way to change the schema is to change the document. You are guaranteeing that the specification, schema, and code all agree. You minimize the amount of work you have to do for each change, and you can update the views of the change automatically.

---

10. See *It's Just a View*, page 157, for more on models and views.

<u>**What if My Document Isn't Plain Text?**</u>

Unfortunately, more and more project documents are now being written using word processors that store the file on disk in some proprietary format. We say "unfortunately" because this severely restricts your options to process the document automatically. However, you still have a couple of options:

- **Write macros.** Most sophisticated word processors now have a macro language. With some effort you can program them to export tagged sections of your documents into the alternative forms you need. If programming at this level is too painful, you could always export the appropriate section into a standard format plain text file, and then use a tool such as Perl to convert this into the final forms.

- **Make the document subordinate.** Rather than have the document as the definitive source, use another representation. (In the database example, you might want to use the schema as the authoritative information.) Then write a tool that exports this information into a form that the document can import. Be careful, however. You need to ensure that this information is imported every time the document is printed, rather than just once when the document is created.

We can generate API-level documentation from source code using tools such as JavaDoc and DOC++ in a similar fashion. The model is the source code: one view of the model can be compiled; other views are meant to be printed out or viewed on the Web. Our goal is always to work on the model—whether the model is the code itself or some other document—and have all views updated automatically (see *Ubiquitous Automation*, page 230, for more on automatic processes).

Suddenly, documentation isn't so bad.

Technical Writers

Up until now, we've talked only about internal documentation—written by the programmers themselves. But what happens when you have professional technical writers involved in the project? All too often, programmers just throw material "over the wall" to technical writers and let them fend for themselves to produce user manuals, promotional pieces, and so on.

This is a mistake. Just because programmers aren't writing these documents doesn't mean that we can forsake pragmatic principles. We want the writers to embrace the same basic principles that a Pragmatic Programmer does—especially honoring the *DRY* principle, orthogonality, the model-view concept, and the use of automation and scripting.

Print It or Weave It

One problem inherent with published, paper documentation is that it can become out of date as soon as it's printed. Documentation of any form is just a snapshot.

So we try to produce all documentation in a form that can be published online, on the Web, complete with hyperlinks. It's easier to keep this view of the documentation up to date than to track down every existing paper copy, burn it, and reprint and redistribute new copies. It's also a better way to address the needs of a wide audience. Remember, though, to put a date stamp or version number on each Web page. This way the reader can get a good idea of what's up to date, what's changed recently, and what hasn't.

Many times you need to present the same documentation in different formats: a printed document, Web pages, online help, or perhaps a slide show. The typical solution relies heavily on cut-and-paste, creating a number of new independent documents from the original. This is a bad idea: a document's presentation should be independent of its content.

If you are using a markup system, you have the flexibility to implement as many different output formats as you need. You can choose to have

```
<H1>Chapter Title</H1>
```

generate a new chapter in the report version of the document and title a new slide in the slide show. Technologies such as XSL and CSS[11] can be used to generate multiple output formats from this one markup.

---

11. eXtensible Style Language and Cascading Style Sheets, two technologies designed to help separate presentation from content.

If you are using a word processor, you'll probably have similar capabilities. If you remembered to use styles to identify different document elements, then by applying different style sheets you can drastically alter the look of the final output. Most word processors now allow you to convert your document to formats such as HTML for Web publishing.

Markup Languages

Finally, for large-scale documentation projects, we recommend looking at some of the more modern schemes for marking up documentation.

Many technical authors now use DocBook to define their documents. DocBook is an SGML-based markup standard that carefully identifies every component in a document. The document can be passed through a DSSSL processor to render it into any number of different formats. The Linux documentation project uses DocBook to publish information in RTF, TEX, info, PostScript, and HTML formats.

As long as your original markup is rich enough to express all the concepts you need (including hyperlinks), translation to any other publishable form can be both easy and automatic. You can produce online help, published manuals, product highlights for the Web site, and even a tip-a-day calendar, all from the same source—which of course is under source control and is built along with the nightly build (see *Ubiquitous Automation*, page 230).

Documentation and code are different views of the same underlying model, but the view is *all* that should be different. Don't let documentation become a second-class citizen, banished from the main project workflow. Treat documentation with the same care you treat code, and the users (and maintainers who follow) will sing your praises.

Related sections include:

Challenges

- Did you write an explanatory comment for the source code you just wrote? Why not? Pressed for time? Not sure if the code will really work—are you just trying out an idea as a prototype? You'll throw the code away afterwards, right? It won't make it into the project uncommented and experimental, will it?

- Sometimes it is uncomfortable to document the design of source code because the design isn't clear in your mind; it's still evolving. You don't feel that you should waste effort describing what something does until it actually does it. Does this sound like programming by coincidence (page 172)?

 # Great Expectations

Be astonished, O ye heavens, at this, and be horribly afraid...
  ▶ **Jeremiah 2:12**

A company announces record profits, and its share price drops 20%. The financial news that night explains that the company failed to meet analysts' expectations. A child opens an expensive Christmas present and bursts into tears—it wasn't the cheap doll the child was hoping for. A project team works miracles to implement a phenomenally complex application, only to have it shunned by its users because it doesn't have a help system.

In an abstract sense, an application is successful if it correctly implements its specifications. Unfortunately, this pays only abstract bills.

In reality, the success of a project is measured by how well it meets the *expectations* of its users. A project that falls below their expectations is deemed a failure, no matter how good the deliverable is in absolute terms. However, like the parent of the child expecting the cheap doll, go too far and you'll be a failure, too.

> TIP 69
> **Gently Exceed Your Users' Expectations**

However, the execution of this tip requires some work.

Communicating Expectations

Users initially come to you with some vision of what they want. It may be incomplete, inconsistent, or technically impossible, but it is *theirs*, and, like the child at Christmas, they have some emotion invested in it. You cannot just ignore it.

As your understanding of their needs develops, you'll find areas where their expectations cannot be met, or where their expectations are perhaps too conservative. Part of your role is to communicate this. Work with your users so that their understanding of what you'll be delivering is accurate. And do this throughout the development process. Never lose sight of the business problems your application is intended to solve.

Some consultants call this process "managing expectations"—actively controlling what users should hope to get from their systems. We think this is a somewhat elitist position. Our role is not to control the hopes of our users. Instead, we need to work with them to come to a common understanding of the development process and the final deliverable, along with those expectations they have not yet verbalized. If the team is communicating fluently with the outside world, this process is almost automatic; everyone should understand what's expected and how it will be built.

There are some important techniques that can be used to facilitate this process. Of these, *Tracer Bullets*, page 48, and *Prototypes and Post-it Notes*, page 53, are the most important. Both let the team construct something that the user can see. Both are ideal ways of communicating your understanding of their requirements. And both let you and your users practice communicating with each other.

The Extra Mile

If you work closely with your users, sharing their expectations and communicating what you're doing, then there will be few surprises when the project gets delivered.

This is a BAD THING. Try to surprise your users. Not scare them, mind you, but *delight* them.

Give them that little bit more than they were expecting. The extra bit of effort it requires to add some user-oriented feature to the system will pay for itself time and time again in goodwill.

Listen to your users as the project progresses for clues about what features would really delight them. Some things you can add relatively easily that look good to the average user include:

- Balloon or ToolTip help
- Keyboard shortcuts
- A quick reference guide as a supplement to the user's manual
- Colorization
- Log file analyzers
- Automated installation
- Tools for checking the integrity of the system
- The ability to run multiple versions of the system for training
- A splash screen customized for their organization

All of these things are relatively superficial, and don't really overburden the system with feature bloat. However, each tells your users that the development team cared about producing a great system, one that was intended for real use. Just remember not to break the system adding these new features.

Related sections include:
- *Good-Enough Software*, page 9
- *Tracer Bullets*, page 48
- *Prototypes and Post-it Notes*, page 53
- *The Requirements Pit*, page 202

Challenges
- Sometimes the toughest critics of a project are the people who worked on it. Have you ever experienced disappointment that your own expectations weren't met by something you produced? How could that be? Maybe there's more than logic at work here.

- What do your users comment on when you deliver software? Is their attention to the various areas of the application proportional to the effort you invested in each? What delights them?

Pride and Prejudice

You have delighted us long enough.
▶ **Jane Austen, *Pride and Prejudice***

Pragmatic Programmers don't shirk from responsibility. Instead, we rejoice in accepting challenges and in making our expertise well known. If we are responsible for a design, or a piece of code, we do a job we can be proud of.

> **TIP 70**
>
> Sign Your Work

Craftsmen of an earlier age were proud to sign their work. You should be, too.

Project teams are still made up of people, however, and this rule can cause trouble. On some projects, the idea of *code ownership* can cause cooperation problems. People may become territorial, or unwilling to work on common foundation elements. The project may end up like a bunch of insular little fiefdoms. You become prejudiced in favor of your code and against your coworkers.

That's not what we want. You shouldn't jealously defend your code against interlopers; by the same token, you should treat other people's code with respect. The Golden Rule ("Do unto others as you would have them do unto you") and a foundation of mutual respect among the developers is critical to make this tip work.

Anonymity, especially on large projects, can provide a breeding ground for sloppiness, mistakes, sloth, and bad code. It becomes too easy to see yourself as just a cog in the wheel, producing lame excuses in endless status reports instead of good code.

While code must be owned, it doesn't have to be owned by an individual. In fact, Kent Beck's successful eXtreme Programming method [URL 45] recommends communal ownership of code (but this also requires additional practices, such as pair programming, to guard against the dangers of anonymity).

We want to see pride of ownership. "I wrote this, and I stand behind my work." Your signature should come to be recognized as an indicator of quality. People should see your name on a piece of code and expect it to be solid, well written, tested, and documented. A really professional job. Written by a real professional.

A Pragmatic Programmer.

Appendix A

Resources

The only reason we were able to cover so much ground in this book is that we viewed many of our subjects from a high altitude. If we'd given them the in-depth coverage they deserved, the book would have been ten times longer.

We started the book with the suggestion that Pragmatic Programmers should always be learning. In this appendix we've listed resources that may help you with this process.

In the section *Professional Societies*, we give details of the IEEE and the ACM. We recommend that Pragmatic Programmers join one (or both) of these societies. Then, in *Building a Library*, we highlight periodicals, books, and Web sites that we feel contain high-quality and pertinent information (or that are just plain fun).

Throughout the book we referenced many software resources accessible via the Internet. In the *Internet Resources* section, we list the URLs of these resources, along with a short description of each. However, the nature of the Web means that many of these links may well be stale by the time you read this book. You could try one of the many search engines for a more up-to-date link, or visit our Web site at www. pragmaticprogrammer.com and check our links section.

Finally, this appendix contains the book's bibliography.

Professional Societies

There are two world-class professional societies for programmers: the Association for Computing Machinery (ACM)[1] and the IEEE Computer Society.[2] We recommend that all programmers belong to one (or both) of these societies. In addition, developers outside the United States may want to join their national societies, such as the BCS in the United Kingdom.

Membership in a professional society has many benefits. The conferences and local meetings give you great opportunities to meet people with similar interests, and the special interest groups and technical committees give you the opportunity to participate in setting standards and guidelines used around the world. You'll also get a lot out of their publications, from high-level discussions of industry practice to low-level computing theory.

Building a Library

We're big on reading. As we noted in *Your Knowledge Portfolio*, page 12, a good programmer is always learning. Keeping current with books and periodicals can help. Here are some that we like.

Periodicals

If you're like us, you'll save old magazines and periodicals until they're piled high enough to turn the bottom ones to flat sheets of diamond. This means it's worth being fairly selective. Here are a few periodicals we read.

- **IEEE Computer.** Sent to members of the IEEE Computer Society, *Computer* has a practical focus but is not afraid of theory. Some issues are oriented around a theme, while others are simply col-

---

1. ACM Member Services, PO Box 11414, New York, NY 10286, USA.
   ⇒ www.acm.org

2. 1730 Massachusetts Avenue NW, Washington, DC 20036-1992, USA.
   ⇒ www.computer.org

lections of interesting articles. This magazine has a good signal-to-noise ratio.

- **IEEE Software.** This is another great bimonthly publication of the IEEE Computer Society aimed at software practitioners.

- **Communications of the ACM.** The basic magazine received by all members of the ACM, *CACM* has been a standard in the industry for decades, and has probably published more seminal articles than any other source.

- **SIGPLAN.** Produced by the ACM Special Interest Group on Programming Languages, *SIGPLAN* is an optional addition to your ACM membership. It is often used for publishing language specifications, along with articles of interest to everyone who likes looking deeply into programming.

- **Dr. Dobbs Journal.** A monthly magazine, available by subscription and on newsstands, *Dr. Dobbs* is quirky, but has articles ranging from bit-level practice to heavy theory.

- **The Perl Journal.** If you like Perl, you should probably subscribe to *The Perl Journal* (www.tpj.com).

- **Software Development Magazine.** A monthly magazine focusing on general issues of project management and software development.

Weekly Trade Papers

There are several weekly newspapers published for developers and their managers. These papers are largely a collection of company press releases, redressed as articles. However, the content is still valuable—it lets you track what is going on, keep abreast of new product announcements, and follow industry alliances as they are forged and broken. Don't expect a lot of in-depth technical coverage, though.

Books

Computing books can be expensive, but choose carefully and they're a worthwhile investment. You may want to check out our Pragmatic Bookshelf titles at `http://pragmaticprogrammer.com`. Additionally, here are a handful of the many other books we like.

Analysis and Design

- ***Object-Oriented Software Construction, 2nd Edition.*** Bertrand Meyer's epic book on the fundamentals of object-oriented development, all in about 1,300 pages [Mey97b].

- ***Design Patterns.*** A design pattern describes a way to solve a particular class of problems at a higher level than a programming language idiom. This now-classic book [GHJV95] by the *Gang of Four* describes 23 basic design patterns, including Proxy, Visitor, and Singleton.

- ***Analysis Patterns.*** A treasure trove of high-level, architectural patterns taken from a wide variety of real-world projects and distilled in book form. A relatively quick way to gain the insight of many years of modeling experience [Fow96].

Teams and Projects

- ***The Mythical Man Month.*** Fred Brooks' classic on the perils of organizing project teams, recently updated [Bro95].

- ***Dynamics of Software Development.*** A series of short essays on building software in large teams, focusing on the dynamics between team members, and between the team and the rest of the world [McC95].

- ***Surviving Object-Oriented Projects: A Manager's Guide.*** Alistair Cockburn's "reports from the trenches" illustrate many of the perils and pitfalls of managing an OO project—especially your first one. Mr. Cockburn provides tips and techniques to get you through the most common problems [Coc97b].

Specific Environments

- **Unix.** W. Richard Stevens has several excellent books including *Advanced Programming in the Unix Environment* and the *Unix Network Programming* books [Ste92, Ste98, Ste99].

- **Windows.** Marshall Brain's *Win32 System Services* [Bra95] is a concise reference to the low-level APIs. Charles Petzold's *Programming Windows* [Pet98] is the bible of Windows GUI development.

- **C++.** As soon as you find yourself on a C++ project, run, don't walk, to the bookstore and get Scott Meyer's *Effective C++*, and possibly *More Effective C++* [Mey97a, Mey96]. For building systems of any appreciable size, you need John Lakos' *Large-Scale C++ Software Design* [Lak96]. For advanced techniques, turn to Jim Coplien's *Advanced C++ Programming Styles and Idioms* [Cop92].

In addition, the O'Reilly *Nutshell* series (www.ora.com) gives quick, comprehensive treatments of miscellaneous topics and languages such as perl, yacc, sendmail, Windows internals, and regular expressions.

The Web

Finding good content on the Web is hard. Here are several links that we check at least once a week.

- **Slashdot.** Billed as "News for nerds. Stuff that matters," Slashdot is one of the net homes of the Linux community. As well as regular updates on Linux news, the site offers information on technologies that are cool and issues that affect developers.
  ⇒ www.slashdot.org

- **Cetus Links.** Thousands of links on object-oriented topics.
  ⇒ www.cetus-links.org

- **WikiWikiWeb.** The Portland Pattern Repository and patterns discussion. Not just a great resource, the WikiWikiWeb site is an interesting experiment in collective editing of ideas.
  ⇒ www.c2.com

Internet Resources

The links below are to resources available on the Internet. They were valid at the time of writing, but (the Net being what it is) they may well be out of date by the time you read this. If so, you could try a general search for the filenames, or come to the Pragmatic Programmer Web site (www.pragmaticprogrammer.com) and follow our links.

Editors

Emacs and vi are not the only cross-platform editors, but they are freely available and widely used. A quick scan through a magazine such as *Dr. Dobbs* will turn up several commercial alternatives.

Emacs

Both Emacs and XEmacs are available on Unix and Windows platforms.

[URL 1] **The Emacs Editor**
> ⇒ www.gnu.org
> The ultimate in big editors, containing every feature that any editor has ever had, Emacs has a near-vertical learning curve, but repays handsomely once you've mastered it. It also makes a great mail and news reader, address book, calendar and diary, adventure game, ...

[URL 2] **The XEmacs Editor**
> ⇒ www.xemacs.org
> Spawned from the original Emacs some years ago, XEmacs is reputed to have cleaner internals and a better-looking interface.

vi

There are at least 15 different vi clones available. Of these, vim is probably ported to the most platforms, and so would be a good choice of editor if you find yourself working in many different environments.

[URL 3] **The Vim Editor**
> ⇒ ftp://ftp.fu-berlin.de/misc/editors/vim
> From the documentation: "There are a lot of enhancements above vi: multi level undo, multi windows and buffers, syntax highlighting, command line editing, filename completion, on-line help, visual selection, etc...."

[URL 4] **The elvis Editor**

⇒ `elvis.the-little-red-haired-girl.org`

An enhanced vi clone with support for X.

[URL 5] **Emacs Viper Mode**

⇒ `http://www.cs.sunysb.edu/~kifer/emacs.html`

Viper is a set of macros that make Emacs look like vi. Some may doubt the wisdom of taking the world's largest editor and extending it to emulate an editor whose strength is its compactness. Others claim it combines the best of both worlds.

Compilers, Languages, and Development Tools

[URL 6] **The GNU C/C++ Compiler**

⇒ `www.fsf.org/software/gcc/gcc.html`

One of the most popular C and C++ compilers on the planet. It also does Objective-C. (At the time of writing, the egcs project, which previously splintered from gcc, is in the process of merging back into the fold.)

[URL 7] **The Java Language from Sun**

⇒ `java.sun.com`

Home of Java, including downloadable SDKs, documentation, tutorials, news, and more.

[URL 8] **Perl Language Home Page**

⇒ `www.perl.com`

O'Reilly hosts this set of Perl-related resources.

[URL 9] **The Python Language**

⇒ `www.python.org`

The Python object-oriented programming language is interpreted and interactive, with a slightly quirky syntax and a wide and loyal following.

[URL 10] **SmallEiffel**

⇒ `SmallEiffel.loria.fr`

The GNU Eiffel compiler runs on any machine that has an ANSI C compiler and a Posix runtime environment.

[URL 11] **ISE Eiffel**

⇒ `www.eiffel.com`

Interactive Software Engineering is the originator of Design by Contract, and sells a commercial Eiffel compiler and related tools.

[URL 12] **Sather**

⇒ www.icsi.berkeley.edu/~sather

Sather is an experimental language that grew out of Eiffel. It aims to support higher-order functions and iteration abstraction as well as Common Lisp, CLU, or Scheme, and to be as efficient as C, C++, or Fortran.

[URL 13] **VisualWorks**

⇒ www.cincom.com

Home of the VisualWorks Smalltalk environment. Noncommercial versions for Windows and Linux are available for free.

[URL 14] **The Squeak Language Environment**

⇒ squeak.cs.uiuc.edu

Squeak is a freely available, portable implementation of Smalltalk-80 written in itself; it can produce C code output for higher performance.

[URL 15] **The TOM Programming Language**

⇒ www.gerbil.org/tom

A very dynamic language with roots in Objective-C.

[URL 16] **The Beowulf Project**

⇒ www.beowulf.org

A project that builds high-performance computers out of networked clusters of inexpensive Linux boxes.

[URL 17] **iContract—Design by Contract Tool for Java**

⇒ www.reliable-systems.com

Design by Contract formalism of preconditions, postconditions, and invariants, implemented as a preprocessor for Java. Honors inheritance, implements existential quantifiers, and more.

[URL 18] **Nana—Logging and Assertions for C and C++**

⇒ www.gnu.org/software/nana/nana.html

Improved support for assertion checking and logging in C and C++. It also provides some support for Design by Contract.

[URL 19] **DDD—Data Display Debugger**

⇒ http://www.gnu.org/software/ddd/

A free graphical front end for Unix debuggers.

[URL 20] **John Brant's Refactoring Browser**

⇒ st-www.cs.uiuc.edu/users/brant/Refactory

A popular refactoring browser for Smalltalk.

[URL 21] **DOC++ Documentation Generator**
> ⇒ `www.zib.de/Visual/software/doc++/index.html`
> DOC++ is a documentation system for C/C++ and Java that generates both LaTeX and HTML output for sophisticated online browsing of your documentation directly from the C++ header or Java class files.

[URL 22] **xUnit—Unit Testing Framework**
> ⇒ `www.XProgramming.com`
> A simple but powerful concept, the xUnit unit testing framework provides a consistent platform for testing software written in a variety of languages.

[URL 23] **The Tcl Language**
> ⇒ `www.scriptics.com`
> Tcl ("Tool Command Language") is a scripting language designed to be easy to embed into an application.

[URL 24] **Expect—Automate Interaction with Programs**
> ⇒ `expect.nist.gov`
> An extension built on Tcl [URL 23], `expect` allows you to script interaction with programs. As well as helping you write command files that (for example) fetch files from remote servers or extend the power of your shell, `expect` can be useful when performing regression testing. A graphical version, `expectk`, lets you wrap non-GUI applications with a windowing front end.

[URL 25] **T Spaces**
> ⇒ `www.almaden.ibm.com/cs/TSpaces`
> From their Web page: "T Spaces is a network communication buffer with database capabilities. It enables communication between applications and devices in a network of heterogeneous computers and operating systems. T Spaces provides group communication services, database services, URL-based file transfer services, and event notification services."

[URL 26] **javaCC—Java Compiler-Compiler**
> ⇒ `www.webgain.com/products/java_cc`
> A parser generator that is tightly coupled to the Java language.

[URL 27] **The bison Parser Generator**
> ⇒ `www.gnu.org/software/bison/bison.html`
> `bison` takes an input grammar specification and generates from it the C source code of a suitable parser.

[URL 28] **SWIG—Simplified Wrapper and Interface Generator**

⇒ www.swig.org

SWIG is a software development tool that connects programs written in C, C++, and Objective-C with a variety of high-level programming languages such as Perl, Python, and Tcl/Tk, as well as Java, Eiffel, and Guile.

[URL 29] **The Object Management Group, Inc.**

⇒ www.omg.org

The OMG is the steward of various specifications for producing distributed object-based systems. Their work includes the Common Object Request Broker Architecture (CORBA) and the Internet Inter-ORB Protocol (IIOP). Combined, these specifications make it possible for objects to communicate with each other, even if they are written in different languages and run on different types of computers.

Unix Tools Under DOS

[URL 30] **The UWIN Development Tools**

⇒ www.gtlinc.com/uwin.html

Global Technologies, Inc., Old Bridge, NJ

The UWIN package provides Windows Dynamic Link Libraries (DLLs) that emulate a large portion of the Unix C level library interface. Using this interface, GTL has ported a large number of Unix command-line tools to Windows. See also [URL 31].

[URL 31] **The Cygnus Cygwin Tools**

⇒ sourceware.cygnus.com/cygwin/

Cygnus Solutions, Sunnyvale, CA

The Cygnus package also emulates the the Unix C library interface, and provides a large array of Unix command-line tools under the Windows operating system.

[URL 32] **Perl Power Tools**

⇒ www.perl.com/pub/language/ppt/

A project to reimplement the classic Unix command set in Perl, making the commands available on all platforms that support Perl (and that's a lot of platforms).

Source Code Control Tools

[URL 33] **RCS—Revision Control System**
> ⇒ www.cs.purdue.edu/homes/trinkle/RCS/
>
> GNU source code control system for Unix and Windows NT.

[URL 34] **CVS—Concurrent Version System**
> ⇒ www.cvshome.com
>
> Freely available source code control system for Unix and Windows NT. Extends RCS by supporting a client-server model and concurrent access to files.

[URL 35] **Aegis Transaction-Based Configuration Management**
> ⇒ http://www.canb.auug.org.au/~millerp/aegis.html
>
> A process-oriented revision control tool that imposes project standards (such as verifying that checked-in code passes tests).

[URL 36] **ClearCase**
> ⇒ www.rational.com
>
> Version control, workspace and build management, process control.

[URL 37] **MKS Source Integrity**
> ⇒ www.mks.com
>
> Version control and configuration management. Some versions incorporate features allowing remote developers to work on the same files simultaneously (much like CVS).

[URL 38] **PVCS Configuration Management**
> ⇒ www.merant.com
>
> A source code control system, very popular for Windows systems.

[URL 39] **Visual SourceSafe**
> ⇒ www.microsoft.com
>
> A version control system that integrates with Microsoft's visual development tools.

[URL 40] **Perforce**
> ⇒ www.perforce.com
>
> A client-server software configuration management system.

Other Tools

[URL 41] WinZip—Archive Utility for Windows

⇒ www.winzip.com

Nico Mak Computing, Inc., Mansfield, CT

A Windows-based file archive utility. Supports both zip and tar formats.

[URL 42] The Z Shell

⇒ sunsite.auc.dk/zsh

A shell designed for interactive use, although it is also a powerful scripting language. Many of the useful features of bash, ksh, and tcsh were incorporated into zsh; many original features were added.

[URL 43] A Free SMB Client for Unix Systems

⇒ samba.anu.edu.au/pub/samba/

Samba lets you share files and other resources between Unix and Windows systems. Samba includes:

- An SMB server, to provide Windows NT and LAN Manager-style file and print services to SMB clients such as Windows 95, Warp Server, smbfs, and others.
- A Netbios nameserver, which among other things gives browsing support. Samba can be the master browser on your LAN if you wish.
- An ftp-like SMB client that allows you to access PC resources (disks and printers) from Unix, Netware, and other operating systems.

Papers and Publications

[URL 44] The comp.object FAQ

⇒ www.cyberdyne-object-sys.com/oofaq2

A substantial and well-organized FAQ for the comp.object newsgroup.

[URL 45] eXtreme Programming

⇒ www.XProgramming.com

From the Web site: "In XP, we use a very lightweight combination of practices to create a team that can rapidly produce extremely reliable, efficient, well-factored software. Many of the XP practices were created and tested as part of the Chrysler C3 project, which is a very successful payroll system implemented in Smalltalk."

[URL 46] Alistair Cockburn's Home Page

⇒ members.aol.com/acockburn

Look for "Structuring Use Cases with Goals" and use case templates.

[URL 47] **Martin Fowler's Home Page**

⇒ ourworld.compuserve.com/homepages/martin_fowler

Author of *Analysis Patterns* and co-author of *UML Distilled* and *Refactoring: Improving the Design of Existing Code*. Martin Fowler's home page discusses his books and his work with the UML.

[URL 48] **Robert C. Martin's Home Page**

⇒ www.objectmentor.com

Good introductory papers on object-oriented techniques, including dependency analysis and metrics.

[URL 49] **Aspect-Oriented Programming**

⇒ www.parc.xerox.com/csl/projects/aop/

An approach to adding functionality to code, both orthogonally and declaratively.

[URL 50] **JavaSpaces Specification**

⇒ java.sun.com/products/javaspaces

A Linda-like system for Java that supports distributed persistence and distributed algorithms.

[URL 51] **Netscape Source Code**

⇒ www.mozilla.org

The development source of the Netscape browser.

[URL 52] **The Jargon File**

⇒ www.jargon.org

Eric S. Raymond

Definitions for many common (and not so common) computer industry terms, along with a good dose of folklore.

[URL 53] **Eric S. Raymond's Papers**

⇒ www.tuxedo.org/~esr

Eric's papers on *The Cathedral and the Bazaar* and *Homesteading the Noosphere* describing the psychosocietal basis for and implications of the Open Source movement.

[URL 54] **The K Desktop Environment**

⇒ www.kde.org

From their Web page: "KDE is a powerful graphical desktop environment for Unix workstations. KDE is an Internet project and truly open in every sense."

[URL 55] **The GNU Image Manipulation Program**
⇒ `www.gimp.org`
Gimp is a freely distributed program used for image creation, composition, and retouching.

[URL 56] **The Demeter Project**
⇒ `www.ccs.neu.edu/research/demeter`
Research focused on making software easier to maintain and evolve using Adaptive Programming.

Miscellaneous

[URL 57] **The GNU Project**
⇒ `www.gnu.org`
Free Software Foundation, Boston, MA
The Free Software Foundation is a tax-exempt charity that raises funds for the GNU project. The GNU project's goal is to produce a complete, free, Unix-like system. Many of the tools they've developed along the way have become industry standards.

[URL 58] **Web Server Information**
⇒ `www.netcraft.com/survey/servers.html`
Links to the home pages of over 50 different web servers. Some are commercial products, while others are freely available.

Bibliography

[Bak72]   F. T. Baker. Chief programmer team management of production programming. *IBM Systems Journal*, 11(1):56–73, 1972.

[BBM96]   V. Basili, L. Briand, and W. L. Melo. A validation of object-oriented design metrics as quality indicators. *IEEE Transactions on Software Engineering*, 22(10):751–761, October 1996.

[Ber96]   Albert J. Bernstein. *Dinosaur Brains: Dealing with All Those Impossible People at Work.* Ballantine Books, New York, NY, 1996.

[Bra95]   Marshall Brain. *Win32 System Services*. Prentice Hall, Englewood Cliffs, NJ, 1995.

[Bro95]   Frederick P. Brooks, Jr. *The Mythical Man Month: Essays on Software Engineering*. Addison-Wesley, Reading, MA, anniversary edition, 1995.

[CG90]   N. Carriero and D. Gelenter. *How to Write Parallel Programs: A First Course*. MIT Press, Cambridge, MA, 1990.

[Cla04]   Mike Clark. *Pragmatic Project Automation*. The Pragmatic Programmers, LLC, Raleigh, NC, and Dallas, TX, 2004.

[CN91]   Brad J. Cox and Andrex J. Novobilski. *Object-Oriented Programming, An Evolutionary Approach*. Addison-Wesley, Reading, MA, 1991.

[Coc97a]   Alistair Cockburn. Goals and use cases. *Journal of Object Oriented Programming*, 9(7):35–40, September 1997.

[Coc97b]   Alistair Cockburn. *Surviving Object-Oriented Projects: A Manager's Guide*. Addison Wesley Longman, Reading, MA, 1997.

[Cop92]   James O. Coplien. *Advanced C++ Programming Styles and Idioms*. Addison-Wesley, Reading, MA, 1992.

[DL99]   Tom Demarco and Timothy Lister. *Peopleware: Productive Projects and Teams*. Dorset House, New York, NY, second edition, 1999.

[FBB⁺99]   Martin Fowler, Kent Beck, John Brant, William Opdyke, and Don Roberts. *Refactoring: Improving the Design of Existing Code*. Addison Wesley Longman, Reading, MA, 1999.

[Fow96]   Martin Fowler. *Analysis Patterns: Reusable Object Models*. Addison Wesley Longman, Reading, MA, 1996.

[FS99]   Martin Fowler and Kendall Scott. *UML Distilled: Applying the Standard Object Modeling Language*. Addison Wesley Longman, Reading, MA, second edition, 1999.

[GHJV95]   Erich Gamma, Richard Helm, Ralph Johnson, and John Vlissides. *Design Patterns: Elements of Reusable Object-Oriented Software*. Addison-Wesley, Reading, MA, 1995.

[Gla99a]   Robert L. Glass.   Inspections—Some surprising findings. *Communications of the ACM*, 42(4):17–19, April 1999.

[Gla99b]   Robert L. Glass. The realities of software technology payoffs. *Communications of the ACM*, 42(2):74–79, February 1999.

[Hol78]   Michael Holt. *Math Puzzles and Games*. Dorset Press, New York, NY, 1978.

[HT03]   Andy Hunt and Dave Thomas.   *Pragmatic Unit Testing In Java with JUnit*. The Pragmatic Programmers, LLC, Raleigh, NC, and Dallas, TX, 2003.

[Jac94]   Ivar Jacobson. *Object-Oriented Software Engineering: A Use-Case Driven Approach*. Addison-Wesley, Reading, MA, 1994.

[KLM+97]   Gregor Kiczales, John Lamping, Anurag Mendhekar, Chris Maeda, Cristina Videira Lopes, Jean-Marc Loingtier, and John Irwin.   Aspect-oriented programming.   In *European Conference on Object-Oriented Programming (ECOOP)*, volume LNCS 1241. Springer-Verlag, June 1997.

[Knu97a]   Donald Ervin Knuth. *The Art of Computer Programming: Fundamental Algorithms*, volume 1. Addison Wesley Longman, Reading, MA, third edition, 1997.

[Knu97b]   Donald Ervin Knuth.   *The Art of Computer Programming: Seminumerical Algorithms*, volume 2. Addison Wesley Longman, Reading, MA, third edition, 1997.

[Knu98]   Donald Ervin Knuth.   *The Art of Computer Programming: Sorting and Searching*, volume 3. Addison Wesley Longman, Reading, MA, second edition, 1998.

[KP99]   Brian W. Kernighan and Rob Pike. *The Practice of Programming*. Addison Wesley Longman, Reading, MA, 1999.

[Kru98]   Philippe Kruchten. *The Rational Unified Process: An Introduction*. Addison Wesley Longman, Reading, MA, 1998.

[Lak96]   John Lakos.   *Large-Scale C++ Software Design*.   Addison Wesley Longman, Reading, MA, 1996.

[LH89]   Karl J. Lieberherr and Ian Holland. Assuring good style
           for object-oriented programs. *IEEE Software*, pages 38–48,
           September 1989.

[Lis88]   Barbara Liskov. Data abstraction and hierarchy. *SIGPLAN
           Notices*, 23(5), May 1988.

[LMB92]   John R. Levine, Tony Mason, and Doug Brown. *Lex and
           Yacc*. O'Reilly & Associates, Inc., Sebastopol, CA, second
           edition, 1992.

[McC95]   Jim McCarthy. *Dynamics of Software Development*. Mi-
           crosoft Press, Redmond, WA, 1995.

[Mey96]   Scott Meyers. *More Effective C++: 35 New Ways to Improve
           Your Programs and Designs*. Addison-Wesley, Reading, MA,
           1996.

[Mey97a]   Scott Meyers. *Effective C++: 50 Specific Ways to Improve
           Your Programs and Designs*. Addison Wesley Longman,
           Reading, MA, second edition, 1997.

[Mey97b]   Bertrand Meyer. *Object-Oriented Software Construction*.
           Prentice Hall, Englewood Cliffs, NJ, second edition, 1997.

[Pet98]   Charles Petzold. *Programming Windows, The Definitive
           Guide to the Win32 API*. Microsoft Press, Redmond, WA, fifth
           edition, 1998.

[Sch95]   Bruce Schneier. *Applied Cryptography: Protocols, Algo-
           rithms, and Source Code in C*. John Wiley & Sons, New York,
           NY, second edition, 1995.

[Sed83]   Robert Sedgewick. *Algorithms*. Addison-Wesley, Reading,
           MA, 1983.

[Sed92]   Robert Sedgewick. *Algorithms in C++*. Addison-Wesley,
           Reading, MA, 1992.

[SF96]   Robert Sedgewick and Phillipe Flajolet. *An Introduction to
           the Analysis of Algorithms*. Addison-Wesley, Reading, MA,
           1996.

[Ste92]   W. Richard Stevens. *Advanced Programming in the Unix En-
           vironment*. Addison-Wesley, Reading, MA, 1992.

[Ste98]   W. Richard Stevens. *Unix Network Programming, Volume 1: Networking APIs: Sockets and Xti.* Prentice Hall, Englewood Cliffs, NJ, second edition, 1998.

[Ste99]   W. Richard Stevens. *Unix Network Programming, Volume 2: Interprocess Communications.* Prentice Hall, Englewood Cliffs, NJ, second edition, 1999.

[Str35]   James Ridley Stroop. Studies of interference in serial verbal reactions. *Journal of Experimental Psychology,* 18:643–662, 1935.

[TFH04]   Dave Thomas, Chad Fowler, and Andy Hunt. *Programming Ruby, The Pragmatic Programmers' Guide.* The Pragmatic Programmers, LLC, Raleigh, NC, and Dallas, TX, 2004.

[TH03]   Dave Thomas and Andy Hunt. *Pragmatic Version Control Using CVS.* The Pragmatic Programmers, LLC, Raleigh, NC, and Dallas, TX, 2003.

[WK82]   James Q. Wilson and George Kelling. The police and neighborhood safety. *The Atlantic Monthly,* 249(3):29–38, March 1982.

[YC86]   Edward Yourdon and Larry L. Constantine. *Structured Design: Fundamentals of a Discipline of Computer Program and Systems Design.* Prentice Hall, Englewood Cliffs, NJ, second edition, 1986.

[You95]   Edward Yourdon. When good-enough software is best. *IEEE Software,* May 1995.

Appendix B

Answers to Exercises

Exercise 1: *from Orthogonality on page 43*
You are writing a class called Split, which splits input lines into fields. Which of the following two Java class signatures is the more orthogonal design?

```
class Split1 {
  public Split1(InputStreamReader rdr) { ...
  public void readNextLine() throws IOException { ...
  public int numFields() { ...
  public String getField(int fieldNo) { ...
}
class Split2 {
  public Split2(String line) { ...
  public int numFields()     { ...
  public String getField(int fieldNo) { ...
}
```

Answer 1: To our way of thinking, class Split2 is more orthogonal. It concentrates on its own task, splitting lines, and ignores details such as where the lines are coming from. Not only does this make the code easier to develop, but it also makes it more flexible. Split2 can split lines read from a file, generated by another routine, or passed in via the environment.

Exercise 2: *from Orthogonality on page 43*
Which will lead to a more orthogonal design: modeless or modal dialog boxes?

Answer 2: If done correctly, probably modeless. A system that uses modeless dialog boxes will be less concerned with what is going on at any particular moment in time. It will likely have a better intermodule communications infrastructure than a modal system, which may have built-in assumptions about the state of the system—assumptions that lead to increased coupling and decreased orthogonality.

Exercise 3: *from Orthogonality on page 43*
How about procedural languages versus object technology? Which results in a more orthogonal system?

Answer 3: This is a little tricky. Object technology *can* provide a more orthogonal system, but because it has more features to abuse, it is actually easier to create a *nonorthogonal* system using objects than it is using a procedural language. Features such as multiple inheritance, exceptions, operator overloading, and parent-method overriding (via subclassing) provide ample opportunity to increase coupling in nonobvious ways.

With object technology and a little extra effort, you can achieve a much more orthogonal system. But while you can always write "spaghetti code" in a procedural language, object-oriented languages used poorly can add meatballs to your spaghetti.

Exercise 4: *from Prototypes and Post-it Notes on page 56*
Marketing would like to sit down and brainstorm a few Web-page designs with you. They are thinking of clickable image maps to take you to other pages, and so on. But they can't decide on a model for the image—maybe it's a car, or a phone, or a house. You have a list of target pages and content; they'd like to see a few prototypes. Oh, by the way, you have 15 minutes. What tools might you use?

Answer 4: Low-tech to the rescue! Draw a few cartoons with markers on a whiteboard—a car, a phone, and a house. It doesn't have to be great art; stick-figure outlines are fine. Put Post-it notes that describe the contents of target pages on the clickable areas. As the meeting progresses, you can refine the drawings and placements of the Post-it notes.

Exercise 5: *from Domain Languages on page 63*
We want to implement a mini-language to control a simple drawing package (perhaps a turtle-graphics system). The language consists of single-letter commands. Some commands are followed by a single number. For example, the following input would draw a rectangle.

```
P 2   # select pen 2
D     # pen down
W 2   # draw west 2cm
N 1   # then north 1
E 2   # then east 2
S 1   # then back south
U     # pen up
```

Implement the code that parses this language. It should be designed so that it is simple to add new commands.

Answer 5: Because we want to make the language extendable, we'll make the parser table driven. Each entry in the table contains the command letter, a flag to say whether an argument is required, and the name of the routine to call to handle that particular command.

```c
typedef struct {
    char  cmd;                  /* the command letter */
    int hasArg;                 /* does it take an argument */
    void (*func)(int, int); /* routine to call */
} Command;

static Command cmds[] = {
    { 'P',  ARG,       doSelectPen },
    { 'U',  NO_ARG,  doPenUp },
    { 'D',  NO_ARG,  doPenDown },
    { 'N',  ARG,       doPenDir },
    { 'E',  ARG,       doPenDir },
    { 'S',  ARG,       doPenDir },
    { 'W',  ARG,       doPenDir }
};
```

The main program is pretty simple: read a line, look up the command, get the argument if required, then call the handler function.

```c
while (fgets(buff, sizeof(buff), stdin)) {
    Command *cmd = findCommand(*buff);
    if (cmd) {
        int    arg = 0;
        if (cmd->hasArg && !getArg(buff+1, &arg)) {
            fprintf(stderr, "'%c' needs an argument\n", *buff);
            continue;
        }
        cmd->func(*buff, arg);
    }
}
```

The function that looks up a command performs a linear search of the table, returning either the matching entry or NULL.

```c
Command *findCommand(int cmd) {
    int i;
    for (i = 0; i < ARRAY_SIZE(cmds); i++) {
        if (cmds[i].cmd == cmd)
            return cmds + i;
    }
    fprintf(stderr, "Unknown command '%c'\n", cmd);
    return 0;
}
```

Finally, reading the numeric argument is pretty simple using sscanf.

```c
int getArg(const char *buff, int *result) {
    return sscanf(buff, "%d", result) == 1;
}
```

Exercise 6: *from Domain Languages on page 63*

Design a BNF grammar to parse a time specification. All of the following examples should be accepted.

> 4pm, 7:38pm, 23:42, 3:16, 3:16am

Answer 6: Using BNF, a time specification could be

<time>   ::= *<hour> <ampm>* |
         <hour> : *<minute> <ampm>* |
         <hour> : *<minute>*

<ampm> ::= **am** | **pm**

<hour > ::= *<digit>* |
          <digit> <digit>

<minute> ::= *<digit> <digit>*

<digit>   ::= **0** | **1** | **2** | **3** | **4** | **5** | **6** | **7** | **8** | **9**

Exercise 7: *from Domain Languages on page 63*

Implement a parser for the BNF grammar in Exercise 6 using yacc, bison, or a similar parser-generator.

Answer 7: We coded our example using bison, the GNU version of yacc. For clarity, we're just showing the body of the parser here. Look at the source on our Web site for the full implementation.

```
time:      spec END_TOKEN
           { if ($1 >= 24*60) yyerror("Time is too large");
             printf("%d minutes past midnight\n", $1);
             exit(0);
           }
         ;
spec:      hour ':' minute
           { $$ = $1 + $3;
           }
         | hour ':' minute ampm
           { if ($1 > 11*60) yyerror("Hour out of range");
             $$ = $1 + $3 + $4;
           }
         | hour ampm
           { if ($1 > 11*60) yyerror("Hour out of range");
             $$ = $1 + $2;
           }
         ;
hour:      hour_num
           { if ($1 > 23) yyerror("Hour out of range");
             $$ = $1 * 60;
           };
```

```
minute:     DIGIT DIGIT
            { $$ = $1*10 + $2;
              if ($$ > 59) yyerror("minute out of range");
            };
ampm:       AM                      {  $$ = AM_MINS; }
          | PM                      {  $$ = PM_MINS; }
          ;
hour_num:   DIGIT                   {  $$ = $1; }
          | DIGIT DIGIT             {  $$ = $1*10 + $2; }
          ;
```

Exercise 8: *from Domain Languages on page 63*
Implement the time parser using Perl. [*Hint:* Regular expressions make good parsers.]

Answer 8:

```
$_ = shift;
/^(\d\d?)(am|pm)$/          && doTime($1, 0,   $2, 12);
/^(\d\d?):(\d\d)(am|pm)$/ && doTime($1, $2, $3, 12);
/^(\d\d?):(\d\d)$/          && doTime($1, $2,  0, 24);
die "Invalid time $_\n";
#
# doTime(hour, min, ampm, maxHour)
#
sub doTime($$$$) {
  my ($hour, $min, $offset, $maxHour) = @_;
  die "Invalid hour: $hour" if ($hour >= $maxHour);
  $hour += 12 if ($offset eq "pm");
  print $hour*60 + $min, " minutes past midnight\n";
  exit(0);
}
```

Exercise 9: *from Estimating on page 69*
You are asked "Which has a higher bandwidth: a 1Mbps communications line or a person walking between two computers with a full 4GB tape in their pocket?" What constraints will you put on your answer to ensure that the scope of your response is correct? (For example, you might say that the time taken to access the tape is ignored.)

Answer 9: Our answer must be couched in several assumptions:

- The tape contains the information we need to be transferred.
- We know the speed at which the person walks.
- We know the distance between the machines.
- We are not accounting for the time it takes to transfer information to and from the tape.

- The overhead of storing data on a tape is roughly equal to the overhead of sending it over a communications line.

Exercise 10: *from Estimating on page 69*
So, which has the higher bandwidth?

Answer 10: Subject to the caveats in Answer 9: A 4GB tape contains 32×10^9 bits, so a 1Mbps line would have to pump data for about 32,000 seconds, or roughly 9 hours, to transfer the equivalent amount of information. If the person is walking at a constant $3\frac{1}{2}$ mph, then our two machines would need to be at least 31 miles apart for the communications line to outperform our courier. Otherwise, the person wins.

Exercise 11: *from Text Manipulation on page 102*
Your C program uses an enumerated type to represent one of 100 states. You'd like to be able to print out the state as a string (as opposed to a number) for debugging purposes. Write a script that reads from standard input a file containing

```
name
state_a
state_b
  :    :
```

Produce the file *name.h*, which contains

```
extern const char* NAME_names[];
typedef enum {
    state_a,
    state_b,
      :    :
  } NAME;
```

and the file *name.c*, which contains

```
const char* NAME_names[] = {
    "state_a",
    "state_b",
      :    :
  };
```

Answer 11:   We implemented our answer using Perl.

```perl
my @consts;

my $name = <>;
die "Invalid format - missing name" unless defined($name);
chomp $name;
# Read in the rest of the file
while (<>) {
  chomp;
  s/^\s*//; s/\s*$//;
  die "Invalid line: $_" unless /^(\w+)$/;
  push @consts, $_;
}
# Now generate the file
open(HDR, ">$name.h") or die "Can't open $name.h: $!";
open(SRC, ">$name.c") or die "Can't open $name.c: $!";
my $uc_name = uc($name);
my $array_name = $uc_name . "_names";
print HDR "/* File generated automatically - do not edit */\n";
print HDR "extern const char *$ {array_name}[];";
print HDR "typedef enum {\n  ";
print HDR join ",\n  ", @consts;
print HDR "\n} $uc_name;\n\n";

print SRC "/* File generated automatically - do not edit */\n";
print SRC "const char *$ {array_name}[] = {\n  \"";
print SRC join "\",\n  \"", @consts;
print SRC "\"\n};\n";
close(SRC);
close(HDR);
```

Using the *DRY* principle, we won't cut and paste this new file into our code. Instead, we'll #include it—the flat file is the master source of these constants. This means that we'll need a makefile to regenerate the header when the file changes. The following extract is from the test bed in our source tree (available on the Web site).

```
etest.c etest.h:  etest.inc enumerated.pl
                  perl enumerated.pl etest.inc
```

Exercise 12:   *from Text Manipulation on page 102*

Halfway through writing this book, we realized that we hadn't put the use strict directive into many of our Perl examples. Write a script that goes through the .pl files in a directory and adds a use strict at the end of the initial comment block to all files that don't already have one. Remember to keep a backup of all files you change.

Answer 12: Here's our answer, written in Perl.

```perl
my $dir = shift or die "Missing directory";
for my $file (glob("$dir/*.pl")) {
  open(IP, "$file") or die "Opening $file: $!";
  undef $/;           # Turn off input record separator --
  my $content = <IP>; # read whole file as one string.
  close(IP);
  if ($content !~ /^use strict/m) {
    rename $file, "$file.bak" or die "Renaming $file: $!";
    open(OP, ">$file") or die "Creating $file: $!";
    # Put 'use strict' on first line that
    # doesn't start '#'
    $content =~ s/^(?!#)/\nuse strict;\n\n/m;

    print OP $content;
    close(OP);

    print "Updated $file\n";
  }
  else {
    print "$file already strict\n";
  }
}
```

Exercise 13: *from Code Generators on page 106*
Write a code generator that takes the input file in Figure 3.4, page 106, and generates output in two languages of your choice. Try to make it easy to add new languages.

Answer 13: We use Perl to implement our solution. It dynamically loads a module to generate the requested language, so adding new languages is easy. The main routine loads the back end (based on a command-line parameter), then reads its input and calls code generation routines based on the content of each line. We're not particularly fussy about error handling—we'll get to know pretty quickly if things go wrong.

```perl
my $lang = shift or die "Missing language";
$lang .= "_cg.pm";
require "$lang" or die "Couldn't load $lang";
# Read and parse the file
my $name;
while (<>) {
  chomp;
  if    (/^\s*$/)       { CG::blankLine(); }
  elsif (/^\#(.*)/)     { CG::comment($1); }
  elsif (/^M\s*(.+)/) { CG::startMsg($1); $name = $1; }
  elsif (/^E/)          { CG::endMsg($name); }
  elsif (/^F\s*(\w+)\s+(\w+)$/)
                        { CG::simpleType($1,$2); }
```

```perl
    elsif (/^F\s*(\w+)\s+(\w+)\[(\d+)\]$/)
                           { CG::arrayType($1,$2,$3); }
    else {
      die "Invalid line: $_";
    }
  }
}
```

Writing a language back end is simple: provide a module that implements the required six entry points. Here's the C generator:

```perl
#!/usr/bin/perl -w
package CG;
use strict;
# Code generator for 'C' (see cg_base.pl)
sub blankLine() { print "\n"; }
sub comment()   { print "/*$_[0] */\n"; }
sub startMsg()  { print "typedef struct {\n"; }
sub endMsg()    { print "} $_[0];\n\n"; }
sub arrayType() {
  my ($name, $type, $size) = @_;
  print "    $type $name\[$size];\n";
}
sub simpleType() {
  my ($name, $type) = @_;
  print "    $type $name;\n";
}
1;
```

And here's the one for Pascal:

```perl
#!/usr/bin/perl -w
package CG;
use strict;
# Code generator for 'Pascal' (see cg_base.pl)
sub blankLine() { print "\n"; }
sub comment()   { print "{$_[0] }\n"; }
sub startMsg()  { print "$_[0] = packed record\n"; }
sub endMsg()    { print "end;\n\n"; }
sub arrayType() {
  my ($name, $type, $size) = @_;
  $size--;
  print "    $name: array[0..$size] of $type;\n";
}
sub simpleType() {
  my ($name, $type) = @_;
  print "    $name: $type;\n";
}
1;
```

Exercise 14: *from Design by Contract on page 118*

What makes a good contract? Anyone can add preconditions and postconditions, but will they do you any good? Worse yet, will they actually do more harm than good? For the example below and for those in Exercises 15 and 16, decide whether the specified contract is good, bad, or ugly, and explain why.

First, let's look at an Eiffel example. Here we have a routine for adding a STRING to a doubly linked, circular list (remember that preconditions are labeled with require, and postconditions with ensure).

```
-- Add a unique item to a doubly linked list,
-- and return the newly created NODE.
add_item (item : STRING) : NODE is
   require
      item /= Void                      -- '/=' is 'not equal'.
      find_item(item) = Void            -- Must be unique
   deferred                             -- Abstract base class.
   ensure
      result.next.previous = result  -- Check the newly
      result.previous.next = result  -- added node's links.
      find_item(item) = result       -- Should find it.
   end
```

Answer 14: This Eiffel example is *good*. We require non-null data to be passed in, and we guarantee that the semantics of a circular, doubly linked list are honored. It also helps to be able to find the string we stored. Because this is a deferred class, the actual class that implements it is free to use whatever underlying mechanism it wants to. It may choose to use pointers, or an array, or whatever; as long as it honors the contract, we don't care.

Exercise 15: *from Design by Contract on page 119*

Next, let's try an example in Java—somewhat similar to the example in Exercise 14. insertNumber inserts an integer into an ordered list. Pre- and postconditions are labeled as in iContract (see [URL 17]).

```
private int data[];
/**
 * @post data[index-1] < data[index] &&
 *       data[index] == aValue
 */
public Node insertNumber (final int aValue)
{
   int index = findPlaceToInsert(aValue);
   ...
```

Answer 15: This is *bad*. The math in the index clause (index-1) won't work on boundary conditions such as the first entry. The postcondition assumes a particular implementation: we want contracts to be more abstract than that.

Exercise 16:   *from Design by Contract on page 119*

Here's a fragment from a stack class in Java. Is this a good contract?

```
/**
  * @pre anItem != null   // Require real data
  * @post pop() == anItem  // Verify that it's
  *                        // on the stack
  */
public void push(final String anItem)
```

Answer 16:   It's a good contract, but a bad implementation. Here, the infamous "Heisenbug" [URL 52] rears its *ugly* head. The programmer probably just made a simple typo—pop instead of top. While this is a simple and contrived example, side effects in assertions (or in any unexpected place in the code) can be very difficult to diagnose.

Exercise 17:   *from Design by Contract on page 119*

The classic examples of DBC (as in Exercises 14–16) show an implementation of an ADT (Abstract Data Type)—typically a stack or queue. But not many people really write these kinds of low-level classes.

So, for this exercise, design an interface to a kitchen blender. It will eventually be a Web-based, Internet-enabled, CORBA-fied blender, but for now we just need the interface to control it. It has ten speed settings (0 means off). You can't operate it empty, and you can change the speed only one unit at a time (that is, from 0 to 1, and from 1 to 2, not from 0 to 2).

Here are the methods. Add appropriate pre- and postconditions and an invariant.

```
int getSpeed()
void setSpeed(int x)
boolean isFull()
void fill()
void empty()
```

Answer 17:   We'll show the function signatures in Java, with the pre- and postconditions labeled as in iContract.

First, the invariant for the class:

```
/**
  * @invariant getSpeed() > 0
  *        implies isFull()           // Don't run empty
  * @invariant getSpeed() >= 0 &&
  *        getSpeed() < 10            // Range check
  */
```

Next, the pre- and postconditions:

```
/**
 * @pre Math.abs(getSpeed() - x) <= 1  // Only change by one
 * @pre x >= 0 && x < 10               // Range check
 * @post getSpeed() == x              // Honor requested speed
 */
public void setSpeed(final int x)
/**
 * @pre !isFull()                     // Don't fill it twice
 * @post isFull()                     // Ensure it was done
 */
void fill()
/**
 * @pre isFull()                      // Don't empty it twice
 * @post !isFull()                    // Ensure it was done
 */
void empty()
```

Exercise 18:   *from Design by Contract on page 119*
How many numbers are in the series $0, 5, 10, 15, \ldots, 100$?

Answer 18:   There are 21 terms in the series. If you said 20, you just experienced a fencepost error.

Exercise 19:   *from Assertive Programming on page 125*
A quick reality check. Which of these "impossible" things can happen?

1. A month with fewer than 28 days
2. `stat(".",&sb) == -1` (that is, can't access the current directory)
3. In C++:   `a = 2; b = 3; if (a + b != 5) exit(1);`
4. A triangle with an interior angle sum $\neq 180°$
5. A minute that doesn't have 60 seconds
6. In Java: `(a + 1) <= a`

Answer 19:
1. September, 1752 had only 19 days. This was done to synchronize calendars as part of the Gregorian Reformation.

2. The directory could have been removed by another process, you might not have permission to read it, &sb might be invalid—you get the picture.

3. We sneakily didn't specify the types of a and b. Operator overloading might have defined +, =, or != to have unexpected behavior. Also, a and b may be aliases for the same variable, so the second assignment will overwrite the value stored in the first.

4. In non-Euclidean geometry, the sum of the angles of a triangle will not add up to $180°$. Think of a triangle mapped on the surface of a sphere.

5. Leap minutes may have 61 or 62 seconds.

6. Overflow may leave the result of a + 1 negative (this can also happen in C and C++).

Exercise 20: *from Assertive Programming on page 125*
Develop a simple assertion checking class for Java.

Answer 20: We chose to implement a very simple class with a single static method, TEST, that prints a message and a stack trace if the passed condition parameter is false.

```
package com.pragprog.util;
import java.lang.System;        // for exit()
import java.lang.Thread;        // for dumpStack()
public class Assert {
  /** Write a message, print a stack trace and exit if
    * our parameter is false.
    */
  public static void TEST(boolean condition) {
    if (!condition) {
      System.out.println("==== Assertion Failed ====");
      Thread.dumpStack();
      System.exit(1);
    }
  }
  // Testbed. If our argument is 'okay', try an assertion that
  // succeeds, if 'fail' try one that fails
  public static final void main(String args[]) {
    if (args[0].compareTo("okay") == 0) {
      TEST(1 == 1);
    }
    else if (args[0].compareTo("fail") == 0) {
      TEST(1 == 2);
    }
    else {
      throw new RuntimeException("Bad argument");
    }
  }
}
```

Exercise 21: *from When to Use Exceptions on page 128*
While designing a new container class, you identify the following possible error conditions:

1. No memory available for a new element in the add routine

2. Requested entry not found in the fetch routine

3. null pointer passed to the add routine

How should each be handled? Should an error be generated, should an exception be raised, or should the condition be ignored?

Answer 21: Running out of memory is an exceptional condition, so we feel that case (1) should raise an exception.

Failure to find an entry is probably quite a normal occurrence. The application that calls our collection class may well write code that checks to see if an entry is present before adding a potential duplicate. We feel that case (2) should just return an error.

Case (3) is more problematic—if the value null is significant to the application, then it may be justifiably added to the container. If, however, it makes no sense to store null values, an exception should probably be thrown.

Exercise 22: *from How to Balance Resources on page 136*
Some C and C++ developers make a point of setting a pointer to NULL after they deallocate the memory it references. Why is this a good idea?

Answer 22: In most C and C++ implementations, there is no way of checking that a pointer actually points to valid memory. A common mistake is to deallocate a block of memory and reference that memory later in the program. By then, the memory pointed to may well have been reallocated to some other purpose. By setting the pointer to NULL, the programmers hope to prevent these rogue references—in most cases, dereferencing a NULL pointer will generate a runtime error.

Exercise 23: *from How to Balance Resources on page 136*
Some Java developers make a point of setting an object variable to NULL after they have finished using the object. Why is this a good idea?

Answer 23: By setting the reference to NULL, you reduce the number of pointers to the referenced object by one. Once this count reaches zero, the object is eligible for garbage collection. Setting the references to NULL can be significant for long-running programs, where the programmers need to ensure that memory utilization doesn't increase over time.

Exercise 24: *from Decoupling and the Law of Demeter on page 143*
We discussed the concept of physical decoupling in the box on page 142. Which of the following C++ header files is more tightly coupled to the rest of the system?

person1.h:
```
#include "date.h"
class  Person1 {
private:
  Date myBirthdate;
public:
  Person1(Date &birthDate);
  // ...
```

person2.h:
```
class Date;
class  Person2 {
private:
  Date *myBirthdate;
public:
  Person2(Date &birthDate);
  // ...
```

Answer 24: A header file is supposed to define the interface between the corresponding implementation and the rest of the world. The header file itself has no need to know about the internals of the Date class—it merely needs to tell the compiler that the constructor takes a Date as a parameter. So, unless the header file uses Dates in inline functions, the second snippet will work fine.

What's wrong with the first snippet? On a small project, nothing, except that you are unnecessarily making everything that uses a Person1 class also include the header file for Date. Once this kind of usage gets common in a project, you soon find that including one header file ends up including most of the rest of the system—a serious drag on compilation times.

Exercise 25: *from Decoupling and the Law of Demeter on page 143*
For the example below and for those in Exercises 26 and 27, determine if the method calls shown are allowed according to the Law of Demeter. This first one is in Java.

```
public void showBalance(BankAccount acct) {
  Money amt = acct.getBalance();
  printToScreen(amt.printFormat());
}
```

Answer 25: The variable acct is passed in as a parameter, so the getBalance call is allowed. Calling amt.printFormat(), however, is not. We don't "own" amt and it wasn't passed to us. We could eliminate showBalance's coupling to Money with something like this:

```
void showBalance(BankAccount b) {
  b.printBalance();
}
```

Exercise 26: *from Decoupling and the Law of Demeter on page 143*
This example is also in Java.

```
public class Colada {
  private Blender myBlender;
  private Vector myStuff;

  public Colada() {
    myBlender = new Blender();
    myStuff = new Vector();
  }
  private void doSomething() {
    myBlender.addIngredients(myStuff.elements());
  }
}
```

Answer 26: Since Colada creates and owns both myBlender and myStuff, the calls to addIngredients and elements are allowed.

Exercise 27: *from Decoupling and the Law of Demeter on page 143*
This example is in C++.

```
void processTransaction(BankAccount acct, int) {
  Person *who;
  Money amt;

  amt.setValue(123.45);
  acct.setBalance(amt);
  who = acct.getOwner();
  markWorkflow(who->name(), SET_BALANCE);
}
```

Answer 27: In this case, processTransaction owns amt—it is created on the stack. acct is passed in, so both setValue and setBalance are allowed. But processTransaction does not own who, so the call who->name() is in violation. The Law of Demeter suggests replacing this line with

```
markWorkflow(acct.name(), SET_BALANCE);
```

The code in processTransaction should not have to know which subobject within a BankAccount holds the name—this structural knowledge should not show through BankAccount's contract. Instead, we ask the BankAccount for the name on the account. It knows where it keeps the name (maybe in a Person, in a Business, or in a polymorphic Customer object).

Exercise 28: *from Metaprogramming on page 149*
Which of the following things would be better represented as code within a program, and which externally as metadata?

1. Communication port assignments
2. An editor's support for highlighting the syntax of various languages
3. An editor's support for different graphic devices
4. A state machine for a parser or scanner
5. Sample values and results for use in unit testing

Answer 28:   There are no definitive answers here—the questions were intended primarily to give you food for thought. However, this is what we think:

1. **Communication port assignments.** Clearly, this information should be stored as metadata. But to what level of detail? Some Windows communications programs let you select only baud rate and port (say COM1 to COM4). But perhaps you need to specify word size, parity, stop bits, and the duplex setting as well. Try to allow the finest level of detail where practical.

2. **An editor's support for highlighting the syntax of various languages.** This should be implemented as metadata. You wouldn't want to have to hack code just because the latest version of Java introduced a new keyword.

3. **An editor's support for different graphic devices.** This would probably be difficult to implement strictly as metadata. You would not want to burden your application with multiple device drivers only to select one at runtime. You could, however, use metadata to specify the name of the driver and dynamically load the code. This is another good argument for keeping the metadata in a human-readable format; if you use the program to set up a dysfunctional video driver, you may not be able to use the program to set it back.

4. **A state machine for a parser or scanner.** This depends on what you are parsing or scanning. If you are parsing some data that is rigidly defined by a standards body and is unlikely to change without an act of Congress, then hard coding it is fine. But if you are faced with a more volatile situation, it may be beneficial to define the state tables externally.

5. **Sample values and results for use in unit testing.**   Most applications define these values inline in the testing harness, but you can get better flexibility by moving the test data—and the definition of the acceptable results—out of the code itself.

Exercise 29: *from It's Just a View on page 164*

Suppose you have an airline reservation system that includes the concept of a flight:

```
public interface Flight {
  // Return false if flight full.
  public boolean addPassenger(Passenger p);
  public void addToWaitList(Passenger p);
  public int getFlightCapacity();
  public int getNumPassengers();
}
```

If you add a passenger to the wait list, they'll be put on the flight automatically when an opening becomes available.

There's a massive reporting job that goes through looking for overbooked or full flights to suggest when additional flights might be scheduled. It works fine, but it takes hours to run.

We'd like to have a little more flexibility in processing wait-list passengers, and we've got to do something about that big report—it takes too long to run. Use the ideas from this section to redesign this interface.

Answer 29: We'll take `Flight` and add some additional methods for maintaining two lists of listeners: one for wait-list notification, and the other for full-flight notification.

```
public interface Passenger {
  public void waitListAvailable();
}
public interface Flight {
  . . .
  public void addWaitListListener(Passenger p);
  public void removeWaitListListener(Passenger p);

  public void addFullListener(FullListener b);
  public void removeFullListener(FullListener b);
  . . .
}
public interface BigReport extends FullListener {
  public void FlightFullAlert(Flight f);
}
```

If we try to add a `Passenger` and fail because the flight is full, we can, optionally, put the `Passenger` on the wait list. When a spot opens up, `waitList-Available` will be called. This method can then choose to add the `Passenger` automatically, or have a service representative call the customer to ask if they are still interested, or whatever. We now have the flexibility to perform different behaviors on a per-customer basis.

Next, we want to avoid having the `BigReport` troll through tons of records looking for full flights. By having `BigReport` registered as a listener on `Flight`s, each individual `Flight` can report when it is full—or nearly full, if we want. Now users can get live, up-to-the-minute reports from `BigReport` instantly, without waiting hours for it to run as it did previously.

Exercise 30: *from Blackboards on page 170*
For each of the following applications, would a blackboard system be appropriate or not? Why?

1. **Image processing.**   You'd like to have a number of parallel processes grab chunks of an image, process them, and put the completed chunk back.

2. **Group calendaring.**   You've got people scattered across the globe, in different time zones, and speaking different languages, trying to schedule a meeting.

3. **Network monitoring tool.**   The system gathers performance statistics and collects trouble reports. You'd like to implement some agents to use this information to look for trouble in the system.

Answer 30:
1. **Image processing.**   For simple scheduling of a workload among the parallel processes, a shared work queue may be more than adequate. You might want to consider a blackboard system if there is feedback involved—that is, if the results of one processed chunk affect other chunks, as in machine vision applications, or complex 3D image-warp transforms.

2. **Group calendaring.**   This might be a good fit. You can post scheduled meetings and availability to the blackboard. You have entities functioning autonomously, feedback from decisions is important, and participants may come and go.

   You might want to consider partitioning this kind of blackboard system depending on who is searching: junior staff may care about only the immediate office, human resources may want only English-speaking offices worldwide, and the CEO may want the whole enchilada.

   There is also some flexibility on data formats: we are free to ignore formats or languages we don't understand. We have to understand different formats only for those offices that have meetings with each other, and we do not need to expose all participants to a full transitive closure of all possible formats. This reduces coupling to where it is necessary, and does not constrain us artificially.

3. **Network monitoring tool.**   This is very similar to the mortgage/loan application program described on page 168. You've got trouble reports sent in by users and statistics reported automatically, all posting to the blackboard. A human or software agent can analyze the blackboard to diagnose

network failures: two errors on a line might just be cosmic rays, but 20,000 errors and you've got a hardware problem. Just as the detectives solve the murder mystery, you can have multiple entities analyzing and contributing ideas to solve the network problems.

Exercise 31:   *from Programming by Coincidence on page 176*

Can you identify some coincidences in the following C code fragment? Assume that this code is buried deep in a library routine.

```
fprintf(stderr, "Error, continue?");
gets(buf);
```

Answer 31:   There are several potential problems with this code. First, it assumes a `tty` environment. That may be fine if the assumption is true, but what if this code is called from a GUI environment where neither `stderr` nor `stdin` is open?

Second, there is the problematic `gets`, which will write as many characters as it receives into the buffer passed in. Malicious users have used this failing to create *buffer overrun* security holes in many different systems. Never use `gets()`.

Third, the code assumes the user understands English.

Finally, no one in their right mind would ever bury user interaction such as this in a library routine.

Exercise 32:   *from Programming by Coincidence on page 176*

This piece of C code might work some of the time, on some machines. Then again, it might not. What's wrong?

```
/* Truncate string to its last maxlen chars */
void string_tail(char *string, int maxlen) {
  int len = strlen(string);
  if (len > maxlen) {
    strcpy(string, string + (len - maxlen));
  }
}
```

Answer 32:   POSIX `strcpy` isn't guaranteed to work for overlapping strings. It might happen to work on some architectures, but only by coincidence.

Exercise 33:   *from Programming by Coincidence on page 177*

This code comes from a general-purpose Java tracing suite. The function writes a string to a log file. It passes its unit test, but fails when one of the Web developers uses it. What coincidence does it rely on?

```java
public static void debug(String s) throws IOException {
  FileWriter fw = new FileWriter("debug.log", true);
  fw.write(s);
  fw.flush();
  fw.close();
}
```

Answer 33:   It won't work in an applet context with security restrictions against writing to the local disk. Again, when you have a choice of running in GUI contexts or not, you may want to check dynamically to see what the current environment is like. In this case, you may want to put a log file somewhere other than the local disk if it isn't accessible.

Exercise 34:   *from Algorithm Speed on page 183*

We have coded a set of simple sort routines, which can be downloaded from our Web site (www.pragmaticprogrammer.com). Run them on various machines available to you. Do your figures follow the expected curves? What can you deduce about the relative speeds of your machines? What are the effects of various compiler optimization settings? Is the radix sort indeed linear?

Answer 34:   Clearly, we can't give any absolute answers to this exercise. However, we can give you a couple of pointers.

If you find that your results don't follow a smooth curve, you might want to check to see if some other activity is using some of your processor's power. You probably won't get good figures on a multiuser system, and even if you are the only user you may find that background processes periodically take cycles away from your programs. You might also want to check memory: if the application starts using swap space, performance will nose dive.

It is interesting to experiment with different compilers and different optimization settings. We found some that pretty startling speed-ups were possible by enabling aggressive optimization. We also found that on the wider RISC architectures the manufacturer's compilers often outperformed the more portable GCC. Presumably, the manufacturer is privy to the secrets of efficient code generation on these machines.

Exercise 35: *from Algorithm Speed on page 183*

The routine below prints out the contents of a binary tree. Assuming the tree is balanced, roughly how much stack space will the routine use while printing a tree of 1,000,000 elements? (Assume that subroutine calls impose no significant stack overhead.)

```
void printTree(const Node *node) {
  char buffer[1000];
  if (node) {
    printTree(node->left);

    getNodeAsString(node, buffer);
    puts(buffer);

    printTree(node->right);
  }
}
```

Answer 35: The `printTree` routine uses about 1,000 bytes of stack space for the `buffer` variable. It calls itself recursively to descend through the tree, and each nested call adds another 1,000 bytes to the stack. It also calls itself when it gets to the leaf nodes, but exits immediately when it discovers that the pointer passed in is NULL. If the depth of the tree is D, the maximum stack requirement is therefore roughly $1000 \times (D + 1)$.

A balanced binary tree holds twice as many elements at each level. A tree of depth D holds $1+2+4+8+\cdots+2^{(D-1)}$, or $2^D - 1$, elements. Our million-element tree will therefore need $\lceil \lg(1,000,001) \rceil$, or 20 levels.

We'd therefore expect our routine to use roughly 21,000 bytes of stack.

Exercise 36: *from Algorithm Speed on page 183*

Can you see any way to reduce the stack requirements of the routine in Exercise 35 (apart from reducing the size of the buffer)?

Answer 36: A couple of optimizations come to mind. First, the `printTree` routine calls itself on leaf nodes, only to exit because there are no children. That call increases the maximum stack depth by about 1,000 bytes. We can also eliminate the tail recursion (the second recursive call), although this won't affect the worst-case stack usage.

```
while (node) {
  if (node->left) printTree(node->left);

  getNodeAsString(node, buffer);
  puts(buffer);

  node = node->right;
}
```

The biggest gain, however, comes from allocating just a single buffer, shared by all invocations of printTree. Pass this buffer as a parameter to the recursive calls, and only 1,000 bytes will be allocated, regardless of the depth of recursion.

```
void printTreePrivate(const Node *node, char *buffer) {
  if (node) {
    printTreePrivate(node->left, buffer);
    getNodeAsString(node, buffer);
    puts(buffer);
    printTreePrivate(node->right, buffer);
  }
}

void newPrintTree(const Node *node) {
  char buffer[1000];
  printTreePrivate(node, buffer);
}
```

Exercise 37: *from Algorithm Speed on page 183*
On page 180, we claimed that a binary chop is $O(lg(n))$. Can you prove this?

Answer 37:   There are a couple of ways of getting there. One is to turn the problem on its head. If the array has just one element, we don't iterate around the loop. Each additional iteration doubles the size of the array we can search. The general formula for the array size is therefore $n = 2^m$, where m is the number of iterations. If you take logs to the base 2 of each side, you get $lg(n) = lg(2^m)$, which by the definition of logs becomes $lg(n) = m$.

Exercise 38: *from Refactoring on page 188*
The following code has obviously been updated several times over the years, but the changes haven't improved its structure. Refactor it.

```
if (state == TEXAS) {
  rate = TX_RATE;
  amt  = base * TX_RATE;
  calc = 2*basis(amt) + extra(amt)*1.05;
}
else if ((state == OHIO) || (state == MAINE)) {
  rate = (state == OHIO) ? OH_RATE : ME_RATE;
  amt  = base * rate;
  calc = 2*basis(amt) + extra(amt)*1.05;
  if (state == OHIO)
    points = 2;
}
else {
  rate = 1;
  amt  = base;
  calc = 2*basis(amt) + extra(amt)*1.05;
}
```

Answer 38:   We might suggest a fairly mild restructuring here: make sure that every test is performed just once, and make all the calculations common. If the expression `2*basis(...)*1.05` appears in other places in the program, we should probably make it a function. We haven't bothered here.

We've added a `rate_lookup` array, initialized so that entries other than Texas, Ohio, and Maine have a value of 1. This approach makes it easy to add values for other states in the future. Depending on the expected usage pattern, we might want to make the `points` field an array lookup as well.

```
rate = rate_lookup[state];
amt  = base * rate;
calc = 2*basis(amt) + extra(amt)*1.05;
if (state == OHIO)
  points = 2;
```

Exercise 39:   *from Refactoring on page 188*

The following Java class needs to support a few more shapes. Refactor the class to prepare it for the additions.

```
public class Shape {
  public static final int SQUARE    = 1;
  public static final int CIRCLE    = 2;
  public static final int RIGHT_TRIANGLE = 3;

  private int    shapeType;
  private double size;

  public Shape(int shapeType, double size) {
    this.shapeType = shapeType;
    this.size      = size;
  }
  // ... other methods ...

  public double area() {
    switch (shapeType) {
    case SQUARE:    return size*size;
    case CIRCLE:    return Math.PI*size*size/4.0;
    case RIGHT_TRIANGLE: return size*size/2.0;
    }
    return 0;
  }
}
```

Answer 39: When you see someone using enumerated types (or their equivalent in Java) to distinguish between variants of a type, you can often improve the code by subclassing:

```java
public class Shape {
  private double size;
  public Shape(double size) {
    this.size = size;
  }
  public double getSize() { return size; }
}
public class Square extends Shape {
  public Square(double size) {
    super(size);
  }
  public double area() {
    double size = getSize();
    return size*size;
  }
}
public class Circle extends Shape {
  public Circle(double size) {
    super(size);
  }
  public double area() {
    double size = getSize();
    return Math.PI*size*size/4.0;
  }
}
// etc...
```

Exercise 40: *from Refactoring on page 189*
This Java code is part of a framework that will be used throughout your project. Refactor it to be more general and easier to extend in the future.

```java
public class Window {
  public Window(int width, int height) { ... }
  public void setSize(int width, int height) { ... }
  public boolean overlaps(Window w) { ... }
  public int getArea() { ... }
}
```

Answer 40: This case is interesting. At first sight, it seems reasonable that a window should have a width and a height. However, consider the future. Let's imagine that we want to support arbitrarily shaped windows (which will be difficult if the Window class knows all about rectangles and their properties).

We'd suggest abstracting the shape of the window out of the Window class itself.

```
public abstract class Shape {
  // ...
  public abstract boolean overlaps(Shape s);
  public abstract int getArea();
}
public class Window {
  private Shape shape;
  public Window(Shape shape) {
    this.shape = shape;
    ...
  }
  public void setShape(Shape shape) {
    this.shape = shape;
    ...
  }
  public boolean overlaps(Window w) {
    return shape.overlaps(w.shape);
  }
  public int getArea() {
    return shape.getArea();
  }
}
```

Note that in this approach we've used delegation rather than subclassing: a window is not a "kind-of" shape—a window "has-a" shape. It uses a shape to do its job. You'll often find delegation useful when refactoring.

We could also have extended this example by introducing a Java interface that specified the methods a class must support to support the shape functions. This is a good idea. It means that when you extend the concept of a shape, the compiler will warn you about classes that you have affected. We recommend using interfaces this way when you delegate all the functions of some other class.

Exercise 41:   *from Code That's Easy to Test on page 197*
Design a test jig for the blender interface described in the answer to Exercise 17 on page 289. Write a shell script that will perform a regression test for the blender. You need to test basic functionality, error and boundary conditions, and any contractual obligations. What restrictions are placed on changing the speed? Are they being honored?

Answer 41: First, we'll add a main to act as a unit test driver. It will accept a very small, simple language as an argument: "E" to empty the blender, "F" to fill it, digits 0-9 to set the speed, and so on.

```java
public static void main(String args[]) {
  // Create the blender to test
  dbc_ex blender = new dbc_ex();
  // And test it according to the string on standard input
  try {
    int a;
    char c;
    while ((a = System.in.read()) != -1) {
      c = (char)a;
      if (Character.isWhitespace(c)) {
        continue;
      }
      if (Character.isDigit(c)) {
        blender.setSpeed(Character.digit(c, 10));
      }
      else {
        switch (c) {
          case 'F': blender.fill();
                    break;
          case 'E': blender.empty();
                    break;
          case 's': System.out.println("SPEED: " +
                                       blender.getSpeed());
                    break;
          case 'f': System.out.println("FULL " +
                                       blender.isFull());
                    break;
          default: throw new RuntimeException(
                    "Unknown Test directive");
        }
      }
    }
  }
  catch (java.io.IOException e) {
    System.err.println("Test jig failed: " + e.getMessage());
  }
  System.err.println("Completed blending\n");
  System.exit(0);
}
```

Next comes the shell script to drive the tests.

```sh
#!/bin/sh
CMD="java dbc.dbc_ex"
failcount=0
expect_okay() {
    if echo "$*" | $CMD #>/dev/null 2>&1
    then
        :
    else
      echo "FAILED! $*"
      failcount=`expr $failcount + 1`
    fi
}
expect_fail() {
    if echo "$*" | $CMD >/dev/null 2>&1
    then
      echo "FAILED! (Should have failed): $*"
      failcount=`expr $failcount + 1`
    fi
}
report() {
  if [ $failcount -gt 0 ]
  then
    echo -e "\n\n*** FAILED $failcount TESTS\n"
    exit 1 # In case we are part of something larger
  else
    exit 0 # In case we are part of something larger
  fi
}
#
# Start the tests
#
expect_okay F123456789876543210E # Should run thru
expect_fail F5     # Fails, speed too high
expect_fail 1      # Fails, empty
expect_fail F10E1  # Fails, empty
expect_fail F1238  # Fails, skips
expect_okay FE     # Never turn on
expect_fail F1E    # Emptying while running
expect_okay F10E   # Should be ok
report             # Report results
```

The tests check to see if illegal speed changes are detected, if you try to empty the blender while running, and so on. We put this in the makefile so we can compile and run the regression test by simply typing

```
% make
% make test
```

Note that we have the test exit with 0 or 1 so we can use this as part of a larger test as well.

There was nothing in the requirements that spoke of driving this component via a script, or even using a language. End users will never see it. But we have a powerful tool that we can use to test our code, quickly and exhaustively.

Exercise 42: *from The Requirements Pit on page 211*
Which of the following are probably genuine requirements? Restate those that are not to make them more useful (if possible).

1. The response time must be less than 500 ms.
2. Dialog boxes will have a gray background.
3. The application will be organized as a number of front-end processes and a back-end server.
4. If a user enters non-numeric characters in a numeric field, the system will beep and not accept them.
5. The application code and data must fit within 256kB.

Answer 42:

1. This statement sounds like a real requirement: there may be constraints placed on the application by its environment.
2. Even though this may be a corporate standard, it isn't a requirement. It would be better stated as "The dialog background must be configurable by the end user. As shipped, the color will be gray." Even better would be the broader statement "All visual elements of the application (colors, fonts, and languages) must be configurable by the end user."
3. This statement is not a requirement, it's architecture. When faced with something like this, you have to dig deep to find out what the user is thinking.
4. The underlying requirement is probably something closer to "The system will prevent the user from making invalid entries in fields, and will warn the user when these entries are made."
5. This statement is probably a hard requirement.

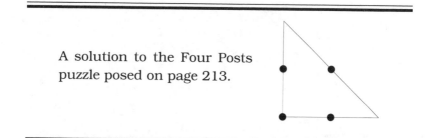

A solution to the Four Posts puzzle posed on page 213.

Index

D

G

F

H

Checklists

✔ **Languages to Learn** . . . . page 17
Tired of C, C++, and Java? Try CLOS, Dylan, Eiffel, Objective C, Prolog, Smalltalk, or TOM. Each of these languages has different capabilities and a different "flavor." Try a small project at home using one or more of them.

✔ **The WISDOM Acrostic** . . . . page 20
What do you want them to learn?
What is their **i**nterest in what you've got to say?
How **s**ophisticated are they?
How much **d**etail do they want?
Whom do you want to **o**wn the information?
How can you **m**otivate them to listen to you?

✔ **How to Maintain Orthogonality** . . . . . page 34
• Design independent, well-defined components.
• Keep your code decoupled.
• Avoid global data.
• Refactor similar functions.

✔ **Things to prototype** . . . . page 53
• Architecture
• New functionality in an existing system
• Structure or contents of external data
• Third-party tools or components
• Performance issues
• User interface design

✔ **Architectural Questions** . . . . page 55
• Are responsibilities well defined?
• Are the collaborations well defined?
• Is coupling minimized?
• Can you identify potential duplication?
• Are interface definitions and constraints acceptable?
• Can modules access needed data—*when* needed?

✔ **Debugging Checklist** . . . . page 98
• Is the problem being reported a direct result of the underlying bug, or merely a symptom?
• Is the bug *really* in the compiler? Is it in the OS? Or is it in your code?
• If you explained this problem in detail to a coworker, what would you say?
• If the suspect code passes its unit tests, are the tests complete enough? What happens if you run the unit test with *this* data?
• Do the conditions that caused this bug exist anywhere else in the system?

✔ **Law of Demeter for Functions** . . . . . page 141
An object's method should call only methods belonging to:
• Itself
• Any parameters passed in
• Objects it creates
• Component objects

✔ **How to Program Deliberately** . . . . . . page 172
• Stay aware of what you're doing.
• Don't code blindfolded.
• Proceed from a plan.
• Rely only on reliable things.
• Document your assumptions.
• Test assumptions as well as code.
• Prioritize your effort.
• Don't be a slave to history.

✔ **When to Refactor** . . . . page 185
• You discover a violation of the *DRY* principle.
• You find things that could be more orthogonal.
• Your knowledge improves.
• The requirements evolve.
• You need to improve performance.

✔ **Cutting the Gordian Knot** . . . . page 212
When solving *impossible* problems, ask yourself:
• Is there an easier way?
• Am I solving the right problem?
• *Why* is this a problem?
• What makes it hard?
• Do I have to do it this way?
• Does it have to be done at all?

✔ **Aspects of Testing** . . . . page 237
• Unit testing
• Integration testing
• Validation and verification
• Resource exhaustion, errors, and recovery
• Performance testing
• Usability testing
• Testing the tests themselves

Checklists from *The Pragmatic Programmer*, by Andrew Hunt and David Thomas. Visit www.pragmaticprogrammer.com.

Copyright © 2000 by Addison Wesley Longman, Inc.

2

The Pragmatic Programmer

This card summarizes the tips and checklists found in *The Pragmatic Programmer.*

For more information about THE PRAGMATIC PROGRAMMERS LLC, source code for the examples, up-to-date pointers to Web resources, and an online bibliography, visit us at www.pragmaticprogrammer.com.

Quick Reference Guide

TIPS 1 TO 22